DATE DUE

AG 3 '95			
JE 9 '04			
AP 5 '06			
AP 28 '06			
AU 12 '10			

DEMCO 38-296

COMMUNITY TELEVISION
IN THE
UNITED STATES

Community Television in the United States

A Sourcebook on Public, Educational, and Governmental Access

Linda K. Fuller

GREENWOOD PRESS
Westport, Connecticut • London

Library of Congress Cataloging-in-Publication Data

Fuller, Linda K.
    Community television in the United States : a sourcebook on
public, educational, and governmental access / Linda K. Fuller.
        p.   cm.
    Includes bibliographical references and index.
    ISBN 0–313–28601–9 (alk. paper)
    1. Cable television—Social aspects—United States.   2. Television
programs, Public service—United States.   3. Television in
education—United States.   4. Television broadcasting—Social
aspects—United States.   I. Title.
HE8700.72.U6F84   1994
384.55′0973—dc20   93–31612

British Library Cataloguing in Publication Data is available.

Library of Congress Catalog Card Number: 93–31612
ISBN: 0–313–28601–9

First published in 1994

Greenwood Press, 88 Post Road West, Westport, CT 06881
An imprint of Greenwood Publishing Group, Inc.

Printed in the United States of America

The paper used in this book complies with the
Permanent Paper Standard issued by the National
Information Standards Organization (Z39.48–1984).

10 9 8 7 6 5 4 3 2 1

Lynne Tower Combs, a special friend since undergraduate days, saw me through my dissertation on the topic of community television and later played her own part in the process by hosting first "Mayor's Corner" and later "Administrator's Alley" on her public access channel in New Jersey. To her, and to all the thousands of other volunteer activists working toward video democracy, this book is dedicated

Contents

Illustrations

FIGURES

Acknowledgments

Throughout its nearly quarter-century existence in the United States, community television has had a number of loyal proponents and practitioners. More than 150 pioneer advocates and activists for grassroots media contributed to this book, many of whom are included here. Like its subject, this compilation is of the people, by the people, and for the people.

Ben Achtenberg, IMDA (Independent Media Distributors' Alliance) and Plainsong/ Fanlight Productions, Boston

Bruce Adams, the Charles F. Kettering Foundation, Dayton, OH

Laura Adams, marketing manager, TI-IN Network, San Antonio

Alison Amoroso, editor, *Women's Express*

Patricia Aufderheide, American University, Washington, DC

Liz Bartucci, community outreach assistant, Queens Public Access Television, Bronx, NY

Terri Baur, director, ESN (Education Satellite Network), Missouri School Boards Association, Columbia, MO

Leigh Beaulieu, manager, ASTS, Oklahoma State University

Sam Behrend, executive director, Tucson (AZ) Community Cable Corp.

Greg Bell, Satellite Scholar, Missoula, MT

Emily Bent, executive director, PACTL, Longmeadow, MA

Lisa Berg, executive director, SPAC (Shrewsbury [MA] Public Access Coalition)

Andrew Blau, policy analyst, Electronic Frontier Foundation, Washington, DC

David Bloch, International Mobile Video, Sierra City, CA

Keith Brand, spokesperson, Citizens for Public Access Cable Coalition, Philadelphia

Celia Braswell, associate director, SWAMP (Southwest Alternate Media Project), Houston, TX

Rosalind Brinkley, community services officer, Austin (TX) Community Television

Joan Burke, executive director, Community Access of Kalamazoo, MI

Sue Buske and Randy VanDalsen, The Buske Group, Sacramento, CA

Mark Canty, assistant director, Missoula (MT) Community Access TV

Martha S. Carrell, president, board of directors, Pacific Islanders in Communications, Honolulu

Fred Carroll, chair, UPPNET, Santa Monica, CA

Lynn Chadwick, president, National Federation of Community Broadcasters, Washington, DC

Beverly J. Chain, director, Office of Communications, United Church of Christ, Cleveland, OH

James Chefchis, assistant director, Cable Access of Dallas

Don Christensen, coordinator, Center for Democratic Renewal, Atlanta

Rick Collin, videoconference coordinator, NASA Educational Services, Oklahoma State University, Stillwater

Lynne Tower Combs, Administrator's Alley, Millington, NJ

Dawnn Cooper, video production specialist, (Raleigh, NC) Community Access TV

Ron Cooper, executive director, Coloma Community Center, Sacramento, CA

Genya Copen, Copen & Lind, Amherst, MA

Katie Corrigan, distribution director, Communication for Change/Martha Stuart, New York

Bill Crawford, Austin, TX

Patrick Creadon, The 90's, Chicago

Bruce Crest, cable communications coordinator, Yakima (WA) Community Television

Ginna Crosby, Development/PR, Talcott Mountain Science Center for Student Involvement, Inc., Avon, CT

Kelley Culmer, administrator for AlterNet, Washington, DC

Bob Daley, the Kettering Foundation, Dayton, OH

Jim Daniels, administrator, Lake Minnetonka Cable Communications Commission, Excelsior, MN

J. R. David and Jonni Erickson, *Womyn's Press*

Everette E. Dennis, executive director, the Freedom Forum, Media Studies Center, New York

Mauro DePasquale, station manager, Access Worcester (MA)

Dan Derosu, Media Network, New York

Joel Desprez, executive director, Cable Access Community TV, Eau Claire, WI

Robert H. Devine, chair, Communications & Media Arts, Antioch University, Yellow Springs, OH

Richard V. Ducey, Research and Planning Department, NAB (National Association of Broadcasters), Washington, DC

Roxanne Earnest, administrative coordinator, Community Access TV of Salina (KS)

Dan Eichler, public relations associate, Northwest Film Center, Portland, OR

W. Douglas Eisele, executive vice president and director of programming, National Community Network, Houston, TX

Greg Farmer, Pioneer Valley Planning Commission, Springfield, MA

Linda Feldman, media program advisor, the John D. and Catherine T. MacArthur Foundation, Chicago

Oleathia Gadsden, Research Development, National Cable Television Association, Washington, DC

Jay Galvan, National Academy of Cable Programming, Washington, DC

Shirley Gazdi and Paul Eisenberg, Freedom Forum, New York

Karen George, the CMR Group (Communications/Media Relations), City of Fremont (CA)

George Gerbner, dean emeritus, the Annenberg School of Communications, University of Pennsylvania, Philadelphia

Joan Gerten, volunteer and community relations coordinator, North Suburbs Community TV, Roseville, MN

Jon E. Giannetti, Fitchburg (MA) Access TV

Helen Granger, Paper Tiger TV, New York

Kathleen Greenwood, Hudson (WI) Community Access

George Grimmett, editor, *Media in Education and Development*

Linda Grote, Cupertino (CA) Community TV

Glenn Guttmacher, executive director, NACB (National Association of College Broadcasters), Providence, RI

Rick Hayes, ACPL (Allen County Public Library), Fort Wayne, IN

Karen Helmerson, director of finance, Film/Video Arts, New York, and chair of the International Committee for The Alliance

Adrian E. Herbst, Moss & Barnett, Minneapolis

Kathy High, editor, *Felix/A Journal of Media Arts and Communication*

Irwin Hipsman, executive director, Cambridge (MA) Community TV

Dr. Renee Hobbs, professor of communication, Babson College, Wellesley, MA

Nelda Holder, executive director, MCTV (Middlebury [VT] Community TV)

Luke Matthew Hones, program director, Bay Area Video Center, San Francisco

James Horwood, Spiegel & McDirmid, Washington, DC

Bryan House, Visions, Boston Center for the Arts

Sharon B. Ingraham, CPG (The Communications Policy Group), Acton, MA

Heidi Irgens, operations manager, Bay Area Video Collective

Michael Jensen, USTEC (US Telecommunications Experts Center), University of Nebraska at Omaha, International Center for Telecommunications Management

Mike Johnson, assistant executive director, Northwest Community TV, Brooklyn Park, MN

Doug Kellner, Department of Philosophy, University of Texas/Austin

Larry Kirkman, executive director of the Benton Foundation, Washington, DC

Adam Knee, the New School for Social Research, New York

Dirk Koning, GRTV (Grand Rapids [MI] Television)

Lori Konopka, public relations coordinator, CNN (Cable News Network), Atlanta

Carl Kucharski, executive director, ACTV/Cable 21, Columbus, OH

Kimberly Anne Kyle, municipal assistance coordinator, Commonwealth of Massachusetts, Cable TV Commission

Louise Lamphere, editor, *Frontiers: A Journal of Women Studies*

Avis Lang, managing editor, *Heresies*

Joseph Langhan, director of programming, Colony Communications, Providence, RI

Gary Larson, access coordinator, Moorhead (MN) Community Access TV

Eric Latzky, the Kitchen, New York

Craig Leddy, editor, *Cablevision*

Maggie Lee, Media Arts Center manager, Little City Foundation, Chicago

Myra L. Lenburg, executive director, Amherst (MA) Community TV

Carla Leshne and Jesse Drew, Paper Tiger TV-West, San Francisco

T. Andrew Lewis, executive director of The Alliance for Community Media, Washington, DC

Nell Lundy, special projects coordinator, Video Data Bank, Chicago

Deborah M. Luppold, general manager, Portland (OR) Cable Access

Marilyn S. Mann, president, NMCLC (National Missing Children's Locate Center), Gresham, OR

Paula Manley, Tualatin Valley Community Access, Beaverton, OR

Byron Marchant, Office of Andrew Barnett, Federal Communications Commission, Washington, DC

Garrett McCarey, executive director, Pittsfield (MA) Community TV

Loretta J. Metcalf, publisher/editor, *The New Voice*

Ralph F. Meuter, dean for regional and continuing education, California State University, Chico

Michael I. Meyerson, University of Baltimore Law School

Dr. Inabeth Miller, executive director, MCET (The Mass LearnPike), Cambridge, MA

Paul A. E. Moeller, director of operations and training, Calaveras Community TV, Avery, CA

Andrea Montoni, public relations director, Mind Extension University, Englewood, CO

Frank Morrow, Alternative Information Network, Austin, TX

Deanna Morse, president, ASIFA, Chicago

Craig M. Muckle, director of public relations and communications, BET (Black Entertainment Television)

Julianne Murrary, manager, WHBC, Willowbrook, IL

Carol J. Naff, executive director, Denver Community TV

Joyce Nako, administrative assistant, Visual Communications, Los Angeles

Congressman Richard Neal, Springfield, MA, and Washington, DC

Barbara Newhouse, associate director, academic programs, Kansas Regents ECC (Educational Communications Center), Manhattan, KS

Margie A. Nicholson, Public Service Media & Marketing, Chicago

Ann Niehaus, Mid-Peninsula Access Corp., Palo Alto, CA

Mary Nordstrom, GTC–3, Columbus, OH

Elsa Norris, Fairfax (VA) County Public Schools

Merrill Oltchick, M-PACT (Municipal Public Access Cable TV), Monson, MA

K. Erin O'Meara, MATA (Milwaukee Access Telecommunications Authority)

Larry Pankratz, director of continuing education, College of Technology, Kansas State University, Salina

Gregory A. Pasi, director, Creative Services, ECI (Executive Communications, Inc.), Pittsburgh, PA

Fred Peniche, Continental Cablevision, Milford (MA) Community TV

Lenny Perry, Lights by Lenny, Tucson, AZ

Debra Pettis, editor, *Fighting Woman News*

Cyrille Phipps, Not Channel Zero, Bronx, NY

Cathy Phoenix, Film and Videomaker Services, American Film Institute, Los Angeles

Barbara Popovich, Chicago Access Corporation

Peggy Psahos, assistant program manager, Ann Arbor (MI) Community Access TV

Robert D. Purvis, legal director, National Institute Against Prejudice & Violence, Baltimore

Tracy Quinn, vice president, communications, Freedom Forum, Arlington, VA

Jeanie Rhoades, education satellite network support assistant, Columbia, MO

John Risk, president, Communications Support Group, Santa Ana, CA

Rosetta Rogers, director, special projects, XPress Information Services, Inc., Denver, CO

Caryn Rogoff and Cynthia Lopez, Deep Dish TV, New York

Temi Rose, Perceptions, Missoula, MT

Jan Rosenthal, director of communications, SCC (Suburban Community Channels), Maplewood, MN

Arlene C. Rubin, executive director, Project LEAP (Legal Elections in All Precincts Educational & Research Fund, Inc.), Chicago

Beverly Salera, executive director, NVYSC (Northern Virginia Youth Services Coalition), Fairfax, VA

Kanti Sandhu, Western Michigan University Media Services Department, Kalamazoo

Lawrence M. Sapadin, president and chair, ITVS (Independent TV Service), St. Paul, MN

Steve Scharl, executive director, WTV–46, Wilbraham, MA

Herb Schiller, Department of Communication, University of California, San Diego

Jennifer Scott, Women Make Movies, New York

Wm. Drew Shaffer, president, RTC (Response TV Corp.), Oakdale, IA

Cynthia Shearer, English Department, Mankato State University, Mankato, MN

Chuck Sherwood, executive director, C3TV (Cape Cod Community TV), South Yarmouth, MA

Paul E. Simon, director, Pocatello (ID) Vision 12/Community Access TV

Judy Skele-Voss, government coordinator, Northern Dakota County Cable Communications Commission, West St. Paul, MN

Faithe Smith, Fairfax County Public Schools, Annandale, VA

Lisa Sporledger, access manager, and Sharon Mooney, board member, Buffalo (NY) Cable Access Media

Steven Rathger Smith, Terry Sanford Institute of Public Policy, Duke University, Durham, NC

Sue Myers Smith, "America's Children," Mountain View (CA) Community TV-KMVT

Windy Spencer, Job Corps Coordinator, AFL-CIO Appalachian Council, Chicago

Lawrence Spotted Bird, development and marketing manager, Native American Public Broadcasting Consortium, Inc., Lincoln, NE

Lisa Stiller, Flying Focus Video Collective, Portland, OR

George Stoney, New York University Department of Film and TV, New York

Carolyn Sturgill, Appalshop Film & Video, Whitesburg, KY

Grace Sullivan, Manchester (NH) Community TV

Polly Taylor and Mickey Spencer, editors, *Broomstick: Options for Women over 40*, San Francisco

Fred Thomas, Alliance for Communications Democracy, Fairfax, VA

Patsy S. Tinsley, publisher/executive editor, Satellite Learning, Alvin, TX

Francene Tobias, community outreach coordinator, QPTV (Queens Public Access TV), Flushing, NY

Shelley A. Treacy, coordinator of community development, A&E (Arts & Entertainment Network), New York

Eric Utne, president and editor-in-chief, *Utne Reader*

Joseph Van Eaton, Miller & Holbrooke, Washington, DC

Kenn Venit, vice president/senior consultant, Primo Newsservice, Inc., Old Greenwich, CT

Kenneth Vest, director of communication resources, AARP (American Association of Retired Persons), Washington, DC

Randy Visser, director, SPTV (Spring Point Community TV Center), South Portland, ME

David Vogel, CTV, Knoxville (TN)

Susan Waller, office manager, *Hot Wire*

Bill Wassmuth, NW (Northwest) Coalition Against Malicious Harassment, Seattle, WA

Margaret Weinstein, Film in the Cities, St. Paul, MN

Rika Welsh, executive director, MATV (Malden [MA] Access Television) and chair of the Northeast Region, the Alliance for Community Media

Rob Wilson, executive producer, Gay Fairfax, Springfield, VA

Mimi Zarsky, program coordinator, NAMAC (National Alliance of Media Arts Centers), Oakland, CA

Pedro Zurita, executive director, Videoteca del Sur, New York

My appreciation also extends to the many libraries and librarians who helped in this effort, particularly Krishna DasGupta of Worcester State College, who guided a computer bibliographic search. Particular thanks also go to the following persons: Tony Lewis of the Alliance for Community Media, who helped inform my overview on the topic; Merrill Oltchick, for keeping it all in perspective; members of the Northeast Region of what was known as NFLCP, especially the Massachusetts group that I chaired; my walking partner, Bitty Tenbrook, for supplying me with an invaluable list of abbreviations for the states; Nolan Bowie, Telecommunications professor at Temple University, for an extensive, careful, and invaluable reading of Chapter 6; the working group on Local Radio and Television of IAMCR, who provided some great suggestions during our last get-together in Guaraja, Brazil; of course my whole family, but especially my oldest son, Will, who took the training and volunteered for the Simsbury, Connecticut, station; and most of all, the devoted group in my town of Wilbraham, Massachusetts, who have been struggling to start up our own community television.

Originally, this book was under the enthusiastic auspices of Lynn Taylor at Greenwood Press, whose hometown was just undertaking community efforts at local programming. Mim Vasan then became its editor, and she has ably seen to the many details necessary to documenting such an ambitious project. Just as they were with my book *The Cosby Show: Audiences, Impact, and Implications* (Greenwood Press, 1992), everyone has been delightful to work with, especially Eric LeStrange and Judy Martin in Marketing, and Maureen Melino in Editorial Administration, who helped with the myriad copyright issues. And it was again a pleasure to work with Sally M. Scott, Production Editor.

Most of all, however, this book owes a debt to the many thousands of volunteers across this country who are actively involved in contributing their expertise to the betterment of their communities, supplying a video voice for access.

COMMUNITY TELEVISION
IN THE
UNITED STATES

Considerations on the Promises and Problems of Community Television

> If electronic media policy is to fortify the public sphere, members of
> the public must be able to use this resource as a public space and in
> support of other spaces. . . . One of the many potential resources already
> exists: public, educational, and governmental (PEG) access channels.
> They exist thanks largely to grassroots activism.[1]
>
> Patricia Aufderheide, The American University, 1992

In this time of general disappointment and disillusionment with media in
general and television in particular, it is instructive to examine the phenomenon of community television in the United States.

While most of us are aware that we are living in a postindustrial Infor-
mation/Communications Age, we simultaneously have to face the fact that
we are living in an age when the movie *Wayne's World*[2] is a top box office
and video rental draw, when television shows like "America's Funniest Home
Videos" and "I Witness Video" get high Nielsen ratings, when computer
and videocassette recorder (VCR) usage continues to climb, and when,
thanks to the Rodney King case of 1991–92,[3] we have become a nation of
video vigilantes, carrying our 12.5 million camcorders around with us practically everywhere.

Local television programming efforts have existed in this country for more
than twenty years, officially so since the Federal Communications Commission (FCC) promulgated rules in its 1972 *Cable Television Report and
Order*[4] mandating cable systems in the Top 100 television markets with
more than 3,500 subscribers to originate community programming. From
the start, the idea has been to promote localism by providing media access.
Yet also from the start there has been a schism between the promise of that
access and its actual implementation and reception. Although the potential
for public, educational, and governmental (PEG) access has been vigorously

addressed and advocated by a number of individuals and groups, its understanding and utilization at a wider level of our society have been seriously deficient.

This book proposes to fill that gap. It begins by introducing the notion of contemporary local television programming efforts, in which more than 2,000 community groups provide some 15,000 hours of original programming per week—more than the annual output of ABC, CBS, and NBC combined and at a cost of about $200 million per year. It defines different types of community television, examines the intrinsic promises and problems of the system, reviews the literature on this subject, and discusses both PEG access and other forms of community television from six perspectives: physical/technical characteristics, history, legal aspects, economic-political factors, social concerns, and shortcomings.

An attempt to compare community television, which typically is associated with cablecasting, is included in Figure 1.1, which discusses similarities and differences between it and traditional American broadcasting. Graphically, this model aims to draw invaluable distinctions between the two systems.

Further chapters discuss organizations affiliated with community television (civic, media, and business), programming types and technicalities, and production and producers; they also include, interspersed in all these discussions, numerous case studies of various operations in the United States. The organic approach—including source(s), content(s), audience(s), product(s), and response(s) to community television—seems critical to its understanding. Emphasis throughout is on a clear presentation of how the many diverse aspects of community television can best be channeled for use by both individuals and groups, and what the implications of all this are both currently and for the future.

The approach of this book is based on the notion of participatory action research, focusing on the social scientific method of observation and insight that can inform the process of change. With historical roots extending to Aristotle and his notion of self-reflection as a way of informing practice, this perspective has been called "praxis," a Greek term equated with the idea of "critically informed practice." Praxis is said to require reflection on three levels: "the exact nature of the action as conducted (and as perceived and understood by its practitioners), the impact or consequences of the action, and its context."[5] The rationale is that reflection can help transform the knowledge base, serving as a guide to further action. Much of the inspiration for community television, after all, derives from the Canadian documentarian Robert Flaherty and his immersion in the environment to produce the 1921 film *Nanook of the North*.

The "participation principle" is certainly operative here. As will be made clear later, my involvement as an activist in and spokesperson for the PEG access movement dates well over a decade. Beginning with a participant observation study of a public access channel that became the subject of my

Figure 1.1
Distinctions between Broadcasting and Cablecasting/Access

	Broadcasting	Cablecasting/Access
Physical/technical		
Transmission	Electromagnetic airwaves	Coaxial wire
Channels	Single/network	Spectrum--infinite
Services	Developed	Auxiliary, but potential
History		
Inception	1930s	Late 1940s
Development	Outlet for advertisers	Improve reception
Legal		
Regulation	FCC and self	Limited FCC; state, local
Economic-political		
Audience type	Mass	Narrow, fragmented
Audience size	Largest possible	Specialized
Market penetration	98+% of all U.S. households	75+% of all U.S. households
Measurement	Ratings	Number of subscribers
Economic feasibility	Highly profitable	Profitable and growing
Economic support	Advertisers	Subscribers' fees, some adv
Means of control	Networks, advertisers	Public
Social concerns		
Public participation	Limited, closed	Encouraged
Access rights	Contingent	Affirmative
Shortcomings		
Limits to growth	Physical--wavelengths	Economic
Style	Slick, professional	Amateurish, unprofessional
Promises	International programming	Diversity, localism, access

doctoral dissertation—I was a scriptwriter, producer, editor, trainer and trainee, fundraiser, volunteer recognition organizer, policy analyst, and then some—my later contributions to the field have mainly been academic. Today I sit on my town's Cable Commission, and I have been instrumental as a volunteer in helping to launch its first-ever community television channel. These experiences have proven invaluable for both a sensitivity to and an appreciation of group dynamics in the process of developing and maintaining PEG access.

In notes to an article that states that public access television provides "not only one of the few existing possibilities for alternative television but also the best possibility for using the broadcast media to serve the interests of popular democracy" (Kellner, 1992, p. 100), Douglas Kellner bemoans the fact that "there is no interventionist consideration of the potential progressive uses of public-access television" (p. 111) and that overviews on the topic are scarce.

I hope this book will address these issues and more, representing a breakthrough for understanding one's rights and responsibilities regarding media, and reconceptualizing attitudes toward how television can be used for positive citizen action.

COMMUNITY TELEVISION—AN OVERVIEW

Evolving as a natural outgrowth to the revolutionary "rights" and countercultural climate of the 1960s, the call for media access was instantly embraced by wide-eyed liberals who saw it as the perfect solution to their desires for disseminating information, particularly to the disenfranchised. Ever since the FCC held its landmark hearings on cable television at the National Academy of Sciences in Washington, D.C., in 1971,[6] a clamor for access to this new communications medium has gathered strength. And, as Johnson and Gerlach (1972, p. 218) have pointed out, that demand came from diverse groups: public broadcasting, the cable industry itself, religious groups, civil rights groups, foundations, lawyers, academics, and especially minority groups. Diversity still marks the movement.

Philosophically, the concept of public access has its roots in John Stuart Mill's social libertarian theory; politically, in First Amendment guarantees of free speech[7]; legally, in FCC and Supreme Court mandates for localism and viewer rights. Aiming to extend the marketplace of ideas beyond those who own the media, Jerome A. Barron (1973) makes the case for access to media for its true proprietors: readers, viewers, and listeners. Kahin and Neuman (1985, p. 6) claim that support for access is rationalized on four related grounds:

1. *Freedom of expression*—Access ensures that diverse ideas can be expressed on television.

2. *Media education*—Access provides an opportunity for individuals and small organizations to learn to use video and television.
3. *Localism*—Access strengthens the local infrastructure by increasing and enhancing local communications.
4. *Public service*—Access provides informative, educational, and cultural programming which is not otherwise available on television.

Noncommercial access to cable television is not affected by the "scarcity of the airwaves" spectrum model. Although it involves a wire-based, point-to-point, subscriber-supported local monopoly, and although its main function is public consumption, the philosophy and the target market differ greatly. Over time, the main function of community television in this form has been as a "bid" item in the franchising process. Control over access channels and resources is addressed by Jesuale and colleagues (1982, p. 88), who say it can be exercised by a city, an advisory board appointed by city officials, the cable company, or an independent, nonprofit, community-based organization. That controlling entity, then, has responsibility for the following:

1. Allocating space on the channels
2. Allocating facilities
3. Developing and managing funding sources and revenues
4. Providing a forum for public input into policy
5. Ensuring that training and technical assistance are available to all sectors of the community
6. Initiating public education and outreach to ensure use of the resources committed

From the beginning, the FCC stipulated that access channels should be made available to the citizenry on a first-come, first-served, nondiscriminatory basis. In 1971, the Center for Analysis of Public Issues declared: "Free public access television channels have the potential to revolutionize the communication patterns of service organizations, consumer groups, and political parties, and could provide an entirely new forum for neighborhood dialogue and artistic expression."[8] "Guidelines for Access,"[9] as outlined by the National Cable Television Association, typically include the following: free air time for at least five minutes, technical equipment and staff, and studio and production facilities for public access channels. While copyrighted material must be cleared and documented to relieve the cable system from liability, typically there are also inherent prohibitions on commercial, service, or political advertisements, lottery information, and/or the presentation of "obscene and indecent" subject matter in programming.

Although the Supreme Court in 1979 abrogated the FCC decision on access channels in the *Midwest Video*[10] case, stating that the FCC had no jurisdiction imposing origination requirements, and that access requirements were outside its regulatory authority, many cable television operators continue to honor franchise agreements that already contained the programming provision, and many local negotiations today continue to include it. There are many reasons for this ongoing process. Preeminently, there is the promise of decentralized media; the promise of grassroots video, where people talk to people, neighbors learn about one another and their common concerns, and minority groups can speak out. There is the promise of personal programming, immediate feedback, and democratic dialogue. The prospects are infinite and intriguing: "Access channels accomplish for cable television a much broader version of what fairness and equal time were intended to accomplish on broadcast television. Access gives a television voice to the dissenter, the unpopular, and the minority as well as to organizations working in the public sector and in the public interest. Access is a video voice for the people."[11]

Second, consider the fact that many diverse citizens and community groups continue to take steps toward getting organized and involved, learning to reorient their attitudes toward television as an active medium for their interests and causes. The next chapter, in fact, is completely devoted to the notion of alternative media and/or using media for agenda-setting and advocacy purposes. Some media organizations, it will be discovered, also provide training far beyond the technical.

Furthermore, many franchise agreements continue to be honored because the cable television industries themselves are by necessity supporting PEG access as attractive "bid" items in their frantic franchising proposals for lucrative major urban markets. And finally, as will be discussed later, with the prospect of video dial tone breathing down their competitive necks, cable companies want to position themselves in as positive a light as possible for community relations.

John R. Bittner (1991, p. 141) describes the cable television's local access concept this way:

Local-access programming is not the glittering lights of Hollywood. Nor is it the elaborate production studios of a major network. It more than likely materializes as one program did, on an October day in a small community of 8,000 people and 1,500 cable subscribers. It is evening, and on a drive in the country a local resident spots a poster tacked to a utility pole: "Halloween Parade—Everyone Welcome—6:30 P.M. October 31, The Fire House Parking Lot." The perfect opportunity for local-access programming.

This is what local-access cable is all about. It is the grass-roots side of television, one that is not possible to incorporate in standard broadcasting stations.

The story of *Community Television in the United States*, as you can already surmise, is one blending far-flung economic, political, and sociocultural interests. Within the last decade, nearly every major communications corporation in the country—including the television networks, print and film industries, and even telephone companies—has invested in the fields of cable television and/or cable technology. Andrew Blau (1991, p. 7), then president of The Alliance for Community Television, has this perspective: "Stripped to the essentials, access centers are education and communication centers in community settings. . . . Perhaps access centers are the laboratories where the future of electronic communications is being developed by tens of thousands of unpaid researchers."

DEFINITIONS REGARDING COMMUNITY TELEVISION

Of the 11,000 cable systems in the United States, serving some 57.2 million households, only about one quarter originate their own television programs; it is those operations that are the focus of this investigation. Since many people are unclear about differentiations between community television types, the following definitions are meant to shed some light on how public access, the grassroots phenomenon being underscored here, differs from other programming, like local origination or leased access. But as Dirk Koning, onetime chair of the *CTR* (*Community Television Review*) editorial review board,[12] reminds us, "The Latin root for words community and communication are almost identical based on the description of them: To share."[10]

Public Access

While access can be public, educational, or governmental (PEG), noncommercial channels programmed by private citizens and/or nonprofit groups and institutions such as schools and municipal governments make up the bulk of public access television. The idea is freedom from the cable operator for grassroots, decentralized media. In its purest form, public access is operated nonhierarchically by artistic and/or advocacy-oriented volunteers.

Francis J. Berrigan (1977, p. 15) finds a basic paradox in the concept of access, as its advocates "share a common mood and tone, at once romantic, radical, and missionary"; yet, the reality is that access is "a matter of operation as well as ideology. Its forms and its tools are electronically based. It involves practitioners, technicians, entrepreneurs, as well as thinkers and social reformers."

The focus in public access tends to be on informational and cultural programming, with about half of the airtime taken up with public affairs topics, such as city or county council meetings, the school board, and/or various community issues. Community calendars and bulletin boards account for the greatest exposure and success of public access. Margot Hardenbergh (1986, p. 6) has written about the difficulty of defining public access, saying it defies a generic description: "For the producer it is a channel to be used on a first come, first-served basis, but . . . the goal is to create unexpected programming, to include people not normally seen on the screen—to provide an outlet for the community to communicate with itself."

Local Origination[14]

Fewer in number nationally than public access channels, local origination is programmed by cable operators, who control program content, production, and funding. Its offerings tend primarily toward entertainment fare. While they can carry local advertising, the channels also make money for the cable company from sales of local sports events, packaging of old movies and television shows, and other low-cost syndicated programming. Nancy Bicknell (1984, p. 9), director of advertising and program development for American Cablesystems, states it clearly: "Local Origination is a business. We have a product and we have customers. We are in the business of local entertainment and information services. We are an integral part of the cable operation, with a direct umbilical cord to the nerve center."

Leased Access

Cable television channels under this arrangement are made available to a variety of users for hourly fees ranging from $50 to $500. While most of the programming consists of conventional television offerings, leased access might also include security systems, home banking, and data and text services like stock market reports, news tickers, and the like.

The cable operator is permitted to sell channel space on a commercial, first-come, first-served basis on the leased access channel; in turn, the user is allowed to sell advertising spots during programming. The goal, according to Loy Singleton (1986, p. 30), is to prevent the cable operator from monopolizing commercial use of cable channels in the community. To date, this channel has not taken off as much as had been predicted; Timothy Hollins (1984, p. 209) points out that about the only place it has had success is Manhattan, "largely for pornographic shows such as 'Ugly George' and 'Video Blue,' supported by advertising for porn shops, massage parlours, sex clubs, and escort agencies."

Community Cable Channels

It is important to note that on some systems, unlike either public access or local origination, the cable operators provide local subscriber services that are typically in the form of programmed pay television. Most of the offerings here fit under the entertainment category, like movies and sports.

For films, local "art houses" have been popular with particular population niches, especially so in the early days of community cable. Sports pioneers using the medium included Madison Square Garden cable in New York, which offered home games of the Rangers (ice hockey), Knicks (basketball), and other local teams; Philadelphia's Prism (for the 'Sixers [basketball] and Flyers [ice hockey]); and Dodgervision, the Los Angeles–based hometown channel. Lately, however, facing competition from the proliferation of video rental stores and sports overexposure on television, community cable channels have had a hard time sustaining their earlier momentum.

While it is rare for local cable systems to produce their own news programs, *News 12 Long Island* runs a twenty-four-hour all-news channel for residents of its more than one hundred towns and villages. A service of Cablevision Systems in Nassau County, New York, this system has become such an important and integral part of the community that the station has sent its own reporters and crews to both the Democratic and Republican national conventions. Local cable news reporting is a growing phenomenon. *Business Week* reports on a number of such activities, citing a prediction by the chief executive officer of Chicago Cable Network: "Just as the 1980s were the decade of national cable networks, the 1990s will be the decade of local cable news networks."[15]

With local cable television advertising experiencing continually spectacular growth, topping $1.8 billion in 1989,[16] prospects for community cable channels look encouraging. Thinking that some of those revenues will be funneled into programming, Dominick and colleagues (1990, p. 204) point out that "once-costly production equipment is being replaced with cheaper, easy to maintain, smaller format gear. This has the potential to enable cable programs to emulate local television stations in production values, content, and audience appeal." Lyle and McLeod (1993, p. 155) point out that as cable access and origination channels become increasingly used as vehicles for local news reporting, "They do provide the potential for expanding the marketplace of ideas, and, when community interest runs high on an issue or event, they may attract an audience significant in its composition if not in numbers."

REVIEW OF THE LITERATURE ON COMMUNITY TELEVISION

Early investigation of both the promise and procedures of community television was undertaken by the Rand Corporation in the early 1970s under grants supported by the National Science Foundation. Initial cable television research at Rand focused on federal regulatory policy, which in 1969 was still in the formative stages; those studies were sponsored by grants from the Ford Foundation and the John and Mary R. Markle Foundation. Then, after the FCC's 1972 *Cable Television Report and Order* asserted its jurisdictional authority, emphasis was placed on encouraging local participation in franchising and implementing processes.

Particular explorations were made on cable's use in education (Carpenter, 1973; Carpenter-Huffman et al., 1974), local government services (Baer, 1973; Yin, 1973a; Jacobson, 1977), and public access (Kletter, 1973; Bender et al., 1979). Some of the focus was on technological considerations (Pilnick, 1973; Pilnick and Baer, 1973; Baer et al., 1974), especially anticipating complex trade-offs and the need for policy alternatives. Where Steven R. Rivkin (1973) outlined federal regulatory policies and rules for cable in terms of protecting local broadcasters, Leland L. Johnson (1975) discussed the practical aspects of taping programs from local commercial and noncommercial stations and then repeating them on otherwise empty cable channels, and Henry Geller (1974) recommended an industry structure dependent on the marketplace rather than governmental regulation. Special concerns were expressed over copyright liability (Besen et al., 1977), control (Yin, 1973b), audiences (Price and Wicklein, 1972; Price and Botein, 1973; Guinary, 1975; Park, 1979), and the arts (Adler and Baer, 1974).

Legal considerations of cable television technology have also received press, notably the following: Don R. LeDuc's *Cable Television and the FCC: A Crisis in Media Control* (1973), Leonard Ross's *Economic and Legal Foundations of Cable Television* (1974), Richard Olin Berner's *Constraints on the Regulatory Process: A Case Study of the Regulation of Cable Television* (1976), Douglas H. Ginsburg's *Regulation of Broadcasting* (1979), Morton I. Hamburg's *All about Cable: Legal and Business Aspects of Cable and Pay Television* (1979), Esther Rit Sinofsky's *Off-Air Videotaping in Education: Copyright Issues, Decisions, and Implications* (1984), Gary L. Christensen's *The New Era in CATV: The Cable Franchise Policy and Communication Act of 1984* (1985), Linda K. Fuller's "The Constitutionality of Cable Technology" (1986), Brenner and colleagues' *Cable Television and Other Nonbroadcast Video: Law and Policy* (1990), and Phil Miller's *Media Law for Producers* (1990).

Of special interest here is Richard C. Kletter's 1973 study, *Cable Television: Making Public Access Effective*. Although it was written just after the FCC rules requiring the channels were drafted, though later lifted from mandatory franchises, this study is critical in terms of the representative optimism surrounding the phenomenon of community television in its introductory days. Emphasis is on television's "addressing the basic information needs of its audience," yet it also treats problems of training, production, program promotion, funding, and apathetic audiences. Kletter is enthusiastic about the concept of neighborhood organization, with television discovering local issues and local cultures. He wants a return to television of "some qualities that have nearly been refined out of it: spontaneity; originality; controversy; realism; even attractive amateurishness" (p. 1). He would like a viewer to be able to see friends on the screen producing his or her own program, and he wants television to provide a forum for community concerns.

Based on Flaherty's aforementioned "participation mystique" in documentary filmmaking, Gilbert Gillespie (1975) attempted to survey 150 city halls in Canada and the United States to see if public access could affect sociocultural aspects of the community. Although nonresponse was high, he found city government in the United States more actively involved in cable television than city government in Canada, with vitality of the system dependent on the cable owner/operator. Its biggest roadblock, according to Gillespie, would be general ignorance of its existence. Among the factors that are instrumental in corrupting the healthy enlargement of the public access cable television (PACT) idea, he identified these (p. 61):

1. Instability of programming as a result of relying too heavily on one source of funding
2. Failure of "seeding" personnel to develop a strong liaison with the local cable ownership and management
3. Failure of "seeding" personnel to develop grassroots support through production workshops
4. The tendency in large metropolitan areas for the development of monolithic, elitist production units comparable to those of the broadcast networks
5. Insufficient available resources or potential for the development of local resources to ensure purchase and maintenance of quality equipment
6. Failure to provide a studio for PACT producers only
7. Incompatibility of equipment and systems in multi-system markets

John A. Ledingham (1982) surveyed thirty-four public access centers in major markets, indicating the following variables for stations that produced more than the mean hours of programming: identified and continuing sources of funding for a center, the existence of staff to assist with production, and a vigorous program of dissemination of information concerning availability of center and staff.

The more recent publications about community television tend to be how-tos, picking up on H. Allan Frederiksen's *Community Access Video* (1972), Michael Shamberg's 1973 *Guerrilla Television*, or Andrew O. Shapiro's 1976 *Media Access: Your Right to Express Your Views on Radio and Television*. They include Bender and colleagues' *Cable Television: Guide to Public Access* (1979), A. C. Lynn Zelmer's 1979 *Community Media Handbook*, Evonne Ianacone's 1980 *Changing More Than the Channel* for the St. Louis Media Access Group, Schaffer and Wheelwright's (eds.) *Creating Original Programming for Cable TV* (1983), Bortz and colleagues' *Great Expectations: A Television Manager's Guide to the Future* (1986), The Media Institute's *Using New Communications Technologies* (1986), Oringe and Buske's *The*

Access Manager's Handbook (1987), the NFLCP Public Policy Committee's 1988 *Cable Access Advocacy Handbook* (Karwin and colleagues) and 1991 *Controversial Programming: A Guide for PEG Access TV Advocates*, Margie Nicholson's *Cable Access: A Community Communication Resource for Non-profits* (1990), Douglas J. Ostling's *Access Producers Handbook* (1990), *ROAR! The Paper Tiger Television Guide to Media Activism* (1991), and NFLCP's second edition of *Public Access Operating Rules and Procedures* (1992).

Audiences

The audience for public access programming has rarely been surveyed (Fuller, 1985c). Although methodology is not specified, David Othmer's 1973 survey of 250 cable subscribers in New York City reported that 30 percent knew what public access was, 20 percent watched occasionally, 5 percent watched regularly, and 70 percent of the sample reported it didn't watch because of difficulty learning when programs would be shown. Furthermore, the report for the Fund of the City of New York found that 7 percent of its random sample was interested in being on access, and that 10 percent had seen someone they knew on the access channel. Another undocumented survey of fifty users/producers of the channel indicated that most received little or no feedback. The point is made that when public access was first introduced there was little interest in its audience—partly from naïveté and partly from a deep conviction that public access was antichannel, an underground medium that should not be guided by the hated Nielsen ratings.

Rudolf Bretz (1975) reported on the Columbus, Indiana, study performed by the University of Indiana Institute for Communication Research (Johnson et al., 1974) using the diary method of obtaining television-viewing time for one week from a 6 percent sample of cable television homes (200 households, 643 persons, 32 percent of the city); it showed that only 20 persons (3 percent of the total) had watched anything at all on the public access channel, 19 out of those 20 for less than one hour. Total public access–viewing time for the sample audience was 0.2 percent of total television-viewing time for the week. Bretz pointed out that oftentimes the staff and volunteers for public access outnumbered its viewing audience.

A follow-up study by the Columbus Video Access Center (VAC) the next year (Ksobiech et al., 1975) used 325 random names from the city's telephone directory to produce 200 responses indicating that the number of persons using the station were up—but no specifics about those citizens were included in the report. When I contacted the senior authors of the studies for further elaboration, I was informed that the station had gone "belly-up." The reason given was that VAC had been funded by only one foundation, Irwin-Sweeney-Miller, which had decided to withdraw its support—a classic case of exactly what Gillespie had warned about.

As part of a descriptive study testing access production variables, Clive J. Enos III (1979) surveyed 640 cable subscribers and 640 nonsubscribers during 1974–75 in New York City (his report does not mention sample methodology), and found a generally negative attitude toward access: 65 percent responded that access programming would not solve community or personal problems.

Patricia Bellamy Goss (1978) conducted a telephone survey of 400+ subscribers to New York City's Manhattan Cable in December 1977, with results indicating that over half of the subscribers were aware of the concept of public access, one third viewed it regularly, and 15 percent saw public access as a reason for subscribing to cable television. Further results indicated that cable subscribers aware of the concept of public access "view more diverse types of programs, and view public access programs for information and educational reasons in higher percentages than typical subscribers not involved in the concept of public access."

A mail survey conducted by Vernone M. Sparkes (1979) of ninety-one past and present users of public access channels in the Toronto area revealed personal contact to be the most important means of diffusing knowledge about access opportunities. No other particular results are reported, but this study is critical in stressing the importance of promotional and facilitative action by expert or professional groups to spread the word on community utilization of its own medium.

In a report[17] to the International Communication Association in San Francisco and to the International Television Studies Conference in London (Fuller, 1984d), I surveyed the town of Longmeadow, Massachusetts, via participant observation both before and after it got involved in community television. An affluent suburb of Springfield, Longmeadow had 74 percent penetration in a population of approximately 8,000, or 5,200 households. Located geographically in a Top 100 television market, knowledge of and enthusiasm for its public access station (PACTL) was such that it had over 150 volunteers prior to its debut in December 1981.

A telephone survey was conducted of 428 cable subscribers, 11 percent of the designated population. Six pretests were performed, then calls were made from January to March of 1983 via the survey instrument available in Appendix 1, "PACTL Audience Survey." The sample design was determined by the local cable company and included systematic sampling of each tenth household (54 percent of the survey sample), then each ninth household (33 percent of the survey sample); the response rate, in other words, was high. Demographics included 39 percent male, 61 percent female; a mean age of 40; 96 percent Caucasian; a fairly equal religious split among Protestant, Catholic, and Jewish faiths; 73 percent married; 45 percent employed; mean income of $50,000; and 74 percent college educated.

Since the major purpose was to determine whether public access had made a difference in the town, the audience survey was valuable in finding

reportage from 75 percent of the sample that cable had changed their television viewing habits, especially in terms of watching more television overall.
An impressive 94 percent indicated familiarity with the public access channel, 45 percent being regular viewers. That "regular viewing" was found to
be significantly related to knowing people involved with PACTL, thinking
it had increased a sense of community, age, being active in town, being
involved in voluntarism, and being a registered voter. While only 8 percent
of the sample had ever been part of public access, mostly as performers, a
surprising one hundred people indicated they might get involved with the
station in the future.

In response to various opinion questions, 73 percent of the respondents
felt that special interest groups, like "pro-abortion, environment, anti-
nukes," should be allowed to air programs on PACTL. As to whether content
should be educational or entertainment-oriented, 79 percent wanted a combination. Regarding involvement in town government, the predominant
opinion was that the selectmen's meetings should be shown weekly, 57
percent of the sample stating that public access had increased their knowledge of town practices. Highly significant correlations were found between
increase in knowledge of town government and regular viewing of the selectmen's meetings; nearly one third (29 percent) had even spoken to selectmen about issues aired over the channel. To the question on whether
PACTL had increased a sense of community, 49 percent said yes, 36 percent
a thoughtful "don't know." And, keeping Gillespie's criteria for a successful
community television operation in mind, numbers reportedly willing to contribute to fund-raising costs of the station (48 percent yes, 32 percent depends) were most encouraging (Fuller, 1984c).

The Public Awareness Committee of the Raleigh (North Carolina) Telecommunications Commission performed a "Survey of Viewers of Public Access Programming"[18] in 1988. The executive summary stated (p. 1): "Results
of a telephone survey of almost 400 randomly selected cable television subscribers in the Raleigh franchise area in February show widespread awareness of and support for community access programming. A majority of
respondents state that they have watched the community access channels
(CACs); most of the latter, within the previous two weeks." More specifically,
of the 387 respondents, some 76 percent were aware of the CACs, 58 percent
saying they had watched one or more. Conclusions from the study included
"a clear mandate for continued funding and other support by the City of
Raleigh and by Cablevision of Raleigh," additional publicity and promotions
for the channel, continued support, additional staff, and the performance of
viewership surveys on a regular basis (pp. 8–9).

In 1990 Frank Jamison[19] reported on a multisite public access audience
study from Michigan that found 47 percent of television viewers watching
the community channels, a quarter of them at least three times biweekly,
and nearly one half of the sample (46 percent) saying it was "somewhat" to

"very" important in their cable subscribership decision. The next year, a survey of cable viewers of the Colomo Community Center of Sacramento, California, found two thirds of 408 respondents to a telephone survey both knowing of and watching the channel.[20]

Stating that "few media policy issues evoke as much passion as the debate concerning access to community cablevision channels," Atkin and LaRose (1991, p. 354) have used a regionally diversified sample of cable viewers to investigate viewer patronage of community channels. Results revealed that while nearly 60 percent of all homes serviced by cable are also served by at least one community channel, some 16 percent of the audience reported viewing the channel within the week preceding their interview. The authors point out that "even though a minority of cable systems provide community access, they reside in larger markets and are able to reach a majority of subscribers" (p. 357). Their findings suggest that access viewers were likely to be better educated, older, retired, and to have lower incomes, a profile that does not quite fit the upscale information seeker typical of other public affairs consumers; still, they add (p. 361) that "these attributes are likely artifacts of one another, as viewers further along in the lifecycle (and perhaps, retired) would likely be more literate in public affairs and hence interested in PEG programming. . . . It seems that access presents an alternative to people in a lifestyle and socioeconomic phase where opportunities and alternatives for public affairs participation are few (in terms of mobility and money)." Results also suggest that PEG programmers develop a policy of "triage in terms of resource allocation. That is, rather than trying to maximize access, coordinators and access group leaders could focus on a smaller number of higher quality production" (p. 362). The value of this study is its emphasis on national viewership trends, a direction in which survey research in the area of community television needs to move.

PERSPECTIVES ON COMMUNITY TELEVISION

Because the concept of community television can be approached from a variety of vantage points, the remainder of this chapter discusses the medium technically, historically, legally, economically and politically, socially, and with regard to its limitations.

Physical/Technical Characteristics

First, it is critical to keep in mind that community television typically is made possible by means of a cable television technology that involves the transmission by coaxial wire of broadcast services for space in the communications spectrum.

Cable television, James W. Roman (1983, p. x) points out, "has taken the older, more traditional broadcast technology and combined it with satellites and computers to create a new electronic environment that markets enhanced services to the consumer." From its inception, cable television, like other new communications technologies, has been "software-driven"—dependent on public needs and wants.

Physically, this is how cable transmissions operate: Initially, they receive the signals of television broadcasting stations or satellites, and then they amplify those signals for retransmission by the cable wire or microwave to paying subscribers of the system. Instead of going "over the air," cable television sends its signals through the enclosed, artificial environment of coaxial wire on a portion of the VHF spectrum where a wide band of frequencies—as high as 400 MHz—can be used. While both broadcasting and cablecasting are based on the economic principle of competitive free enterprise, while both serve the public by means of private monopolies, and while both systems are regulated by the FCC, there are nevertheless enormous discrepancies.

While Carl Pilnick (1973) called cable a hybrid—an entertainment distribution network, a quasi-public communications system, and a transmission medium for a variety of new "non-broadcast services"—Ralph Lee Smith termed cable television "an electronic highway" in his 1972 ground-breaking book, *The Wired Nation*.[21] The technology certainly is in place for facilitating a number of functions, ranging from home libraries to facsimile data to mail delivery, crime detection and prevention, emergency services, home shopping and banking, travel, and so on. Further, cable television holds infinite promise in terms of instant, immediate viewer interaction with the program source.

The physical aspects of community television's very existence have implications for going beyond the legal arguments of scarcity of the airwaves spectrum. Douglas H. Ginsburg (1979, p. 335), writing about broadcast regulation, has expressed concern: "Because of cable's ability to carry large numbers of channels, interest in its exploitation, and in some quarters fears of its implications, has been intense."

History

Sue Miller Buske (1986, p. 12), former executive director of NFLCP (National Federation of Local Cable Programmers), draws a parallel between the development of community television in the 1970s and the invention of the printing press in the 1450s in terms of access for the people. The technology has been around since the 1930s, when cable technology came into existence as a means to aid reception from conventional broadcast signals, which were poor owing to geographic location. First used in broadcasting to interconnect the television networks with their affiliate stations, coaxial cable evolved as the ideal means of providing television fare to individual homes, although that had never been its intent. Soon it was realized that there was more power in the medium itself than in the programming of what until recently had been called Community Antenna Television (CATV) was transmitting. A whole new industry was born. Mary Alice Phillips (1972), documenting the history of this development, labeled cable television a uniquely American phenomenon. Audiences for the service burgeoned, as did the growth of multiple system operators (MSOs).

Cable's growth began slowly, taking off in the 1960s as the number of operating cable systems expanded along with a continually rising number of subscriber households. Film- and videomaker Helen DeMichiel phrased it this way: "Giddy and smug, passionate and righteous, alternative media activists and artists of the late 60s and 70s dared to predict a future rosy with proliferating visions of a decentralized and creatively intelligent video democracy."[22]

The introduction in 1968 of Sony's portapak, a twenty-pound, handheld, black-and-white video camera and shoulder-carried recorder, accelerated the process, creating "the most powerful form of media accessible to ordinary people. The beginnings of an underground, alternative video community began to form" (Bowe, 1991, p. 53).

Academic attention began when Antioch College initiated its Community Media Department in 1969; two years later, George Stoney and Canadian documentarian Red Burns founded the Alternate Media Center at New York University "to promote use of cable technology by local, nonprofessional communicators." Around that time, media critic John J. O'Connor of the *New York Times* wrote, "The content can be miserable. The technical quality is often atrocious. And, as established television executives insistently note, nobody is watching anyway. Yet the experiments with public access on cable television continue to be among the more significant in contemporary communications."[23]

Guerrilla television, according to Ralph Engelman (1990, p. 24) was yet another force to be reckoned with in the development of public access. Coming from outside both the cable industry and established institutions, radical video collectives in the late 1960s and early 1970s included utopian-minded groups such as Raindance, Videofreeks, People's Communication Network, Video Free America, Ant Farm, Global Village, and the May Day Collective.

With the introduction of satellite communications in 1975, expanding programming and promising diversified services, a great deal of attention focused on the cable industry, and prospects for it increased exponentially. It was concern about how this new technology would be used that caused a group of persons to band together to create the National Federation of Local Cable Programmers in 1976, with fewer than one hundred community centers then in existence. Consider: That number is now more than 2,000. The "magic number" for cable penetration was reached in 1988, when more than half the television households in the United States were cable subscribers; today, according to the National Cable Television Association,[24] there are more than 11,000 cable systems in operation, delivering the service to 61.5 percent of all television homes, more than 57 million households in all. And consider: Revenues from subscribers are approximately $20 billion.

The community access movement, according to Howard Horton (1982), is part of a general media movement that has emerged since the 1966 *United Church of Christ v. FCC* decision that gave citizens' groups authority to intervene in license renewal proceedings, as well as the development of Action for Children's Television (ACT) and other consumer advocacy organizations, plus the advent of inexpensive, easy-to-use, portable video technology and FCC emphasis on deregulation. He distinguishes three different groups who converged in the video movement: video artists, counterculturalists, and community activists who saw television not only as a product but also as a process tool.

Johnson and Gerlach (1972) cite the *Business Executives' Move for Vietnam Peace*[25] case of 1971 as giving the doctrine of outright access to the airwaves its biggest boost. When the group wanted to buy radio time for spot announcements against the Vietnam War, they were turned down by the stations on the grounds that they didn't sell time for discussion of controversial issues, a decision supported by the FCC; later, however, the U.S. Court of Appeals for the District of Columbia reversed that opinion as a violation of First Amendment rights.[26]

More recent trends for community television today include combining local programming with access and the establishment of nonprofit access corporations. To keep all this in perspective, John Downing (1991, p. 7) of the University of Texas at Austin reminds us that the phenomenon is not unique to the United States but is "an integral part of a much wider international movement, a movement with many powerful historical forebears, to open up media communication, to liberate it from the strait jackets imposed subtly or unsubtly by the powers that be, to extend our connections with each other and to expand our awareness of each other's situations and problems." Patricia Aufderheide (1991, p. 62) would add that "access—lacking a national substructure as public television did until 1967—is still in its pre-history."

Legal Aspects

Community television via public access derives its existence legally from the First Amendment notion protecting free speech, a doctrine confirmed in the Supreme Court's 1969 *Red Lion* decision[27]: "It is the right of the public to receive suitable access to social, political, esthetic, moral, and other ideas and experiences which is critical here." Although that provision has not been specifically carried over to cable television, the legal principle of access to the broadcast media has at least been established (Fuller, 1986).

Figure 1.2 lists FCC requirements related to public access channels, requirements that, according to Engelman (1990, p. 39), represent "a milestone in the history of community television (as) a confluence of forces—technological, institutional, and ideological."

As with broadcasting, chief regulatory responsibility for cablecasting and, by default, community television, falls under the jurisdiction of the FCC. The major documents relating to this arrangement are various FCC Reports and Orders, discussed in Benno C. Schmidt's book *Freedom of the Press vs. Public Access* (1976, pp. 202–6).

First Report and Order, 1965: Carriers that served cable systems were required to condition relay service on the cable system's agreement to carry the signal of local stations, and to refrain from duplicating the programs of local stations, both simultaneously and within fifteen days before or after the local broadcast.

Second Report and Order, 1966: Carriage and nonduplication rules were extended beyond microwave relays to the cable system, the FCC asserting its jurisdiction over cablecasting for the first time. By declaring which major markets' distant signals could not be brought into the Top 100 markets (which service almost 90 percent of television households in the country), the FCC virtually froze cable expansion. And although it was hoped that this decision would expand UHF broadcasting, that result did not materialize. These rules were sustained in 1968 by the Supreme Court's decision in *U.S. v. Southwestern Cable Co.*

The next applicable federal case came the same year in *Fortnightly Corp. v. United Artists TV* (later reaffirmed in 1974 with *TelePrompTer Corp. v. Columbia Broadcasting Service*) on the issue of copyrighting. As the FCC was working at the highest jurisdictional level to restrict cable television from the major markets, a lower court tried to rule against cable as an infringement of copyright protection; however, *Fortnightly* claimed that cable systems did not "perform" according to copyright laws, and the FCC affirmed its power over cable. The commission used that power to aid broadcasters, saying that cable's nonpayment for programs was unfair, so it should be kept from the Top 100 markets.

Third Report and Order, 1972: "Cable systems were obliged to carry local broadcasters' signals without simultaneous duplication, but were also allowed to import a number of distant signals measured by reference to the size of the market in which they operated." While cable systems in the Top 100 markets were allowed to import at least two distant signals, complex rules were added for protection of network and syndicated programming.

Some other court cases relevant to community television are outlined in the NFLCP *Yellow Pages* (Cardona, 1992, p. 128), notably the following:

- *Quincy Cable TV v. FCC*, 1985—Scarcity rationale does not apply to cable regulations, and regulatory requirements that cable operators carry "significantly viewed" over-the-air signals violates the First Amendment.

Figure 1.2
FCC Requirements Related to the Public Access Channel

<u>General requirements</u>:
1.The system must maintain at least one such non-commercial channel.

2.At least one public access channel shall always be free.

3.The system must maintain and have available for public use at least minimal equipment and facilities necessary for the production of programming.

4.The system may not assess production costs for live studio presentations of less than five minutes.

5.The system may not exercise any control over program content (except as mentioned below).

6.Finally, the system must establish operating rules for the channel.

<u>Operating rules</u>:
1.Access is to be first-come, first-served, non-discriminatory.

2.A prohibition on the presentation of any advertising material designed to promote the sale of commercial products or services (including advertising by or on behalf of candidates for public office).

3.A prohibition on the presentation of any lottery information (as in the cablecasting rules).

4.A prohibition on presentation of obscene and indecent matter (as in the cablecasting rules).

5.Permission of public inspection of a complete record of the names and addresses of all persons or groups requesting access time. (The record must be retained for two years).

- *City of New York v. FCC*, 1987—FCC has authority to preempt local technical standards for a particular class of cable channels and substitute less onerous standards.

- *Erie Telecommunications, Inc. v. City of Erie*, 1988—City did not violate First or Fourteenth Amendments by requiring cable company to pay fees under its franchise and access agreements with the city.

- *City of Lansing v. Edward Rose Realty, Inc.*, 1992—City did not have authority to demand permanent easements through private apartment complexes for the purpose of allowing cable company to service tenants, because primary benefactor of the proposed easements would be the cable company rather than the public.

Five other selected court cases, from federal district courts, are also briefly discussed:

- *United States v. AT&T*, 1982—Court approved, with some modifications, antitrust consent decree which removed from the Bell system the function of supplying local telephone service, eliminated most line-of-business restrictions, and generally required equal access to interconnection facilities.

- *Berkshire Cablevision of Rhode Island v. Burke*, 1985—City's requirement that cable company provide seven public access stations did not violate First or Fourteenth Amendments; appeal vacated as moot because franchise was awarded to another applicant.

- *Missouri Knights of the Ku Klux Klan v. City of Kansas City, Missouri*, 1989—Cable operators cannot exercise any editorial control over public access channel nor can they eliminate the channel, and city cannot effectively suppress objectionable speech by eliminating the public access channel. (Note: This case is discussed in detail in Chapter 3, under "Controversial Programming.")

- *Preferred Communications, Inc. v. City of Los Angeles*, 1990—Cities may require cable franchises to give the city free use of the cable facilities, may require franchisees to waive all rights to recover from the city for any claims arising out of the franchise or its enforcement, and may require franchisees to pay franchise fees; the city may not require franchisees to provide public access production facilities, equipment and staff, character generators, or portable production facilities.

- *Madison Cablevision, Inc. v. City of Morgantown*, 1991—Where there was physical and economic capacity for only one cable system in the area, the city was not required to grant franchise to incumbent cable operator, but could instead establish municipally owned cable system.

Jurisdiction of cable is encouraged at the local level, then, but it is obviously not very well thought through. Bob Ronka (1981, p. 9) comments: "For all their potential benefits, public access channels also pose a legal and political dilemma. How do we ensure public access while also avoiding controls over content? How do we protect the cable operator from the ire of the city council member who is the subject of political critiques on the air and, simultaneously, is the grantor of the cable franchise and arbitrator on the requests for rate increases and franchise renewals?"

Although the rules were spelled out, their implementation was not delineated. Walter S. Baer (1973, p. 137) encouraged communities to consider these factors during a franchise period and/or through separate negotiations with the cable operator: administering the public access channel, program scheduling, use of production facilities and equipment, "quality" standards for access programming, charges for production costs, funds for public access, and access to grandfathered, or already long-existing, systems and those outside the major markets.

Contending that the FCC mainly wants to protect local broadcasters, Steven R. Rivkin (1973) sees its views of regulatory programs as intuitive and evolutionary. Some of the technical standards imposed by the FCC have included the following: frequency boundaries of cable channels, frequencies of the visual and aural carriers, visual signal levels, variations, rm voltage, peak-to-peak, channel frequency responses, ratio of noise to interference, terminal isolation, and external radiation. Leonard Ross (1974, pp. 52–76) has pointed out how the proposal to change cable television's regulation status from franchised private communications carrier to "common carrier" involves both practical and theoretical problems, but Fuller (1986, p. 125) argues that "while spectrum space has been reserved for use by common carriers, cable operators have had to negotiate rates for their services on a diminished bargaining power basis. According to the FCC's bifurcated jurisdictional structure, there is a dual licensing system recognizing local authorities that issue franchises or licenses, subject to federal standards by means of certificates of compliance."

Calling cable a "regressive mass medium," Don R. LeDuc (1973) considers the role of the FCC as an independent arm of Congress, a quasi-executive agency. Yet, he says the alternative, freeing communications technology from competitive controls, might result in a chaos of techniques incompatible with public needs. A new federal agency would encounter the same problems of bureaucracy, while strengthening the state regulatory role might simply result in balkanizing national systems into narrow sectional services.

There are a number of issues to consider regarding the legality of community television:

Censorship—Beyond the rules and restrictions mentioned in Figure 1.2, the cable operator has no censorship control over either programming content or producers on public access channels. Schmidt (1976, p. 244), in fact, takes this attitude: "Many Commission (FCC) and judicial decisions have pointed to the pre-eminent value of diversity and expression over the air."

Reporting in *The Wired Island: The First Two Years of Public Access to Cable Television in Manhattan* (1973), David Othmer noted that only four programs had been censored: two as pornographic, one as possibly libelous, and another as possibly commercial. While nudity and four-letter words were not uncommon on the channel, no complaints had been filed with either the New York Office of Telecommunications or the cable companies. Both tapes rejected as pornographic were from films in the "Experiments in Art and Technology" series, one of which depicted sexual intercourse and the other an attempt at masturbation by a patient in traction in a hospital; neither producer objected to the censoring. The tape censored as potentially libelous involved a woman's account of what she felt was medical malpractice, but when she redid the tape eliminating individual names it was approved. And the tape questioned on commercial grounds was a Global Village one on transsexuals that was originally rejected not for its subject matter, which included views of transformed genitalia, but for the inclusion of clips from television commercials showing various beauty aids, such as skin lotion and hair remover; once the commercials were removed, the tape was shown on the public access channels with no repercussions.

Yet, as Terry Clifford (1982, pp. 389–90) has pointed out, New York City's public access programming is a phenomenon "outrageous and lively. In these days of unprecedented disgust with network television, public access offers instant exposure and an opportunity to strike back at the media . . . short of actual coitus, pretty much anything can go, as long as it happens after 11 P.M." Censorship remains a hot topic relative to community television, as will be evident in the chapter on programming.

On September 14, 1993, a panel of the U.S. Court of Appeals for the District of Columbia Circuit heard an appeal by The Alliance and its coalition partners regarding the FCC's PEG access and leased access censorship rules challenging the constitutionality of provisions in the 1992 Cable Act. Arguing that if the onus of censorship implementation was on cable operators, who are often inherent competitors of access programmers and hostile to their needs, lawyers for access rights were optimistic with the FCC's reconsiderations of its vague censorship regulations. Still, PEG access censorship issues undoubtedly will continue to need interpretation.

Copyright is yet another matter.[28] Pool and Alexander (1973, p. 98) discuss how abundance brings a wide diversity of tendencies and views, which inevitably increases the amount of irresponsible and even illegal matter that is available; clearly, there is too much to monitor.

As was noted earlier, the *Fortnightly* decision took liability for copyright infringement from cable systems. Since it took effect in 1976, the General Revision of the Copyright Act "provides a compulsory license that permits cable systems to carry those signals currently authorized for retransmission by the FCC upon payment of a specified percentage of revenues" (Besen et al., 1977, p. v). Fees are then distributed among the owners of the copyrighted programs that are carried by the cable system. The National Cable Television Association guidelines on copyright include the following: "Operating rules should specify procedures to insure that copyright clearances have been obtained. To relieve the system from copyright liability, rules could require each user to furnish appropriate documentation that, where copyrighted material is included in the program, clearance had been obtained" (Kletter, 1973, p. 64).

The *certificate of compliance*, according to Price and Botein (1973, p. 6), comes from Section 76.11 of FCC rules stipulating that "no cable television system shall commence operation or add a television broadcast signal to existing operations unless it receives a certificate of compliance from the Commission." The franchisee must submit a document explaining the following:

1. How the system proposes to fulfill the goals of federal regulations establishing a channel for educational uses and a channel for local government uses.
2. How the system's plans are consistent with federal regulations requiring the establishment of a special channel for public access—that is, the right of individuals and groups to reserve time for the distribution of their own television programming.
3. The system's plan for meeting federal requirements that systems in large markets locally originate to a significant extent and that systems in small markets provide certain programming facilities.
4. How the franchise fulfills the federal expectation that cable systems will be built in time and that cable will be equitably spread throughout the franchise area.
5. How initial subscriber rates were set, and the procedure to be followed when subscriber rates are to be amended.
6. How the franchise process met standards requiring a "full public proceeding affording due process."

Although legally the FCC was forced to rescind its requirement for public access in 1979, the Cable Communications Policy Act of 1984 specifically allowed franchises to negotiate for public channels but did not contain any mandate for public access. The House report[29] described public access at that time as "the video equivalent of the speaker's soap box or the electronic parallel to the printed leaflet."

Tom Karwin (1986) has proposed that the growth of community television has been hindered by lack of sufficient and consistent operating resources, and he calls for state regulation of franchise fee usage to support access. Arguing that "policy reform checking the cable industry's power could lay the groundwork for other uses of the service as a public space," Patricia Aufderheide (1992, p. 56) of American University cites PEG access as an already existing resource, a valued community service that helps strengthen the public sphere. She envisions cable television policy positioned in the public interest as improving the "dismal legal situation for access":

• A percentage of channel capacity—in a fixed, low range of numbers—could be reserved for public use on all cable systems.

- Centers should universally have funding for professional staff, which would not mitigate access's value as a public space.
- National public cable channel capacity, with protected funds to avoid both censorship and the distortions of corporate underwriting, could further broaden the public forum.
- Such national channel capacity would boldly raise the perennial problem of who should broker information and how . . . for instance, users might have to meet a minimum standard of organization.
- Another resource for such a reinvigorated public interest could be a national video production fund, with its products available for distribution through all televisual vehicles. (pp. 60–61)

Economic-Political Aspects

More than two decades ago Charles Tate of the Urban Institute (1971, p. 24) declared that the economic success of a cable system is determined by the following factors: (1) total population base, (2) housing density, (3) market saturation, (4) number of channels available, and (5) the quality of reception for over-the-air broadcast television signals. Today, the cable industry is doing incredibly well, having become a multibillion-dollar business.

"Cable programming is cheap compared to broadcast television," Ben Achtenberg (1974, p. 34) reminds us, "but it is not free." What keeps the cost of community television down is the portapak videotape recorder, which can go almost anywhere and record almost anything; it costs less than $1,000, or it can be rented for about $50 a day. Studios run to about $10,000, more or less, depending on what facilities and extras are desired. And videotape itself is quite reasonable, at about $15 per half-hour reel. Consider, too, Atkin and LaRose's (1991, p. 362) comment that community programming operations range anywhere from $10 to $100 per subscriber, depending on the franchise agreement.

Organizationally, community television fits into one of these management models: institution-based, such as schools, libraries, or churches; cable company–managed local origination; urban access management corporations, incorporated as nonprofit, tax-exempt entities separate from the cable company and the city, overseers of access administration and development; and independent citizens' organizations, the traditional grassroots structure where the governing board is elected by its own members and operation is dependent upon the system's townspeople. Support can come from members' contributions, grants, service contracts, and/or the cable company— but is most of all highly dependent on volunteer efforts.

Early "seed" money for public access experiments was provided by grants from the Markle Foundation, the Stern Fund, the Schumann Fund, the Kaplan Fund, the America the Beautiful Foundation, and the New York State Council of the Arts.[30] Michele Raymond (1980, p. 69) suggests as other potential sources of funds "housing grants, federal grants, educational grants, state and local grants, as well as private foundation monies." Some local money might additionally come from cable television tax revenues.

، As cable television is basically a local issue, it is therefore essentially a political phenomenon. Stemming from authorization by the Communications Act of 1934 for Congress to regulate interstate commerce, cablecasting undergoes its federal regulation, as does broadcasting, "in the public interest, convenience, and necessity." State approaches to cable television are discrepant, ranging from imposing more restrictions than the FCC requires to substantial deregulatory policies. States often transmit franchising authority to local governments through legislative grants, receiving financial support from established state fee assignments. They also usually allow local municipalities to decide ownership issues in the franchising process, to determine program content standards, privacy legislation, pole attachment rules, access requirements, service extensions and interconnections, and fraudulent reception laws, and even to maintain ongoing assessments of their cable operations.[31] In most instances, final decisions rest with the local issuing authorities for franchises,[32] although states are increasingly getting involved in the many complex issues surrounding cable television.

In the Commonwealth of Massachusetts, for example, cable is regulated by Massachusetts Cable Antenna Television[33] at 100 Cambridge Street in Boston, a panel established according to the state's General Laws (Chapter 166A) of 1971. The Massachusetts Cable Commission became, in 1980, "the first agency in a regulating state to take rate deregulation action, basing its new policy on the presence of competitive services; that is, the availability of at least three over-the-air television signals" (Jesuale et al., 1982, p. 14). Its stated mission is "to oversee the cable industry in Massachusetts in a manner that will provide a high level of service available across the state; promote consumer protection; and encourage private capital investment and employment in a manner that will expand the service offered to residential consumers, as well as private business and government." Another important goal of the commission is the enhancing and expansion of local programming; in support of the contention that "community television provides significant civic benefits for individual communities," it manages and oversees judging for an annual Community Television Awards Contest.

Yet, as is well-known, citizen advocacy can be incorporated at the local, state, and/or national levels. Price and Wicklein (1972, p. 94) suggest these sources either for obtaining information or, reciprocally, making one's views known:

1. Chairman, FCC

2. Senators and representatives

3. Chair, Subcommittee on Communication of the House Commerce Committee

4. Chair, Subcommittee on Communication, Senate Interstate and Foreign Commerce Committee

5. Office of Telecommunications Policy, White House

6. State public utilities commission

7. Director, CATV Bureau, FCC

8. State legislators

9. Local mayor

10. Local city council

Politically, community television can be invaluable to politicians and constituencies alike. Head and Sterling (1990, p. 348) point out that "on a cable channel, meetings, hearings, and presentations on local issues can be carried to the bitter end without interruption. Live coverage of an issue important to just a few hundred residents may be justified on local cable channels but not on a broadcast station." Both candidates and incumbents alike are increasingly finding their own stations useful tools for being seen and heard by varying past and future potential voters. A recent article in the *Boston Globe* (Iudica, 1991, p. W1) is relevant:

Local cable television shows traditionally have been forums for the weighty and the wacky. Live coverage of selectmen's meetings and zoning board hearings are part of programming lineups that include talk shows on the paranormal, beauty pageant patter and celebrity rap sessions.

In the past few years, however, producers of local access TV have found that the little magic box is a useful medium for educating what they call an apathetic public that expects to be entertained and informed with the flick of a remote control. As a result, more serious shows with political bents—often with local politicians as hosts—are cropping up.

Adrian E. Herbst (1992), an attorney with the law firm Moss & Barnett of Minneapolis, has prepared an invaluable document on this topic: *Restrictions on Public Access Channels: Candidates on Access in an Election Year*.

In March 1982, Senator Barry Goldwater (R-Arizona) introduced Bill S.2172, to "increase the role of the FCC in cable regulation, pre-empting state and local authority in certain areas, set aside a percentage of channel capacity for educational, municipal and public channel programmers, establish a ceiling on franchise fees, and allow state and local governments to regulate basic rates."[34] The bill required cable companies to devote a maximum of 10 percent of their channels to community programming, but would make it illegal for communities to include access as a franchise condition. While some critics complained that the bill could pull the plug on community input, most people knew that most local programming was already so engrained that it wouldn't be much of a threat. S.2172 died, but it was reintroduced as S.66 in April 1983, with amendments such as Section 606, on access channels:

1. A cable system operator may offer in a franchise to dedicate or set aside channels for public, educational, governmental or other channel users.
2. The franchising authority and the cable operator may establish rules and procedures for the use of the channels set aside or dedicated pursuant to this section.
3. Until such time as there is demand for each channel, full time for its designated use, public, educational, governmental, or other channel programming may be combined by the cable system operator on one or more channels, and to the extent time is available on such channels, they may be used by the cable system operator for the provision of other services.[35]

On June 14, 1983, S.66, sponsored by Senate Commerce Committee Chairman Robert Packwood (R-Oregon) passed overwhelmingly 87 to 9. Hailed as the first "national policy" for federal regulation of cable, the bill stripped local government of control of both rate setting and renewals of contracts except under exceptional circumstances. Yet, proponents of access channels were not too worried, as the cable television industry at that point had been heading toward deregulation for some time, and PEG access had not suffered. If anything, they reasoned, the idea would be that local communities would incorporate a concern for public access along with carefully thought-through negotiations in the franchising process for cable.

The Cable Communications Policy Act of 1984 formally freed cable from most regulations under which it had been governed. Codifying many of the cable regulations that had been developed during the period beginning in the 1960s, the Cable Act gave the FCC jurisdiction over cable television. Of particular significance is Section 521, which called for these provisions[36]:

1. Establish a national policy concerning cable communications.
2. Establish franchise procedures and standards which encourage the growth and development of cable systems and assure that cable systems are responsive to the needs and interests of the local community.
3. Establish guidelines for the exercise of federal, state, and local authority with respect to the regulation of cable systems.
4. Assure and encourage that cable communications provide and are encouraged to provide the widest possible diversity of information sources and services to the public.
5. Establish an orderly process for franchise renewal that protects cable operators against unfair denials of renewal where the operator's past performance and proposal for future performance meet the standards established by this title.
6. Promote competition in cable communications and minimize unnecessary regulation that would impose an undue economic burden on cable systems.

The Cable Act of 1984, while permitting a franchising authority to establish requirements to designate channels for PEG use, prohibits the cable operator from exercising any editorial control over the channels. Otherwise, the FCC rules do not contain separate provisions related to PEG access, although the act does establish "conditions under which a cable operator must designate channels for commercial use by persons who are not affiliated with the cable operator."[37] Aufderheide (1992, p. 52) argues that "since passage of The Cable Communications Policy Act of 1984, the cable industry has thoroughly demonstrated its failure to serve the public interest, as measured minimally in diversity of sources." She would add that since Congress overrode President Bush's veto of the Cable Television Consumer Protection and Competition Act of 1992 on October 5, 1992, the first major revision of the 1984 act was a move "intended to rectify some of the egregious results of the cable business' unchecked market power. However, for access cable nationally, the 1992 cable act worsened the already dismal status quo."[38]

With cable operators being allowed to set their own rates, subscribers screamed when most basic rates increased more than 20 percent; however, they generally liked the fact that the federal court system overturned the "must-carry" rules stating that cable systems were required to carry any and all stations that were significantly received in their local markets.

Although the Cable Act did not mandate that local franchises set aside channels for PEG access, it did require systems with more than thirty-five channels to provide commercial, leased access channels; systems with thirty-six to fifty-four channels to set aside 10 percent of their activated channels for the same purpose; and systems with more than fifty-four channels to reserve 15 percent. Liability was to be assumed by program producers, with cable operators relieved of concerns for libel and other content-related suits. Cable companies were also allowed to set rates and conditions for leased access (Fuller, 1987).

PEG access under the Cable Act of 1984 was established so that the local franchising authority is empowered by Section 531 (a), with specific stipulations varying in number and form depending on the franchise agreement. It is important to underscore here that although cable stations were required to provide leased access channels, the Cable Act did not mandate PEG channels, even though local communities might still demand them in franchise negotiations. To help its constituency, NFLCP made available three packages of information: "The Cable Communications Policy Act of 1984: A Balancing Act on the Coaxial Wires," a law review article by Michael Meyerson; *After the Act*, a thirty-minute videotape produced by Fred Johnson; and an educational packet entitled "The Cable Policy."

Re-regulation has been the most recent move for the cable industry; it was approved in October 1992 over President Bush's veto, to take effect as of April 3, 1993. By law after that date, cable companies are required to provide local broadcast stations in addition to public and government access channels on basic cable service, with prices prescribed by the FCC.

Social Concerns

Television plays an enormous role in our society. With 92.1 million television households in the United States, accounting for 98+ percent of the population—a higher percentage than have indoor plumbing!—we not only watch a great deal (the latest Nielsen data reporting the average daily home use to be seven hours and four minutes),[39] we also increasingly turn to television as our major news source. A number of scholars, notably George Gerbner and his colleagues at the University of Pennsylvania, have long been concerned about the long-term "cultivation" effects of too much television viewing, which they contend distorts perceptions of reality to conform to media portrayals rather than actuality.

The advent of interest in cable television paralleled a disillusionment with traditional broadcasting, a general public distrust of media. Then along came public access, offering an answer to those feeling disenfranchised by the system. Benno Schmidt (1976, p. 204) detailed this scenario:

The bland uniformity of broadcast television was blamed for much of the homogenization of American life, and cable became a symbol of pluralism powerfully attractive to media critics both from left and right. Proponents of equality and participatory democracy saw that the abundance of cable channels might provide an opportunity of access to the media for political, ethnic, and cultural groups excluded from the mass merchandising of broadcast television. Others looked to cable as a means of decentralizing television programming and regenerating local communities. Supporters of cable's promises of diversity, localism, and public access found allies among critics of press concentration and bias. Policy planners decried the FCC's protectionist attitudes in behalf of traditional broadcasting. Thus, the Nixon Administration (whose feud with the networks made support of cable an appealing political weapon), communications egalitarians, futurists fascinated with new hardware and technology, critics of government intervention in economic development, and video radicals all combined to form an unusual constituency for change in official attitudes toward cable.

By the end of the 1980s, cable television seemed to have reached maturity, leveling off to more realistic appraisals of its capabilities. As an industry it began to find its prime target niches, while at the same time remaining mostly responsive to community demands from existing franchises.

A number of advocates have underscored the importance for public access groups of ongoing workshops, where decisions are made by consensus, radicals and archconservatives work side by side, and various motivations for involvement, as outlined above in the Schmidt quotation, can be accommodated.

In answer to the question "What activates the process of seeing themselves on videotape?" Henaut of Canada's Challenge for Change has declared: "Public access proponents subscribe to the macroevolutionary theory that the quality of life in a community has been substantially enriched through decentralization of telecommunications program control."[40]

With a different set of purposes and different audiences, programming on public access can become more personal. Chuck Anderson, author of *Video Power: Grass Roots Television* (1975, p. 79), reminds us that "public access can be a community's conscience, because it is not financially answerable to anybody. It can also provide the opportunity for many people to contribute to the collective information bank that we form by storing facts, attitudes, and opinions from the mass media." Emphasis and rationale are based on their own cultures, issues, and interests (Fuller, 1989). The idea is to "offer remarkable opportunities for local communities. Just imagine being able to watch—right in your own living room—crucial meetings of your school board, town government or selectmen, or local athletic or cultural events."[41] Achtenberg (1974, p. 33) phrased it this way: "The public access channel is the place for individuals and community organizations to present *their* ideas, *their* activities, *their* plans."

On wider issues of affirmative rights and nondiscrimination, public access certainly fills the bill. Price and Wicklein (1972, p. 4) talk of the importance of cable for minority and majority dialogue, promoting "mutual understanding of different points of view by developing lines of communication among disparate groups." Charles Tate (1971, p. 3) fantasized: "Imagine television and radio systems where blacks could program for blacks, Chicanos for Chicanos, Indians for Indians, Puerto Ricans for Puerto Ricans—a system that can give the community a communications service as well as the income and profit that the system receives for providing that service." Concerned about community development, Tate saw possibilities for public access in educational, health, legal and consumer, safety, cultural, and entertainment uses.

Churches have long had an interest in cable television and have had a particular stake in public access. Consider the work of the Office of Communication of the United Church of Christ, or the National Council of Churches' "Cable TV and Video Resource List," in terms of comprehensiveness and comprehension of the potential of access for religious groups. Many churches and temples, as will be seen in the chapter on programming, are actively involved with community television in various religious undertakings.

With the emphasis on and encouragement of "community dialogue," community television in America is seen as offering a promise toward addressing social concerns. It offers an opportunity, according to Walter S. Baer (1973, p. vi), for cable to "become a medium for local action instead of a distributor of prepackaged mass-consumption programs to a passive audience."

In the early days of cable television, Townsend and Marlowe (1974, p. 24) said of the term "electronic soap box" that "it doesn't mean that anybody will listen to you or care what you do, but it does mean that you can do it." The first step, according to Allison Longworth (1976, p. 14), is for people to initiate use of their access channels. After a halting beginning, that movement is finally catching on:

The cable soapbox is now a vital part of almost 2,000 CATV systems across the United States. Each week, these channels produce thousands of hours of original programming. Although widely varied in choice of subject and production quality, this video tidal wave unquestionably shakes the fragile notion that television's limits are defined by the glossy commercial networks. There are spokesmen for the homeless to be seen on these channels, salsa festivals, gays and lesbians giving safe-sex advice, radical Marxists and fundamentalist Christian political candidates holding forth, homeopaths hawking herbal concoctions, community news programs and even, on occasion, museum curators walking the viewer through current exhibitions.[42]

Socioculturally, it is also interesting to note that many of the advocates of access have been drawn from the same group of people throughout its nearly quarter-century evolution. George Stoney (1986, p. 7) of New York University, whom many people credit with being the "Founding Father of Public Access," has wryly noted how many of those "pioneers" have learned not only the rules of the process, but also how to play them. He cites what we have learned to make access work: "a clearly defined legitimacy in the franchise and in law; independence from the forever vacillating policies of cable companies; adequate and constant financial support; and a staff of dedicated facilitators who understand and believe in the concept."

"Access has gone establishment," it would appear—dominated more recently by socioeconomically advantaged whites in suits rather than by diverse young people in jeans and concert T-shirts. Many of the players are the same, if with hair shorn and/or bending to the temper of the times; many other new converts to the process "get" the goal and play accordingly. Stephen Manzi and Ivano Brugnoli (1990, p. 55), both producers of community television, characterize it thus: "For the uninitiated, public access is a bizzaro [sic] universe inhabited by harebrained politicos, pseudo-psychics, and other loons who, 20 years ago, would probably have been holding court in your local bus terminal. Now, with the advent of advanced cable communications, you can enjoy the musings of these miscreants and malcontents from the comfort of your living room sofa." Obviously, wide-eyed enthusiasm for the system has prevailed.

Shortcomings

Despite the many promises, there have always been inherent problems with community television. Overriding them all have been money and audiences.

Citing an article in the *New York Times* from 1971, Gillespie says in his annotated bibliography that "its impact, despite widespread initial publicity and the infectious enthusiasm of its advocates, has been muted by such practical realities as high production costs, technical problems, and lack of public awareness."[43] The battle of the budget has been unrelenting.

The concern with drawing an audience is something else again. With limited resources, access channels have difficulty publicizing their programs, and are in fierce competition for the more professional, fast-paced production of commercial broadcasting from both the networks and other cable television offerings. Market Opinion Research has predicted that by the year 2000, 60 percent of television viewers will not put up with ads on their screens.[44] If one problem is actually getting that audience in the first place, another more difficult one—especially in this era of the remote control for zipping, zapping, and grazing—is actually keeping viewers once they do tune in. Yet, say community television proponents, that is just the point: Programming is deliberately geared to specialized audiences, and its aim is at quality, not quantity in terms of viewing numbers.

This brings up the festering of yet another potential problem on community channels: takeovers by organized special interest groups or individuals. As Jerome A. Barron (1973, p. 258) has noted, "On CATV, it is possible for every local Marx, Rasputin, Voltaire, and Hitler to have his own show." This has been the case with stations that have been monopolized by hillbillies, religious fanatics, and various rights groups throughout the country. Any number of individuals and organizations, controversial or otherwise, have the possibility of controlling access channels if wide enough community interest isn't sparked to counter or at least dilute it.

The interest doesn't even have to be that from a group, but can be for a group—witness the case of Ugly George in New York City, who had great "success" with a wide audience for his filmings of obscenity.

Michele Raymond (1980, p. 73) thinks that the primary problem with cable television is penetration—who is wired and how educated the citizenry is with regard to access. She recommends anticipating the penetration by investigating leasing or adding new channels, being in touch with the FCC along the way.

Furthermore, there is the need to get people involved, going beyond being an audience to becoming producers. Community television needs to encourage its constituency not to be psychologically intimidated by participation. Concerned that we are not "systematically training people to use video as a cultural practice, as a means for critique, for developing 'local vernaculars of analysis,' or as a vehicle for creating and sustaining oppositional cultures," Robert H. Devine (1991, p. 10) argues that public access needs to detach itself from some surrounding myths—namely, that it is about television, when "the truth is that access is about speech and has more to do with community, cultural and economic development than it does with television," or that it is about programming, when "access is more grounded in communication and interaction than it is in programs and audiences."

Most people think of television production only in terms of highly trained, well-paid professional entertainers and technicians, according to Baer (1973, pp. 134–35): "Because it is so foreign to their daily lives, many citizens will neither understand nor be interested in public access when the tools become available to them; others will be afraid of it." Michael V. Sedano (1975) urges a skilled public, involved both as video producers and human receivers in the access adventure—especially teachers and civil libertarians. Workshops and training sessions need to be offered continually. Programs might be set aside for those who are involved to explain their project processes and the feelings that went along with them. And one hopes that passing along information by word of mouth will help this problem, as viewers ask their neighbors about experiences with community television.

Interpersonal communication about the medium of public access is particularly important, as it suffers from a long-standing longhair negative image of being "trivial, self-indulgent, and derivative" (Aufderheide, 1992, p. 62). Consider a *New Yorker* cartoon, with the message "Coming soon to a public-access station near you": Titled "Welcome to Deconstructionist Scrabble, 1992!" it shows three persons sitting around a game board, the first pondering, "What does the blank title really represent?," the middle, " 'Dog' spelled backward is 'god,' yet I still get the same number of points, and the third, "Is it only a word?" The understood message of *boring* comes through loud and clear. But the public perception doesn't always have to be negative; consider too the popular NBC choice for the holiday season of the made-for-television movie *The Story Lady*, starring Jessica Tandy as a retired, bored widow who discovers joy, talent, and recognition reading children's stories on her local public access channel. Built into the script was a satiric view of the corrupting influence of network television and its partner, the advertising community.

Even some supporters take a Voltairean attitude, echoing Pamela Doty's (1975) stance: Who cares? To that Aufderheide (1992, pp. 57–58) responds: "The real value of such services has been and must be in helping to build social relationships within which such speech would be meaningful—constructing that 'marketplace of ideas.' Such a service needs to be seen and used not as a pathetic, homemade version of entertainment, but as an arm of community self-structuring."

Beyond all these concerns, what is really needed goes back to the top: Key followers of the cable industry[45] have said all along that the FCC needs to rethink cable's non–common carrier status and develop a national policy on cable television in general.

Despite the discussions on promise, then, community television remains inherently problematic: Will the phenomenon continue, with issues like cable television re-regulation, increasing use of remote-control devices, even possible telephone company intrusion into the fray? Will there be enough programming? Will there be enough producers of that programming? Will there be an audience? And will there be enough ongoing financial support to allow producers to cablecast and fulfill the many promises of community television? The answers can be a resounding affirmative in all instances, but only if an informed citizenry is encouraged to know about and use its own medium and its rights and responsibilities for access. This book represents a start in that direction. After all, at this point only 16.5 percent of all cable television systems have public access, 12.9 percent educational, and 10.7 percent governmental[46]; there is plenty of room for growth.

Since people have traditionally thought of media in general and broadcasting in particular as closed entertainment and information systems, they might need to reorient themselves to notions of narrowcasting and access in terms of what new communications technologies allow. The key variable is control. Instead of being the passive receiver, the individual has the option of being the active program source, or at least interacting with it. Public access restores First Amendment rights to its true proprietors, giving them control over decisions and decision making in terms of "infotainment" (Fuller, 1984b). After all, the Cable Television Consumer Protection Act of 1990[47] represented a congressional approval of First Amendment and constitutional standards for PEG access.

The alternative is allowing large industrial conglomerates simply to use the technology to control the medium as a purely financial enterprise. Schwartz and Watkins (1973, pp. 80–87) have pointed out that cable began not as a product, but a service—an instrument of social change, a paradigm of man evolving under the influence of his existing environment. As the FCC originally put cable jurisdiction at the state and local levels, it is especially critical that control remain with the people, that individual citizens take advantage of this "viable alternative to the monolithic power of broadcast television."[48]

NOTES

1. Patricia Aufderheide, "Cable Television and the Public Interest," *Journal of Communication*, 42, no. 1 (Winter 1992), p. 57.

2. *Wayne's World* is a movie version of the "Saturday Night Live" comedy skit about two teens who host their own cable access show, starring Mike Myers and Dana Carvey.

3. Rodney King is a black man from Los Angeles who received wide media attention when a videotape was released in 1991 showing him being beaten by white police officers.

4. *Federal Register*, 37, no. 30 (February 12, 1972).

5. This approach is informed by a paper entitled "Action Research: Theoretical and Methodological Considerations for Development Communications," presented

by Edna F. Einsiedel of the University of Calgary to the International Association for Mass Communication Research at Guaruja, Brazil, in August 1992.

6. "Official Proceedings concerning Amendment of Part 74, Subpart K of the Commission's Rules and Regulations," Nos. 18397-A, 18891, 18892, 18894 (FCC, March 11, 1971).

7. Volume 14, no. 5 (November/December 1991) of *CTR* is devoted to "Access and the First Amendment." Dirk Koning's article on "45 fighting words" is particularly inspiring. Volume 8, no. 2 discusses "Cable and the First Amendment." The reader is also directed to Patrick Parsons's *Cable Television and the First Amendment* (Lexington, MA: Lexington Books, 1987).

8. Center for Analysis of Public Issues, *Public Issues*, Supplement no. 1 (July 1971), p. 1.

9. Cited in Richard C. Kletter, *Cable Television: Making Public Access Effective* (Santa Monica, CA: Rand, 1973), pp. 62–65.

10. *FCC v. Midwest Video Corporation*, 440 U.S. 689, S. Ct. 1435, 1979.

11. Kristen Beck, *Cultivating the Wasteland: Can Cable Put the Vision Back in TV?* (New York: American Council for the Arts, 1983), p. 113.

12. *CTR* is the official publication of the Alliance for Community Media (formerly, NFLCP).

13. Dirk Koning, "Community and Communication," *CTR* (Spring 1990), p. 1.

14. Volume 7, no. 4 (Winter 1984) of *CTR* is devoted to local origination.

15. Peter Hong, "Fires, School Board Meetings, and Accidents—24 Hours a Day," *Business Week*, no. 3192 (December 17, 1990), p. 32.

16. Still, Dominick and colleagues point out: "This growth is unprecedented and impressive, but a little perspective is in order: ad revenues for broadcast television were estimated at up to $20 billion for 1989, over seven times the volume of cable ad revenue" (1990, p. 73).

17. Linda K. Fuller, "Public Access Cable Television: A Case Study on Source, Contents, Audience, Producers, and Rules-Theoretical Perspective," unpublished doctoral dissertation, University of Massachusetts, 1984.

18. My thanks to Dawnn B. Cooper, video production specialist at Raleigh, NC, Community Access Television, for a copy of the report.

19. Frank R. Jamison, "Community Programming Viewership Study Composite Profile." Unpublished document at the Western Michigan University Media Services Department, Kalamazoo, MI. My thanks to Kanti Sandhu for a copy of the document.

20. Access Sacramento, "1991 Audience Survey Findings Report" (Sacramento, CA: Coloma Community Center, 1991). My thanks to Ron Cooper, executive director of Access Sacramento, for a copy of the document.

21. For a more recent interpretation of this term, see William H. Dutton, Jay G. Blumler, and Kenneth L. Kraemer (eds.), *Wired Cities: Shaping the Future of Communications* (Washington Program of the Annenberg School of Communications, 1987).

22. Helen DeMichiel, "Re-Visioning the Electronic Democracy," in *ROAR: The Paper Tiger Television Guide to Media Activism* (New York: Paper Tiger Television Collective, 1991), p. 14.

23. John J. O'Connor, *New York Times* (June 6, 1972).

24. Telephone conversation with Oleathia Gadsden of the National Cable Tele-

vision Association's research department, August 1992. Thanks to her also for sending me NCTA's "Cable Television Developments, October, 1992."

25. *BEM*—450 F.2d 642 (D.C. Cir. 1971).

26. For a discussion on the recent role of the First Amendment and PEG access, see Aufderheide (1992), p. 62.

27. *Red Lion Broadcasting v. FCC*, 395 U.S. 367, S. Ct. 1794, 1969.

28. The reader should be informed that the NFLCP has put out a document called *Copyright and You*, available from their Washington, DC, offices.

29. Cited in Michael I. Meyerson, "The Cable Communications Policy Act of 1984: A Balancing Act on the Coaxial Wires," *Georgia Law Review* 19, (1985), p. 569.

30. Gilbert Gillespie, *Public Access Cable Television in the United States and Canada* (New York: Praeger, 1975), p. 90. Johnson, Agostino, and Ksobiech (1974) also mention the Noble Foundation and the Irwin-Sweeney-Miller Foundation.

31. Nancy Jesuale, Richard M. Neustadt, and Nicholas P. Miller, *CTIC Cablebooks*, Vol. 2: *A Guide for Local Policy* (Arlington, VA: Cable Television Information Center, 1982), pp. 12–17.

32. A particularly well-presented example is the "Community Television Plan," presented to the Yakima (WA) City Council (August 1982).

33. Response form and materials from Kimberly Anne Kyle, municipal assistance coordinator, Commonwealth of Massachusetts Cable TV Commission.

34. Joan Gudgel, "New Cable Bill," *NFLCP Newsletter* (March/April 1982), p. 1. See also "New Cable Bill Introduced in Senate," *CTIC Cable Reports*, 3, no. 3 (March 1982), p. 1, citing Tom Wheeler, president of the National Cable Television Association (NCTA) commending Goldwater's efforts toward a "comprehensive policy" on cable, supporting the franchise fee ceiling and deregulation of all but basic service rates, but expressing concern about the mandatory leased access provision, the sports ban, and the municipal ownership provision.

35. Cable Telecommunications Act of 1983, Report together with Minority Views of the Senate Committee on Commerce, Science, and Transportation on S.66 to Amend the Communications Act of 1934 (Washington, DC: U.S. Government Printing Office, April 27, 1983), p. 38.

36. 47 U.S.C.A. Title VI, 521.

37. FCC "Information Bulletin: Cable Television" (January 1990), p. 11. Information thanks to the office of Andrew Barnett.

38. Patricia Aufderheide, "Local Access and Cable Re-Regulation," working paper.

39. *Nielsen Report on Television*, 1991.

40. Gillespie (1975), p. 79.

41. "Legislative Boost for Cable TV," *Christian Science Monitor* (June 17, 1983), p. 24.

42. Douglas Davis, "Public-Access TV Is Heard in the Land," *New York Times* (June 11, 1989), H31.

43. George Bent, "Public Access TV Here Undergoing Growing Pains," cited in Gillespie (1975), p. 132.

44. Cited in Carrie Heeter and Bradley S. Greenberg, *Cableviewing* (Norwood, NJ: Ablex, 1988), p. 4.

45. See, for example, Barry Schwartz and Jay-Garfield Watkins, "The Anatomy of Cable Television," in Barry N. Schwartz (ed.), *Human Connection and the New Media* (Englewood Cliffs, NJ: Prentice-Hall, 1973), pp. 80–87; Lawrence A. Wenner, "Cable Television and the Promise of Public Access," paper presented at the Uni-

versity of Iowa, 1976; Morton I. Hamburg, *All about Cable: Legal and Business Aspects of Cable and Pay Television* (New York: Law Journal Seminars-Press, 1979); Linda K. Fuller, "The Constitutionality of Cable Technology," in Ray B. Browne and Glenn J. Browne, *Laws of Our Fathers: Popular Culture and the U.S. Constitution* (Bowling Green, OH: Bowling Green State University, 1986), pp. 123–131.

46. *Television and Cable Factbook* (1990), p. C–384.

47. U.S. Senate, "Cable Television Consumer Protection Act of 1990: Report on S.1880." Report 101–381, 101st Congress, 2nd Session, 1990; and U.S. House of Representatives, "Cable Television Consumer Protection and Competition Act of 1990." House Report H.R. 5267, Report 101–682, 101st Congress, 2nd Session, 1990.

48. Patricia Bellamy Goss, "A Policy Analysis of Subscriber Reaction to Cable TV Access Programming in New York City," unpublished doctoral dissertation, New York University, 1978.

_____

Chapter Two

Related Organizations and Individuals

> The mechanisms that govern the mass media marketplace are those of property and money. Such mechanisms include technology, capital investment needed to enter the communications marketplace, reliance on corporate sponsors, and relative insulation from democratic (public) participation in policy-making.[1]
>
> George Gerbner, Annenberg School for Communication

There are an amazing number of support groups and supportive people associated with the community television phenomenon. This chapter aims to outline some of those organizations and individuals, discussing as well the media that deal with community television and some of the businesses that profit from it.

Information was solicited from a variety of sources. From various resource lists, requests for data were sent out to some four hundred people and places, telling about this project and supplying the form in Appendix 2, "Solicitation for Book Information"; the response rate, as is evidenced in this chapter, was both encouraging and enthusiastic.

NATIONAL AFFILIATIONS

As with most telecommunications policy in the United States, community television comes under the auspices of the federal government through legislation dating from the Communications Act of 1934. Congressional committees today include the Subcommittee on Telecommunications, Consumer Protection, and Finance in the House of Representatives and the Senate Subcommittee on Communications, while the Federal Communications Commission (FCC) is empowered to regulate all interstate communication that is considered broadcast/cablecast. Other regulatory players include the courts, the White House, industry lobbyists, state and local governments, the public, and, of course, the marketplace. See Appendix 3, "National Affiliations," for exact addresses and telephone numbers.

The Alliance for Community Media

The national organization that is most concerned with the topic of this book is The Alliance for Community Media, referred to as "The Alliance," formerly known until its recent name change as the National Federation of Local Cable Programmers (NFLCP). Headquartered in Washington, D.C., the organization was founded in 1976 by community television persons who wanted to form an information network encouraging access to and use of cable television channels. At that point, there were fewer than one hundred community cable programming centers in the United States.

Since its inception in 1976, The Alliance has provided its membership, which has increased more than tenfold, with "information on FCC regulations pertaining to their situations, fund-raising, community involvement in programming, developments in the field, and other matters which affect the day-to-day work of community television."[2] The stated goals of the organization include:

1. To discover and assist user groups of local cable channels.
2. To facilitate the exchange of information between people throughout the country who are concerned with community responsive utilization of cable.
3. To spread innovative programming ideas among community access centers.
4. To assist in effective implementation of local cable channels.

In addition, The Alliance serves as an advocate for its members and the access/local origination community with such agencies as the FCC, the Carnegie Commission on the Future of Public Broadcasting, and the House of Representatives Subcommittee on Communications. Operating on a budget of just over $400,000, its current membership numbers around 1,200 individuals. Members include cable systems, school districts, nonprofit video access centers, local origination programming centers, community producers, city and county governments, universities, libraries, regulatory authorities, religious institutions, and others interested in community uses of cable television.

At its national convention in 1983 the organization adopted an advocacy platform, since amended, which appears in Appendix 4, "NFLCP Public Policy Platform Summary"; the complete text, approved by delegates to the 1988 convention, appears in Appendix 5, since amended only to allow for the organization's name change. The Alliance's promotional brochure lists its activities:

- Provides assistance in the development and operation of PEG access channels and community TV organizations.
- Supports community television advocates with materials and information on community programming and national policy issues.
- Promotes political, regulatory, and industry support for PEG access.
- Facilitates networking and education among people and organizations involved with community media.
- Monitors the latest developments in telecommunications technology and advocates for the public's access to emerging media systems.

The Alliance publishes *Community TV Review* (*CTR*), which serves as the journal of record for professionals in the field. Issues tend to be organized around particular themes, such as "Cable and the First Amendment," "PEG Access—Issues and Answers," "Community Networks," "Focusing on Local Origination," "Social and Political Issues," and various anniversary volumes. The *Medium*, The Alliance's bimonthly newsletter, alternates with *CTR*.

In addition to its own publications, The Alliance serves as a distributor for various other books, directories, and related print and video resources that might help its membership, such as *The PARTICIPATE Report: A Case Study of Public Access TV in New York State*, Douglas Ostling's *The Access Producers Handbook*, the handbook *Controversial Programming*, and *The NFLCP Yellow Pages*.

Continually evolving as a grassroots organization, The Alliance maintains a flexible structure that allows it to be responsive to members at local, regional, and/or national levels. Its twenty-four-member volunteer board of directors, made up of regional chairs, at-large members, standing committee representatives, and up to four discretionary members, oversees the operation—setting policies, allocating resources, initiating new projects, and establishing its direction. Headquarters in Washington also maintains a twenty-four-hour jobline listing current job openings in PEG access and related fields, as well as a twenty-four-hour Bulletin Board System (BBS) with up-to-date information on organizational news and public policy issues.

One of the major projects of The Alliance is the Hometown USA Video Festival, an annual competition judging thousands of entries from PEG volunteers and producers in more than one hundred categories, typically drawing more than two thousand entries from about four hundred cities. The only national video festival that judges the work of both access and local origination producers, it culminates in an awards ceremony that is held during the organization's annual national convention, in which winners are honored and clips of their programs are shown. A subsidiary of the awards is the Hometown Bicycle Tour, a sampler of winning productions from the fields of ethnic expression, documentaries, free speech minutes, talk shows, music videos, and programs for youth and seniors. Other awards sponsored by The Alliance include the following:

- The George Stoney Award for Humanistic Communications—awarded to an organization or individual who has made an outstanding contribution to humanistic community communications. Past recipients have included Dee Dee Halleck, Michael Meyerson, the Benton Foundation, Nicholas Johnson, Sue Miller Buske, Jean Rice, Roxie Cole, Tom Borrup, Reverend Everett Parker, Dianna Peck, and Herbert Schiller.

- The Buske Leadership Award—to a person who has demonstrated leadership in the organization within the last three years; continuing service to The Alliance; a high degree of involvement in the organization on national, regional, and chapter levels; and an undying commitment to the mission and goals of The Alliance. Past recipients have included Jan Lesher, Dirk Koning, Chuck Sherwood, Jerry Field, and Sharon Ingraham.

- The Jewell Ryan-White Award for Cultural Diversity—to an organization(s) or individual(s) in recognition of an outstanding contribution to a *process* that encourages, facilitates, or creates culturally diverse and/or nonmainstream community involvement in the field of community media.

- The Community Communications Award for Public Access—recognizes an access operation that has consistently demonstrated outstanding achievements and promotion of access development over the course of time.

- The Community Communications Award for Institutional Access—recognizes municipal and educational access operations that have consistently demonstrated outstanding achievements in programming and community outreach.

- The Community Communications Award for Local Origination—recognizes an LO operation that produces outstanding diverse and innovative programming that meets the needs and interests of the community and demonstrates the commitment of the cable company to local programming.

Another ongoing Alliance committee that keeps evolving ambitiously is the International Committee, which deals with issues such as multicultural access to media and the global promotion of diversity. Under the leadership of chair Karen Helmerson, the committee has participated in international conferences, cosponsored a Latin American video competition, participated in tape exchanges, attended the 1992 Video Olympics in Albertville, France, and has plans for many more cooperative ventures.

Other standing committees of The Alliance include the Information Services Committee, Organizational Development Committee, Public Policy Committee, Equal Opportunity Committee, Finance and Fundraising Committee, Special Human Interest Committee, nine regional committees (i.e., central states, northwest, northeast, mountain states, midwest, mid-atlantic, far west, southeast, and southwest), and chapter committees.

The Alliance for Communications Democracy (ACD)

In 1988, ten public access organizations got together to form this organization "to represent their interests in federal lawsuits brought by cable companies challenging the constitutionality of access channels and financial responsibility in support of them."[3] Founding members included Access 30 Dayton (Ohio), Boston Community Access and Programming Foundation, Chicago Access Corporation, Columbus (Ohio) Community Cable Access, Fairfax (Virginia) Cable Access Corporation, GRTV (Grand Rapids, Michigan), Milwaukee Television Authority, Montgomery Community TV (Rockville, Maryland), Portland (Oregon) Cable Access, and Staten Island (New York) Community TV.

With the express purpose of increasing awareness of community television by means of educational programs and legal participation in cases involving constitutional questions about cable access television, within just a brief period of time ACD has scored tremendous success in a series of court decisions. In addition to filing briefs opposing challenges to the franchising process in Los Angeles, Santa Cruz, California, and Erie, Pennsylvania, it also filed a brief on behalf of access users in the Kansas City, Missouri, case involving a challenge to a decision by the city to eliminate the public access channel to stop the Ku Klux Klan from using it. In the latter case, the court ruled that public access channels constitute a public forum and an open center for speech, and it ruled that access users have the right to bring lawsuits against operators who try to control their programming content.

National Association of Broadcasters

The largest broadcast trade association in the United States is the National Association of Broadcasters (NAB), counting among its members all the major television and radio networks in addition to some 5,000 radio stations, 950 television stations, and 1,500 associate and international members. Since 1923 the NAB has offered a wide variety of services to its constituency in addition to provision of legal, legislative, and regulatory representation. While it led the opposition to cable television in the 1960s, afraid that cable would undercut the financial base of over-the-air, advertiser-supported television, more recently the NAB has been responsive to the cable industry, particularly as many broadcasting interests have moved into cable ventures.

National Cable Television Association

The National Cable Television Association (NCTA) is the country's largest cable trade association, providing media services and research, scientific and technological assistance, and publications to its members. Located in Washington, D.C., NCTA is involved in government relations at both the state and federal levels.

As a means to help promote and credit excellence in cable television programming, NCTA established the National Academy of Cable Programming in 1985. Each year in the autumn, a local cable programming week is celebrated, supported by an extensive video and print public relations campaign. Nearly one thousand systems participate in this celebration highlighting the value and diversity of locally produced cable programming. Included in the free packet that the National Academy of Cable Programming puts out, geared to a variety of target audiences involved in the industry—employees, government officials, subscribers, nonsubscribers, media, and ad sales—is a "Local Programming Fact Sheet" that includes the following promotional information:

- Individual cable systems air an average of 450 hours of local programming per year.
- The Cable Industry spends over $250 million annually on non-revenue production local origination programming.
- The average annual local programming budget is one-half the average cost of one 30-minute episode of a network sitcom.
- Local cable programming produces a vast array of informational programming geared specifically to the local community: documentaries; public and cultural affairs; news; magazine and talk shows; and civic and government coverage are all examples of the extensive commitment to local programming made by the cable industry.
- Localized coverage of sporting events and other community activities that is cost prohibitive for broadcast has been a cornerstone of local origination programming on cable.

Other national affiliations more distantly related to cable and community television include the following:

The Alliance for Public Technology (APT) is a Washington, D.C.–based organization focusing on socioeconomic issues relative to infrastructure requirements necessary for universal and affordable access to information age technologies and services.

The Alternative Media Information Center, also known as "Media Network,"[4] teaches community groups to use media effectively. It is a multiracial, multiethnic media arts organization based in New York City assisting social-issue media producers and activists as well as individuals and educators. Through its Sponsored Projects Program it has helped independent producers raise more than $6 million in production funding since 1979. Publisher of the quarterly *ImMEDIAte Impact*, its newsletter on alternative media, some of its recent productions have included *Seeing Through AIDS*, *Safe Planet*, *Images of Color*, *Bombs Aren't Cool*, *Choice* (women's reproductive freedom and health), *A Reality Check on the American Dream*, and films and videos empowering women for the future, *In Her Own Image*.

The American Film Institute (AFI, Los Angeles) sponsors an "Independent Film and Videomaker Program," funding up to $20,000 for various projects in these categories: animation, documentary, experimental, and narrative.[5]

The Association of Independent Video and Filmmakers (AIVF) is a national advocacy and information group for independent producers. Since its founding by New York film and video indies, it has been an important influence on public policy for independent media.

The Benton Foundation of Washington, D.C., provides funding for projects relating to communications issues. Founded in 1980 as a legacy of U.S. Senator William Benton, the foundation's *Mission Statement* states that it "encourages the use of techniques and technologies of communications to advance the democratic process." In 1990 it published Margie Nicholson's brochure, "Cable Access: A Community Communications Resource for Nonprofits," a collection of case studies of effective nonprofit uses for public education, community organizing, fund-raising, and issue advocacy. This collection also includes her "Bottom Line on What Cable Access Can Mean to Your Organization" (p. 8):

- Broadcast viewership is dropping while cable viewership is growing.
- You now have access via cable television to, on average, 60 percent of the households in your community.
- Television viewing trends, including the proliferation of channels and fickleness of viewers, have created an opportunity for local programmers.
- Viewers can be reached with "empathy-based" programming or with short, frequently repeated messages.
- Because of their activities and interests, community television viewers are an ideal target audience for nonprofit messages and programming.
- The size of the audience can be less important than the impact or results generated by reaching and persuading your target audience.
- You control the program content.
- Your message or program can be shown in prime-time and can be frequently repeated.
- You may use access channels and equipment and receive training at low or no cost.
- You may use television production equipment to create your own television program, or produce a monthly or weekly series.

The Cable-Television Advertising Bureau (CAB) supplies sales and promotional materials in addition to services to its members.

Cable Television Information Center (CTIC, Arlington, Virginia) is a nonprofit membership organization for local governments providing an array of services relating to cable television decision making through its monitoring of state and federal legislation. Begun in 1972 with funding from the Ford Foundation and the John and Mary Markle Foundation, it publishes issue papers, books, and *CTIC CableReports*, a monthly newsletter for local officials.

The Cable Television Public Affairs Association (CTPAA, Laurel, Maryland) annually salutes the industry's public affairs professionals with its Beacon Awards.

The Center for Media and Values (Los Angeles), a nonprofit membership organization providing resources for teaching critical awareness about media, analyzes trends in both print and electronic media and publishes *Media & Values*, a quarterly resource for media literacy. Of particular relevance to this is the spring 1992 issue, "Rethinking Democracy: Citizenship in the Media Age."

The Committee for Labor Access (Chicago), seeking to encourage and support unionization of cable television employees, both commercial and public access, aims to develop strategies mutually beneficial to public access labor producers and professional broadcast unions. Operated on a budget of under $10,000, its *Labor Beat* is available in both video and print formats.

The Association of Independent Television Stations (INTV) is a trade organization that offers lobbying assistance in addition to sales advice and program information.

The Electronic Frontier Foundation (Cambridge, Massachusetts, and Washington, D.C.), a nonprofit organization founded to educate the public about the democratic potential of computer communications technology, deals with legal policy and technical issues. EFF's stated purpose is "to ensure that the new electronic highways emerging from the convergence of telephone, cable, broadcast, and other communications technologies enhance First and Fourth Amendment rights, encourage new entrepreneurial activity, and are open and accessible to all segments of society."

FAIR (Fairness & Accuracy in Reporting, New York) is a national media watch group focusing on public awareness about the press. Begun in 1986 to shake up the establishment-dominated media, the anticensorship organization publishes *Extra!*, a monthly journal of mainstream media bias.

The Freedom Forum (Arlington, Virginia), devoted to promoting free press, free speech, and free spirit for all people, is the largest media-oriented nonprofit organization in the United States. A promoter of First Amendment freedoms, it is a major national funder of journalism education and is also active in the international area, providing professional development of journalists, and it is a leader in promoting the hiring and advancement of minorities and women in news media professions.

Funding Exchange, part of the Paul Robeson Fund for Film and Video (New York), is a resource for producing and distributing social-issue films and videos.

Global Information Network (New York), a unique news service providing hard-to-find information on underreported regions of the world, operates Inter Press Service (IPS), the world's sixth largest international news wire.

The Independent Television Service[6] (ITVS, St. Paul, Minnesota), created by the community of independent producers and the Corporation for Public Broadcasting under special authorization of Congress, has as its mission bringing innovative programming involving creative risks and addressing the needs of unserved or underserved audiences, particularly minorities and children.

The International Radio and Television Society (IRTS), a membership organization founded in 1939 for communications professionals working for radio or television stations or networks, rep firms, advertising agencies, program distributors, cable companies, and other related support services, is headquartered in New York City.

The Institute for Alternative Journalism (IAJ, Washington, D.C.), a nonprofit organization dedicated to strengthening and advocating for the alternative press and independent media voices, operates AlterNet and publishes *Media Culture Review.*

The Kitchen Center for Video, Music, Dance, Performance, Film and Literature (New York), established as a nonprofit media center in 1971, distributes over three hundred independent videos internationally. Some of its programs have included *Art of Music Video: 10 Years After, D'Ghetto Eyes, South* (the world's first television magazine series made entirely by film- and videomakers from Asia, Africa, Latin America, the Caribbean, and the Arab world), *Hissing and Kissing the Wind, Players Nights* (a "hip hop rock collaborative jam"), and the militantly alternative guerrilla media rock band Emergency Broadcast Network. It recently presented a retrospective and celebration for its *Standby* program, a model for making technically advanced media tools accessible to the arts community.

The National Alliance for Media Arts and Culture (NAMAC),[7] located in Oakland, California, has coordinated a number of arts and video centers since 1980. A nonprofit association of organizations and individuals committed to furthering diversity and participation in all forms of media arts, NAMAC has, through its advocacy efforts, helped form the Independent Media Distributors' Alliance (IMDA),[8] the National Coalition of Multicultural Media Artists (NCMMA), and the National Alliance of Media Educators (NAME). From a field survey of member organizations performed in 1992,[9] the nearly two hundred organizations reported budgets totaling $53 million and 21,470 film, video, and audio presentations to audiences totaling over 4.3 million, providing production facilities and equipment to 58,884 people and instruction and training to more than 124,000 students and community members. Its 1992 membership directory is an invaluable resource for persons involved in media arts, and NAMAC's newsletter *MAIN* provides interesting case studies and reports.

The National Association of Telecommunications Officers and Advisors (NATOA, Washington, D.C.), an organization of regulatory professionals from local and state levels, is an affiliate of the National League of Cities. Its objectives include providing technical assistance and information services to members, keeping its membership informed of legal, regulatory, and technical developments in telecommunications, and sponsorship of conferences and training sessions to share information and experiences on what local governments are doing in cable and telecommunications planning.

The National Association of Television Program Executives (NATPE) offers opportunities for program selling, buying, and information exchange at its annual conventions.

The National Cable Television Association (NCTA, Washington, D.C.), a major resource for statistics about the industry, provides valuable media services and research.

The National Citizens Committee for Broadcasting (NCCB), a national nonprofit consumer organization chaired by Ralph Nader, aims to protect the public interest in the field of electronic media. The Washington, D.C.– based organization, dedicated to protecting subscriber privacy and preventing media ownership concentration, houses the Cooperative Communications Project, a public education and assistance effort promoting subscriber ownership of cable systems.

The National Coalition of Independent Public Broadcasting Producers (NCIPBP), reflecting a growing consensus among independent producers, serves to voice public policy concerns of both independent producers and media activists for democratic access to broadcasting, cultural diversity, technology, and public participation in emerging telecommunications structures. Chaired by Lillian Jemenez, NCIPBP is located in New York City.

The National Federation of Community Broadcasters (NFCB, Washington, D.C.), a grassroots, nonprofit membership organization representing 170 stations and producers of community-oriented radio[10] in the United States, was founded in 1975. It publishes the monthly newsletter *Community Radio News, Audiocraft: An Introduction to the Tools and Techniques of Audio Production*, and *The Public Radio Legal Handbook*.

The National Institute Against Prejudice & Violence (NIAPV,[11] Baltimore), a response to ethnic violence, was organized as a private nonprofit center in 1984. Its major program efforts involve a clearinghouse, research, response, education, and policy.

The National Videotape Exchange (Olympia, Washington), a resource directory of no-cost, low-cost, noncommercial video programming created by community programmers, nonprofit organizations, government and educational agencies, cable operations, independent producers, and the like, provides information on subject matter, target audience, formats, and associated fees.

The Radio-Television News Directors Association (RTNDA) is a professional association that enrolls individuals for skills training with a focus on media ethics and First Amendment issues.

Third World Newsreel (New York), founded in 1967, is one of the oldest alternative media organizations in the United States. Committed to the creation and appreciation of media by and about people of color in the United States, as well as by Third World and indigenous peoples throughout the world, it produces, distributes, and exhibits social-issue documentaries and experimental media. Some recent examples include the following: *Latin American Voices, Lesbian and Gay Experience, Look at My People: The Salvadoran Revolution, Palestinian Voices, Voices from the Asian Diaspora, Women's Films*, and *Voices from the African Diaspora*.

U Network (Providence, Rhode Island), a division of the National Association of College Broadcasters, is a nonprofit satellite network linking hundreds of college campuses across the United States. The first college radio and television link, it features the best of student-produced programming. Premiering in 1989, the network has over 170 affiliates and about six million subscribers.

The Office of Communication of the United Church of Christ (UCC, Cleveland, Ohio) has long been an advocacy and educational organization that deals with telecommunications issues. Working primarily at the federal level, it has tried to "protect the Fairness Doctrine, to secure equal rights for employment and ownership of stations by women and minorities, keep down costs for telephone and cable residential subscribers, and [has] filed comments with the FCC on proposed rules making to limit diversity of viewpoints in broadcasting and cable transmissions."[12]

Women Make Movies,[13] founded in 1972, which also includes Women Make Videos, is a New York–based producer and distributor of works by and relating to women. A multiracial, multicultural organization with a budget of $650,000, it is the only national nonprofit women's media organization dedicated to the production, promotion, exhibition, and distribution of films and videos by and about women. In addition to its collection of three hundred films and videotapes—documentaries, narratives, experimental and animated films, social-issue videos, and video art—it has sponsored international festivals, artist-in-residencies, workshops, and touring programs.

COOPERATIVES AND COLLECTIVES

While the issue of imported cablecast programming is not a problem in the United States, as rules are determined not by the franchising authority but locally by the cable system or the access organization, networking between systems has great growth potential. Yet, Brian Kahin (1984, p. 31), former coordinator for the Research Program on Communications Policy at the Massachusetts Institute for Technology, brings up some important points for consideration. Predicting that opportunities for importation and exchange will increase significantly, he sees gatekeeping programmers forced to make scheduling decisions as demand for access time increases: "Who gets prime-time slots? Who gets their programming repeated and when? Who gets to import programming and when? And what about repeating imported programming?" This section deals with community television–affiliated organizations that offer models for networking. See Appendix 6, "Cooperatives and Collectives," for exact addresses and telephone numbers.

Bay Area Video Coalition (BAVC)

Formed as a support center for independent film and video producers and artists, Bay Area Video Coalition of San Francisco is a nonprofit, tax-exempt media arts center providing low-cost access to production and post-production facilities. Founded in 1976 by Howard Klein of the Rockefeller Foundation, BAVC is the largest nonprofit media arts center devoted exclusively to video. Its bimonthly newsletter, *Video Networks*, provides information on jobs, grants, events, exhibits, workshops and seminars, and consulting services, and it maintains a library of relevant books, periodicals, and videos.

BAVC's education programs offer two hundred courses each year, specializing in hands-on technical workshops including editing, engineering, lighting, and interactive videodisc production. It also provides seminars on video production management, including legal affairs, fund-raising, budgeting, and distribution. Other programs include its Artists Awards Program, grants management, financing fellowships through Interact, internships, production insurance, project management, a rehabilitation program (to enable individuals injured on the job to retrain for video careers), and a subsidized access program. Half of BAVC's annual operating budget of approximately $260,000 comes from funding, half from operations such as workshops, rental facilities, and some 1,500 memberships.[14]

Although BAVC's founding was not part of the cable access movement, it shares similar fundamental goals for allowing a voice from diverse constituencies, as evidenced in its promotional *A Brief History*: "No other media arts center in the nation matches BAVC's programs in scale, scope and innovation in areas of producing noncommercial programs, pioneering new technologies, providing information and education about video, advocating for artists and independent producers and collaborating with other nonprofit organizations" (p. 2).

Not Channel Zero

Black Planet Production, a collective of African-American and Latino film and video artists, produces Not Channel Zero (NCZ, Bronx, N.Y.), which bills itself as "the revolution, televised."[15] An alternative news/cultural forum focusing on issues concerning its constituency communities, NCZ was conceived as a grassroots television series; it began in the summer of 1990 with the visit of Nelson Mandela to New York. Ideologically, it aims to come from a nonracist, nonsexist, antihomophobic perspective, celebrating the community's diversity. Its programs include *NVZ Goes to War, In Your Own Backyard, The Crown Heights Affair, Gays and Lesbians in the Black Community*, and many more.

All shoots are remotes, including interviews and on-the-street reports, with community screenings held at the Downtown Community Center in Chinatown. Produced by young African-Americans, NCZ is very much influenced by hip-hop music and culture and aims to get viewers to question who constructs and benefits by traditional production "rules" for news reportage. As stated in an NCZ promotional brochure,

Our aesthetic approach attempts to make the point that NCZ, like all media, is an exercise in subjectivity. The difference with NCZ is that we revel in showing the seams. We celebrate demystification. By stressing to our public that our news is just as handmade, subjective, biased and just as valid as mainstream media, we are helping to break down the fourth wall that mainstream TV struggles to maintain between their so-called objective machinations and their audience.

According to one media commentator, "These young videographers do not produce shows that slip into the bland netherworld of generic network news. Rather, their style of editing calls to mind the trademark of a good deejay—the mastery of scratching and mixing. . . . NCZ's artistic flair has been compared to cinema verité and abstract art."[16]

Paper Tiger Television (PTTV) and Deep Dish Television

An alternative media collective producing a weekly half hour of media critiques that airs on Manhattan's public access channel, PTTV aims to expose, not obscure, the workings of television production. Founded in 1981 by pioneer video guerrilla Dee Dee Halleck, it produces programs aimed at demystifying the information industry, such as "Herb Schiller Reads the *New York Times*"[17] and "Do You Know Where Your Brains Are?" Production workshops are offered in collective fashion, with all responsibilities and decisions shared jointly by trainers and trainees. The all-volunteer collective aims to examine mainstream media and their effect on social and political life, claiming that the power of mass culture rests on the public trust—but that legitimacy is a "paper tiger."

Paper Tiger Television—West, located in San Francisco, began as a collective in 1984 by producing and distributing programs for Bay Area stations, and since 1989 it has created a progressive cable news program called "Finally Got the News," covering perspectives normally not included in mainstream newscasts. It describes another part of its programming as follows:

Paper Tiger Television's installation/exhibition "Smashing the Myths of the Information Age" takes the public into the belly of the television beast. Participants pass through the broken screen of a giant television set to encounter some of the great myths of our society, such as the "Myth of Freedom of Choice," or the "Myth of Equality," myths frequently propagated into our homes via the ubiquitous television. These myths are laid out as separate sculptural/installation "circuits" on a giant printed circuit board. As the viewers wind their way past the myths and overgrown electronic components, they pass through the "resister" room, a display of "technology for the people" such as pirate radio and television transmitters. Climbing up a flight of stairs, one attains "media shangri-la," a homey, relaxing space where one can view alternative programming, tap into an interactive database on corporate control of the media, or just hang out. "Smashing the Myths of the Information Age" invites the public to crash through that TV screen, expose the myths of the so called "Information Age," and participate in building an alternative movement of media activism and social change.[18]

The first national grassroots satellite network, Deep Dish Television has been linking community-based producers, programmers, activists, and others who support the movement for a progressive television movement since it was organized by Paper Tiger Television in 1986. Its introductory press release announced: "For the first time in the history of television, local folks will get a chance to see their own programming distributed by satellite nationwide. Deep Dish TV is the merging of democracy and technology— it is the first network to share community produced programming." Frustrated by the limitations of traditional "bicycling" methods for networking, in which stations shared various tapes, Paper Tiger and other groups who wanted to pool programs began that first year's lineup with a show on public access and freedom of speech, followed by others on labor, housing, youth and education, racism, the military, local perspectives on Central America, media by women, the farming crisis, and popular culture.

Devoted to democratizing media, extending the concept of grassroots television to a national scale, Deep Dish TV is a nonprofit, tax-exempt, educational organization supported by donations and grants whose programming is aired on more than three hundred cable systems around the United States. According to Executive Director Steve Pierce, Deep Dish is meant to replace rather than supplement commercial television: "Their first priority is to sell you something, not to challenge people's thinking or get them to communicate with each other. The mainstream media gives you news people reporting the news. We give you the people who are living the news, grassroots organizers telling you the real story."[19]

Helen DeMichiel, a Minneapolis film- and videomaker who helped create the first Deep Dish TV season in 1986, has argued that "the creation of a preserve for dissident television and media production that embraces community engagement, reflection and multi-levelled debate is one of the most important functions of an alternative media culture. As the video illumination permeates virtually every aspect of private and public life, media activism proliferates."[20]

One of Deep Dish's recent productions was the Gulf Crisis TV Project, containing antiwar voices. Paul Wong, editor of the *Video Guide* for the project, comments on how it was an important historical event for media activists: "Through situation reports, chronologies and passionate responses, we can retrace the Gulf crisis through the creative actions of alternative interventions using whatever means possible to counteract the one-sided view of corporate controlled media."[21] Some of the programs, which were picked up by hundreds of cable access channels, included "Manufacturing the Enemy," "News World Order," "Lines in the Sand," "Just Say No," "Global Dissent," and "Bring the War Home." In addition, situation reports were presented from Canada, San Francisco, Japan, Milwaukee, Burlington (Vermont), and New York.

Typically, dissident views are given access on Deep Dish TV. As Marisa Bowe (1991, p. 55) has reported, "The programs may not have been slick or 'balanced,' but they took risks mainstream TV couldn't afford to take. They weren't bland, and they aired views not normally heard on TV. They probably teed a lot of people off, but isn't a little unladylike and ungentlemanly fighting over opinions the very essence of democracy?" More recent productions have included "Behind Censorship: The Assault on Civil Liberties," "Public Access: Spigot for Bigots or Channels for Change?" "News You Can Use," "Youth Speaks," "Video Dialtone: Malling our Free Speech," "Caribbean Voices," and, to celebrate the first World AIDS Day, "We Interrupt This Program." Upcoming projects include "The Nation Erupts: Civil Unrest in the 90s" and a look at health care. Using the "think globally, act locally" notion, Deep Dish's spring 1993 schedule featured "fearless television from around the world," with topics ranging from the International Women's Day Video Festival to the Los Angeles riots, Palestinian statehood, homophobia, the Inkatha Freedom Party, Latin American producers, immigrants, the Waiapi tribe of the Brazilian Amazon, the Cuban embargo, and "Staking a Claim in Cyberspace: Information Policy for the People."

Ralph Engelman (1990, p. 43) has pointed out that "Deep Dish T.V.'s inauguration of a national community television network represented a watershed in the realization of the aspirations of public access pioneers. The task for the next generation wishing to defend and extend community television would be to take advantage of underutilized access channels."

Other Cooperative Operations

Begun in 1969 as an experiment in community-based filmmaking, part of a national program to train poor and minority youth, Appalshop (Whitesburg, Kentucky) is a collective of films and videotapes on culture and social issues from filmmakers in the southern Appalachian area. According to their descriptive brochure about their documentaries, "We try to bring the voices of those who still work with their hands, those who see taking care of the land and water as something more than a passing trend, those who still believe in the power of people to take care of each other into the discussion of what is important in the world."[22]

The goal of the Flying Focus Video Collective (Portland, Oregon) is to promote social change through video. Formed out of outrage at the Gulf War, the all-volunteer collective produces video programming, records informative lectures, and creates interactive media events. Its mission statement says it all: "We support grassroots empowerment: social justice and environmental sustainability; multiculturalism and anti-authoritarianism. We oppose imperialism, tyranny and exploitation from individual to global levels." Some of its shows include: "Videopolitique," "Middle East Peace Talks," "Combatting Homophobia," "Debunking Christmas in America," "Consumerism in the USA," "How to Watch Television," "The Cars That Ate Your Life," and many others.

The 90's, a Chicago-based organization, has positioned itself as an alternative showcase for independent producers. It has a multiweek satellite public broadcast program featuring films and videos that number more than fifty shows to date, 85 percent in portable documentary format.[23]

The Washington, D.C.–based Public Interest Video Network (PIVN) is a nonprofit media center working with various groups to develop media campaigns and to set up satellite distribution networks for programming to public television stations and cable access systems.

Documenting the rising activism regarding reproductive rights, AIDS, and gay and lesbian issues is the Testing the Limits Collective, headquartered in New York.

Established in 1989 to promote prolabor television, video, radio and film production, and programming, Union Producers and Programmers NETwork (UPPNET, Santa Monica, California) was born of a grassroots movement by labor media activists who wanted to create a national network. Its membership numbers over two hundred. One of UPPNET's first actions was to join with Los Angeles Community Access Television to convene the first-ever community-wide conference on the use of local public access television in late 1991. Split into "affinity group" caucuses on how to use community television resources, the groups later reported their findings to the city's Committee of Conveners, charged with administering Los Angeles's PEG access channels. It is now working to establish a National Labor TV Channel.[24]

The largest distributor of tapes by and about contemporary artists in the country, Video Data Bank[25] (VDB, Chicago) is an alternative, nonprofit video distributor that tries to do as much community outreach for the field as possible. Since its founding in 1976, VDB has had many innovative projects, such as its Video Drive-In, an urban "walk-in" that displays free programs on the big screen in a local park; *Video Tape Review*, including more than one thousand titles by two hundred independent videomakers; *Video Against*

AIDS, works by twenty-two independent producers; and *On Art and Artists*, a collection of more than three hundred interviews with and documentaries about contemporary artists. Its current project is a video history catalog, developed to stimulate college curricular development in the field of experimental video. In its Independent Video listings, VDB discusses Paper Tiger Television, stating, "The mandatory provision of public access to cable programming is one of the few vestiges of a non-commercial, public service concept of communication—borrowing a phrase from Fred Glass, 'a crack in the tube.' Access producers around the country often define their work as grassroots, democratic television" (p. 43). In honor of that concept, VDB's 1992 Chicago screening featured the video "A Crack In the Tube," celebrating democracy by bringing television for the people, by the people.

The Video Project of Oakland, California, is a nonprofit distributor of videos and films dealing with peace and environmental issues. Offering "films and videos for a safe & sustainable world" since 1983, its most recent catalog features, among other topics, native peoples, energy, rain forests, global warming, sustainable development, toxics, wildlife, ethics and values, nuclear issues, the arms industry, the wounds of war, and international concerns.

CIVIC, SOCIAL, LOCAL, AND ACADEMIC ORGANIZATIONS

As community television addresses a wide range of audiences, it appeals to a number of very different civic organizations. See Appendix 7, "Civic, Social, Local, and Academic Organizations," for exact addresses and telephone numbers.

The American Association of Retired Persons (AARP, Washington, D.C.), for example, while it has no formal, ongoing program, does have a Communications Division that has produced some programming, and the Consumer Affairs Department issued a video and workbook on community access.[26]

The Appalachian Council Job Corps (Chicago), a community service of the AFL-CIO since 1964 for low-income and disadvantaged youth, offers media and computer training as part of its program.[27]

A national network of community-based activists, artists, and cultural workers, the Alliance for Cultural Democracy (Boston) is founded on the belief that "participatory democracy can only take root and flourish if cultural issues are placed on an equal footing with issues in the political and economic spheres."[28]

ASIFA (Association Internationale du Film d'Animation) was formed in Annecy, France, in 1960 by a group of animation professionals to promote and further their dynamic medium; today, its membership includes over two thousand persons from fifty countries. ASIFA Central,[29] located in Chicago, sponsors and produces a variety of programs, including film screenings, seminars, and workshops, and publishes a quarterly newsletter, *Frame by Frame*.

A nonprofit overseer of the city of Chicago's five cable access channels, Chicago Access Corporation has put together a "Hotline Studio Startup Package," a cost-effective means of supplying nonprofit organizations and educational institutions with a "user-friendly, results-oriented communication service." Included is information on how to construct a hotline studio, develop programming, and use consultation time.

Downtown Community Television in New York City (DCTV) was founded in 1972 as a nonprofit video production and education center with a comprehensive training program for minority and disadvantaged communities. Offering video workshops in Spanish, Chinese, and Korean, among others, it has trained more than six thousand persons. Its Act of Video Festival promotion states, "We are looking for work that plumbs the depths and broadens the scope of the medium of video, whether that work be narrative, documentary, animation, 'video as witness,' PSAs, or any combination or form of electronically-based imaging."

With over twenty years of services in the media arts, Electronic Arts Intermix (EAI, New York) is a nonprofit media arts center, a major international resource for independent video supporting alternative voices and personal visions. Since its founding in 1971 by Howard Wise, it has offered an artists' videotape distribution service, screening room, editing/postproduction facility, and equipment loan service.

Operating on a budget of more than $1 million, since 1970 St. Paul's (Minnesota) Film in the Cities (FITC) has fostered "the creation, appreciation, and understanding of film, video, photography, and audio arts for a public of diverse ages, income levels, and backgrounds"—more than four thousand of them. College credit from Metropolitan State University is available through selected courses.

The only national film and video distribution program exclusively devoted to gay and lesbian media artists, Frameline (San Francisco) sponsors an annual international film festival and publishes a quarterly newsletter, *Frameline News*.

The Institute for Media Analysis (IMA, New York), a nonprofit, educational corporation producing and publishing books, journals, tapes, and monographs on the media and domestic and foreign policy issues, provides research and database services, conducts conferences and seminars, and maintains a research library. IMA's primary mission is "to examine critically the structure and function of commercial, public and government media institutions; to counter misinformation and disinformation from media and government sources; and to foster effective communication of ideas and opinion among those concerned with social change."

Little City Foundation–Media Arts Center (Chicago) is a nonprofit organization that serves people with developmental challenges, providing training in video production skills, artist-in-residence workshops, grant programs, one-on-one consultation, and distribution of completed projects out of its VITAL project (Video Induced Training and Learning) educational program. Operating on a budget of about $100,000, Little City Foundation's overall goals include "fostering the creative self-expression of people with developmental challenges such as mental retardation, educating the public about the abilities of people labeled 'disabled,' and advocating for the full and equal inclusion of people with developmental disabilities in all aspects of society."[30]

Northwest Coalition Against Malicious Harassment, Inc. (NWCAMH, Seattle), a 501(c)3 nonprofit regional organization, was established in 1987 to "address, combat and eradicate harassment and violence . . . based on race, religion or sexual orientation." According to its director, Bill Wassmuth, the use of public access opportunities to respond to racist programs on the various cable networks in the region has been highly encouraged.[31]

A nonprofit entity whose mission since 1977 has been to produce and encourage the production and successful use of quality telecommunications programs by and about its people, the Native American Public Broadcasting Consortium, Inc.[32] (NAPBC, Lincoln, Nebraska) maintains a library offering a wide selection of programs dealing with Native American culture, history, art, multicultural relations, and the like.

Neighborhood Film/Video Project of Philadelphia, founded in 1975, remains dedicated to "the public appreciation for, understanding of, and access to the media arts and to the development of independent media artists in the Delaware Valley."

A newly formed 501(c)3 organization, Pacific Islanders In Communication (Honolulu) is directly funded by the Corporation for Public Broadcasting. It encourages programming by and about people from Hawaii, Guam, the Northern Marianas Islands, and American Samoa.

Response Television Corporation[33] (RT2, Iowa City and Oakdale, Iowa) offers twenty-four-hour action with RT2, its interactive video package that allows viewers to interact with their local cable channels via Touch-Tone telephones. Running on any Amiga computer with two megabytes of memory, RT2 allows participants to design and produce video programs, screens, sounds, information pages, and databases for use in entertainment, access centers, businesses, education, cities, and/or libraries.

Charged with promoting the use of public access television by citizens and civic, cultural, and arts organizations, the San Francisco Community Television Corporation is an independent 501(c)3 corporation with a mandate to reach underserved ethnic and minority communities. It offers workshops on producers' orientation and television lighting and publishes a monthly newsletter.

Committed to the film and video art of its region, the Southwest Alternate Media Project (SWAMP, Houston) offers work from artists producing in dependent images and personal visions, and distributes a quarterly *Media Bulletin.*

Part of Buffalo (New York) Media Resources, Squeaky Wheel[34] is a non-profit service organization for local film/media artists and community leaders. In addition to producing "Axlegrease," a weekly public access program, it publishes a quarterly journal called *The Squealer*, houses a library of film and media work by local artists as well as contemporary art and media journals, and provides consultation to artists and community groups. Recent workshops, for example, included training on camcorders, professional editing, lowel light kit, tascam 4-track, and titling with the Amiga.

Positioning itself beyond either the "cultural elite" or the "average couch potato," TV Dinner of Rochester, New York, offers television for all communities (the Police Review Commission, national health care, abortion rights, labor solidarity, AIDS/HIV). In addition to community workshops and community brunches, it sponsors film series and plays a strong role in media advocacy.

The Union for Democratic Communications (UDC, Department of Communication, Wayne State University, Detroit), an international organization made up of communications scholars and activists who believe in grassroots participation, is dedicated to the critical study of the communications establishment and its policies; the production and distribution of democratically controlled and produced media; the fostering of alternative, oppositional, independent, and experimental production; and the development of democratic communications systems at local, regional, national, and international levels. It publishes *Democratic Communiqué*, a quarterly newsletter, and the *UDC Membership Directory*, as well as maintaining involvement in a number of projects and computer networking.

South Carolina ETV (Columbia) sponsors Video Gallery, an eclectic collection of television programs, such as "The American South Comes of Age," "Cinematic Eye," "Cliffhangers," "Eye of the Storm," "The Hobby Shop," "Ilona's Palette," "Naturescene," "The Playhouse," "Stretch with Priscilla," "Tennis with Van der Meet," and "The Very First Milo Moose Day Celebration," in addition to sponsoring the Writer's Workshop.

Videoteca del Sur (New York) was founded in 1989 as the only cultural organization whose mission is to "foster, expose and disseminate the diverse cultural achievements made by popular video artists of Latin American heritage."[35] Its offerings include screenings and speakers' forums, "Magicamerica," a Latin American video festival, a video archive, a newsletter, and a biweekly radio program.

The oldest Asian Pacific media organization in the United States, Visual Communications[36] (Los Angeles) promotes its history and culture through a comprehensive media arts program. Founded in 1970 from a concept formed in a living room by a group of film and visual arts students, Visual Communications has grown steadily into its current status as a nationally recognized organization. Supported by anywhere from fifty to one hundred volunteers and 150 patrons, it operates on a $300,000 budget.

MAINSTREAM AND ALTERNATIVE MEDIA

See Appendix 8, "Mainstream and Alternative Media," for addresses of the following publications and other media.

While *TV Guide* ranks number one as a weekly in both magazine and newsstand circulation in the United States at 16,800,441 and 8,482,246 respectively,[37] with hardly any close competition, it hardly ever lists specific community television programming unless there is a very special show that might be highlighted. *Cablevision* (New York), a leading magazine for the industry, made quite a splash in the community television community with an editorial by Craig Leddy on May 18, 1992, in which he called for cutbacks on cable public access.[38] Prefacing his remarks by saying they may seem politically incorrect, Leddy urged that "Congress and other supporters of this exercise in TV democracy should realize that it largely has been a failure. It's time to turn over unused public, education and government channels to services that can offer some real programming." NFLCP regional representatives sent out an action alert to their members, urging that letters and faxes be sent to the magazine in response, with the reminder "Don't forget to mention the social value of access in your community." They also encouraged other access users and supporters, as well as "high profile community members" to respond, claiming individual voices were equally important in unison with the official word from the NFLCP office.

Many of the individual cable television networks supply their own program guides, both print and computer-based, but they are typically limited to ownership by subscribers.

Some of the most widely available generic cable television guides include *Cableview*, *Premium Channels*, *Cablewatch*, and *Cabletime*. Electronic Program Guide (EPG), a full-channel service that functions like a basic cable network on a dedicated channel, is the most widely distributed electronic guide, reaching some 7 million homes on 320 cable systems.[39]

Of particular interest to persons involved in noncommercial television is the magazine *Adbusters Quarterly*, a product of the nonprofit Media Foundation in Vancouver.[40] "Here's Your Chance to Break into Television," they offer, providing creative resources, technical skills, and marketing know-how to help people produce posters, print ads, or television spots for various causes. A classic example is "Tubehead," part of an antitelevision campaign, that reads:

Night after night, we sit like zombies in front of the tube while countless social and ecological crises descend upon us. But instead of reaching for solutions, we reach for another potato chip and zap a few more channels. Chronic TV watching has become the number one mental health problem of our age.

Jolt North America out of its TV stupor.

Angles: Women Working in Film & Video is a Milwaukee-based quarterly newsletter focusing on women working in the field at all levels—from directing to distributing, exhibiting, and programming. Since 1978 *Broomstick* (San Francisco) has been a national quarterly feminist political journal by, for, and about women over age forty. *Daughters of Sarah* (Chicago) is a magazine published in the area of Christian feminism. "Women Organizing Economic Solutions" is the theme of *Equal Means* (Berkeley, California), a journal published by the Ms. Foundation for women advocates, labor unionists, legislators, and educators.

The *Feminist Bookstore News* (San Francisco) has a listing of women's bookstores. *Feminist Teacher* (Indiana University, Bloomington) is an educational journal, *Feminist Studies* (Women's Studies, University of Maryland, College Park) a professional journal, *Fighting Woman News* (Theodore, AL) a magazine of martial arts, self-defense, combative sports, and herstory. *Frontiers* (University of New Mexico, Albuquerque) is another journal of women studies; *Heresies* (New York) is a feminist publication on art and politics; *Hikane* (Great Barrington, Massachusetts) includes writing and artwork by disabled "wimmin"; *Hot Wire* (Chicago) is a journal of women's music and culture, dedicated to making the women's community accessible. *Kalliope* (Florida Community College at Jacksonville) is a journal of women's art; *The New VOICE*[41] (Cohasset, California) is a monthly newspaper for women; *North Shore Woman's Newspaper* (Huntington, New York) services its local constituency. Women Express, Incorporated[42] (Boston), a "collective of young women dedicated to helping adolescent girls from at-risk populations successfully navigate the obstacles of sexism, racism, classism, and the troubled waters of adolescence," publishes *Teen Voices*, and *Womyn's Press*[43] (Eugene, Oregon) is a feminist newspaper that has been published by an all-volunteer collective since 1970.

Felix, a Journal of Media Arts and Communications (New York) means to fill a void in the video art field by generating criticism and dialogue about the process of videomaking. Articles are written by artists/producers, poets, communications experts, art critics, and other writers. Issues have included themes of media censorship, video of dissent, and video and the world.

From London, the magazine *Third Text* contains critical articles on culture and media from Europe, the United States, and developing nations. In the United States, the *Utne Reader* (Minneapolis) offers one of the best examples of writing and reporting on alternative media; its president/editor-in-chief, Eric Utne, was keynote speaker for the NFLCP annual conference in 1992. *Visions*[44] (Boston), the only film and television arts quarterly published in New England, focuses on artists beyond the Hollywood spectrum.

AlterNet[45] (Washington, D.C.) is a unique interactive news service catering by nonprint means exclusively to the needs of the alternative press. Linking subscribers via a computer network tying together more than fifty newspapers in the United States and Canada, the service was launched in 1987 by the Institute for Alternative Journalism. It describes itself as unlike other news and syndication services in several ways. First, its mission is to serve nondaily, alternative community media. Second, its structure is bottom-up, with the AlterNet editor responding to input and needs of already existing media, in contrast to the top-down structure of most news services. Third, it offers a variety of copy—in terms of content, style, length, format, and point of view—and tailors those offerings to the individual editors' wants and needs.

BUSINESSES AND FOUNDATIONS RELATED TO COMMUNITY TELEVISION

See Appendix 9, "Businesses and Foundations Related to Community Television," for exact names and addresses of the following organizations.

National Community Network

In operation since the spring of 1993, National Community Network (Denver, Colorado) was envisioned from the start as a public service by the cable television industry in terms of creating a network that will be helpful to access and origination groups, communities, and cable operators alike. Modeled after C-SPAN, it plans to offer the best access programming available both for and from local target communities. Although NCN is positioned as a nonprofit "backdrop," its initial seed money support has come from industry mogul Bill Daniels; eventually, the Denver-based project expects to be a $4–$6 million operating network. Jim Dickson, NCN president, foresees a strong consumer–local access group bond forming, where programs such as a teleconferencing mayors' forum or "Comic Relief"–type coverage can bring grassroots groups together in the national consciousness. The idea is to establish "consumer touch," a groundbreaking experiment allowing access for access.

Economic Opportunities and Offerings

There are a number of communications consultants offering specialized services who specialize in working with PEG access groups and individuals; a number of them have advertised in the NFLCP *Yellow Pages* (Cardona, 1992).

Brewster/Ingraham Consulting Group (Acton, Massachusetts) serves access centers, municipalities, nonprofit organizations, and MSOs in a broad array of cable-related services, including organizational development, community needs ascertainment, franchise/renewal negotiations, performance reviews, long- and short-range financial planning, board development, nonprofit startup assistance, access operating rules, personnel planning and hiring, computer applications, facilities and equipment assessment, and training seminars and workshops. The Buske Group (Sacramento, California) offers a "Community Programming Index" subscription service tracking equipment usage, programming data, training enrollments, and number of producers. Communications Support Group (Santa Ana, California) is made up of a team of professionals who specialize in "comprehensive and unbiased operating evaluations of cable television systems," providing consultant services related to compliance audits, franchise administration, enforcement, and renewal proceedings. The CMR Group (Woodland Hills, California) specializes in news interview survival training, financial media relations, crisis communications, and emergency preparedness. The Communications Policy Group, Incorporated (CPG, Marblehead, Massachusetts) assists policymakers in developing and regulating cable television systems. Genya Copen[46] (Amherst, Massachusetts), with her partner Paul Lind, goes the gamut in her access consultations, including architectural renovations for studios in Greenfield, Massachusetts, and New Haven, Connecticut.

Communication for Change[47] (New York), formerly Martha Stuart Communications, is an independent video production and training company centering around teaching grassroots organizations in developing countries how to use video as a tool to communicate their messages for organizing, training, and advocacy. For example, it has done extensive work with the Self-Employed Women's Association (SEWA) in India, developing a team called Video SEWA, and is currently doing work in Bangladesh and Nigeria. Most famous in the United States for the award-winning human affairs series "Are You Listening"—ordinary people speaking from their own experience—its most recent production is a program called "Patients and Doctors Who Are Partners."

For producers, there are several sources for funding from film and video competitions. The Retirement Research Foundation, part of the Center for New Television (Chicago), for example, offers a $2,000 Community Video Award to the winner of the best entry produced or coproduced by a community group or older people. The Kettering Foundation[48] (Dayton, Ohio), founded in 1927 by Charles F. Kettering in the American tradition of inventive research, particularly addresses itself to the practice of politics, sponsoring, among other projects, "The National Issues Forums" (NIF) that many community television stations air. Created in 1978 for charitable and public service purposes, the John D. and Catherine T. MacArthur Foundation[49] (Chicago) has included community television–related organizations as recipients of their many grants, some of which are the following: Alternative Media Information Center, American Community Service Network, Deep Dish TV Network, Fund for Innovative Television, Fund for New Communications Networks, NAMAC (National Alliance For Media Arts and Culture), National Video Resources, New Images Productions, Original Women's Network, and a number of other media arts centers. The National Council for Research on Women (New York) publishes directories of national women's organizations, work-in-progress and recently published resources, women's media, and opportunities for research and study. Established in 1987 under the direction of his will, the Andy Warhol Foundation for the Visual Arts of New York provides project grants for the "visual/plastic arts."

A number of the major cable television networks have ventures philosophically related to some of the principles of PEG access, especially in the field of education. Cable in the Classroom (Alexandria, Virginia) reports that the cable television industry provides some ten million public secondary students, nearly half of all junior and senior high schoolers, with commercial-free educational programming. For example, the A&E Classroom (New York) provides commercial-free programs in the areas of history, classic dramas, biographies, performing arts, anthropology, and archaeology that can be videotaped and used to complement program schedules. Supplementary reading lists and study guides are also available free of charge, and competitive teacher grants are granted for use of the programs. The first and only network in the United States showcasing black programming twenty-four hours a day, Black Entertainment Television[50] (Rosslyn, Virginia) has drawn on its own constituency from the start. Launched in 1980 as a two-hour weekly service on Friday evenings, in 1991 BET became the first black-owned company to be traded on the New York Stock Exchange; today, it reaches approximately 34 million cable households in the United States. Still, its greatest problem, according to Craig M. Muckle, director of public relations, is getting people to understand BET's wider message and advocating for their communities to carry the channel. "CNN Newsroom,"[51] a product of Turner Broadcasting (Atlanta), is a fifteen-minute, commercial-free news program airing on CNN weekdays at 3:45 A.M. EST, available free of charge to participating schools. And the Learning Channel (Rosslyn, Virginia) has run a series called "The Independents," featuring their productions.

Another cable programmer, although its service does not appear on the television screen, is X*Press Information Services, Limited[52] (Denver, Colorado), an organization that delivers news and information to personal computer users. Offered by more than eight hundred cable systems in the country, in some twelve thousand schools, the method of digital delivery is via cable lines, transmitting information such as stock quotes, in-depth business and financial information, daily news, worldwide weather, and general interest topics. Its educational offerings include "X*Change in the Classroom" and "X*Change-In-The-Schools," as well as "Teacher Champions," a support service of training. When Nickelodeon aired its special edition "A

Conversation with Magic Johnson" in the spring of 1992, Cable in the Classroom developed support materials for use in conjunction with the program. In operation seven days a week, X*Press's latest service is Media Centre, an archiving and catalog indexing tool.

Although there are a number of legal firms that deal with individual community television stations, several law offices and lawyers warrant special attention. Washington lawyers Joe Van Eaton[53] of Miller & Holbrooke and Jim Horwood[54] of Spiegel & McDiarmid have long been valuable to The Alliance. Adrian E. Herbst of Moss & Barnett (Minneapolis) has worked exclusively for cities on cable communication issues for a quarter century, including the following services: initial franchising, refranchising/renewals, franchise administration and enforcement, transfer of ownership, municipal ownership, performance audit, financial audits, rate regulation, litigation, negotiation, ordinance drafting, nonprofit access corporations, programming agreements, and franchise agreements.[55]

In January 1992, one month before the Winter Olympic Games in Albertville, France, another competition took place twenty-seven kilometers away: "The Olympics for Local Television." Participants gathered from both the northern and southern hemispheres to share their experiences of and predictions for community television. One of the participants, Randy Visser, described the event this way: "The common bond between these experiences was video. In some way each of the participants was engaged in the struggle over who would control access to the media in their own countries."[56]

As is evident here, there are a remarkable number of organizations and individuals involved with community television beyond the merely local level—through cooperatives and collectives, civic, social, local, and academic organizations, mainstream and alternative media, and related businesses and foundations. It is a concept with wide ramifications.

NOTES

1. George Gerbner, "Minority Culture, the USA, and the 'Free Marketplace of Ideas," *The National Forum* (Fall 1987), p. 15.

2. I am most appreciative of all the cooperation for both literature and review of this section by Tony Lewis, executive director of The Alliance.

3. "The ACD: Access Strikes Back," *Multichannel News* (February 15, 1988).

4. Telephone conversation with Dan Derosu of Media Network, November 1992.

5. Letter from Cathy Phoenix, Film and Videomaker Services, AFI, November 9, 1992.

6. See a relevant article on the Independent Television Service by Patricia Aufderheide, "Public Television and the Public Sphere," *Critical Studies in Mass Communication* 8 (1991), pp. 168–83.

7. Letter from Mimi Zarsky, NAMAC program coordinator, August 24, 1992.

8. IMDA is located at 47 Halifax St., Boston, MA. Contact Ben Achtenberg for a detailed description of the organization and its activities.

9. "Field Survey," *NAMAC Directory 1992*, p. 3.

10. See also Monika Bauerlein, "Radio Activity: Community Radio Ensures Fresh Airwaves," *Utne Reader* (September/October 1992), pp. 110–12. In addition to NFCB, she mentions these other radio resources: *The Ace* (pirate radio manual), Box 11201, Shawnee Mission, KS; Black Liberation Radio, 333 N. 12th St., Springfield, IL; Earth on the Air, Box 45883, Seattle, WA; and Pacifica Program Service, 3729 Cahuenga Blvd. W., North Hollywood, CA.

11. Letter and materials from Robert D. Purvis of NIAPV, August 26, 1992.

12. Letter and resources from Dr. Beverly J. Chain, director, Office of Communication, UCC, August 13, 1992.

13. Response form and resources from Jennifer Scott, Women Make Movies, September 1992.

14. Response from Heidi Irgens, operations manager, BAVC. Thanks also go to Luke Matthew Hones, BAVC programs director, for his letter of July 28, 1992.

15. Letter and resources from Cyrille Phipps of Not Channel Zero, August 12, 1992. We also had an interview on July 16, 1992 in Minneapolis.

16. LaRose Parris, "Not Channel Zero: The Revolution Televised," *American Visions* (June/July 1992), p. 40.

17. Letter from Herb Schiller, professor of communication at the University of California, San Diego, August 27, 1992.

18. Information from Jesse Drew, Paper Tiger TV-West.

19. David Oestricher, "Activism on the Airwaves: Grassroots TV? You Bet!" *City Limits* (January 1992), p. 8.

20. Helen DeMichiel, "Revisioning the Electronic Democracy," in *ROAR* (New York: Paper Tiger Television Collective, 1992), p. 15.

21. Paul Wong, editor, "Gulf Crisis T.V. Project," *Video Guide*, Vol. 11, no. 3 (Spring 1992), p. 2. Thanks go to Caryn Rogoff for supplying me with this information.

22. Letter from Carolyn Sturgill, film distribution manager for Appalshop, Fall 1992.

23. Fax from Patrick Creadon of September 28, 1992. See also an interesting article, "Chicago's Filmmakers: 'Second' To None," by Carey Lundin, in *StreetWise* (June 1993), pp. 4–6, a nonprofit monthly newspaper to empower the city's homeless through employment.

24. "For a National Labor TV Channel," *UPPNET News* (Jan/Feb/March 1992), p. 4. Thanks to Fred Carroll, chair of UPPNET, for letters and resources August 11, 1992, and September 10, 1992.

25. Letter and resources from Nell Lundy, special projects coordinator, Video Data Bank, August 14, 1992.

26. Letter of September 10, 1992, from Kenneth Vest, director of communication resources of AARP.

27. Response from Windy Spencer, Job Corps coordinator in Chicago.

28. Judy Branfman, "Cultural Rights Declaration: Call for Comments," *The Democratic Communiqué*, Vol. 9, no. 3 (Winter 1990), p. 16.

29. Resources from Deanne Morse, president, ASIFA Central, April 4, 1993.

30. Letter from Maggie Lee, Media Arts Center manager and national training coordinator, Little City Foundation, August 25, 1992.

31. Response from Bill Wassmuth, director, NWCAMH.

32. Letter and resources from Lawrence Spotted Bird, development and marketing manager, Native American Public Broadcasting Consortium, February 11, 1993.

33. Letter and resources from Wm. Drew Shaffer, president of Response Television Corporation and coauthor of "Creating Original Programming for Cable TV," August 1, 1992.

34. Interview with Lisa Sporledger, access manager of Buffalo Cable Access Media, July 16, 1992.

35. Letter and resources from Pedro Zurita, director, Videoteca del Sur, September 1992.

36. Telephone conversation, letter, and resources from Joyce Nako, administration assistant to Linda Mabalot, executive director of Visual Communications, February 1, 1993.

37. Based on the Audit Bureau of Circulation figures.

38. Craig Leddy, "Access Works . . . NOT!" *Cablevision* (May 18, 1992), p. 2.

39. Susan Tyler Eastman, "Basic Cable Networks," in Eastman et al., *Broadcast/ Cable Programming* (Belmont, CA: Wadsworth, 1989), p. 315.

40. Letter of August 21, 1992, from Kalle Lasn, publisher, *Adbusters Quarterly*.

41. Response from Loretta J. Metcalf, publisher/editor, *The New VOICE*, November 1992.

42. Letter and resources from Alison Amoroso, executive director, Women Express, August 13, 1992.

43. Response form and resources from J. R. David and Jonni Erickson, *Womyn's Press*, October 1992.

44. Letter and press release from Carl Germann, *Visions*, August 18, 1992.

45. Letter and resources from Kelley Culmer, administrator for AlterNet, January 28, 1993.

46. Telephone conversation with Genya Copen, November 1992.

47. Letter and resources from Katie Corrigan, distribution director for Communication for Change, January 28, 1993.

48. Letter and resources from Bob Daley of the Kettering Foundation, September 22, 1992.

49. Letter and resources from Linda Feldman, media program advisor for the John D. and Catherine T. MacArthur Foundation, September 16, 1992.

50. Telephone conversation and materials from Craig M. Muckle, director of public relations and communications, BET, February 1993.

51. Letter from Lori Konopka, CNN public relations coordinator, August 5, 1992.

52. Letter and resources from Rosetta Rogers, director of special projects, X*Press Information Services, August 18, 1992.

53. Response form, November 1992.

54. Conversation at Northeast Region NFLCP Conference, Greenfield, MA, November 3, 1991.

55. Letter and resources from Adrian E. Herbst, Moss & Barnett, August 19, 1992.

56. Randy Visser, "Taking Back Television: A Global View," an unpublished grant proposal to *Community Television Review* (*CTR*).

Programming

> In the vast Sahara of television broadcasting there are only a few scattered wadis where authentic, alternative, uncommodified, uncensored programming can live. These oases generally take the form of public access stations, those arcane stops high on the dial that cable companies are compelled, by local governments, to furnish in return for their lucrative monopolies. There's little else.[1]
>
> Editorial, "Censored Air," *The Nation*

As with any number of other issues relating to community television, programming differs enormously according to individual stations and personnel. What follows is a discussion about various program types and technicalities that I hope will be helpful not only in explaining community television programming but also for suggesting ideas for currently operating stations.

TYPES OF PEG ACCESS

By definition, there is no such thing as "typical" community television programming. That is the point of this book—diversity. In an editorial considering the historical roots of access, Fred Johnson commented on access as the merging of two grand American traditions: "One is the long standing tradition of community democracy: local information leaflets and papers, town meetings and gossip; the other tradition is the high flying, stoned radicalism and technological utopianism as expressed in the '60s."[2]

Another key point to be underscored here was best said by Dave Keyes in a *CTR* article on his perspective from working with the Milwaukee Access Telecommunications Authority: "Producing television programs is not the primary goal of a community organization, but access is a great tool for assisting with its mission."[3] As Wm. Drew Schaffer points out in the introduction to his coedited 1983 book *Creating Original Programming for Cable TV*, there are many players in the field: the cable providers, cable controllers, cable programming producers, and suppliers. Citing how "experimentation and variation in approaches to cable are the order of the day" (p. 5), he expands as follows:

An independent producer may attempt to produce commercials for his/her own local show on the local origination channel. A citizen may produce an informational program about the organization he/she belongs to for an access channel. The cable company may create local revenue by setting up an advertising program on its channel. Schools and hospitals may interconnect with the library and utilize the institutional network to search catalog listings or make data transactions. Cities have started to provide public service information on government access channels. Innovators are approaching cable and finding outlets to experiment with the format and style of television such as changing its function to a more participational or interactive medium. The list goes on and on.

And so this chapter on programming, and the following one on production and producers, are about players using various means to reach wider missions.

With so many different forms of community television, and so many different motivations for supporting so many different kinds of programming, exact definitions are hard to specify. Even content categories are difficult to pin down. For New York City, for example, Alan H. Wurtzel (1974, p. 14) constructed the following types: (1) entertainment, (2) news, (3) public affairs, (4) information, (5) religious, (6) instruction, (7) sports, (8) politics, (9) children's, (10) experimental art, and (11) miscellaneous. Since those specifications appeared unique to an urban setting, an alternative choice (Fuller, 1984a) for studying a suburban station included the following: selectmen's meetings, school committee meetings, sports, station promotion, town news/public affairs, entertainment, education/schools, information, instruction, children's programs, and religious programs—see Figure 3.1. Whereas Wurtzel found that "informative" shows dominated others in 76 percent of all programming in Manhattan, and whereas they were also the most dominant category for the suburban station, percentage-wise they commanded less than one quarter of the latter.

Programming on community television, it will be discovered, can cover quite a range, both philosophically and factually. Among the many variables that must be factored in is the external support. For PEG access, "If there is strong city, company, and community support for these channels, the workshops, equipment, and staff necessary to assist the community producers in producing their programming can result in strong, successful access channels."[4]

Figure 3.1
Content Categorization of PACTL Programming—December 1981–December 1982

	Count	%	Hours	Average
PACTL Categories				
Selectmen's meetings	26	16%	57	2 hours
School committee meetings	16	9	32	2 hours
Sports	94	15	53	30 minutes
Station promotion	86	4	15	5 minutes
Town/public affairs	60	13	47	50 minutes
Entertainment	55	7	27	30 minutes
Education/schools	53	10	37	40 minutes
Information	152	22	77	30 minutes
Instruction	9	1	4	25 minutes
Children's programming	2	-	1	60 minutes
Religious programming	3	-	2	40 minutes
Total	556	97%	352	350/60= (50 min. average)

Note: *Count* = number of programs; % = percentage of average programming; *Hours Average* = typical amount of programming hours annually. The average program ran 50 minutes.

Sample Schedules

In one of the first reports on schedules, Johnson and colleagues (1974, pp. 1–18), surveyed ten public access centers in the United States and found an average of fifteen to thirty hours per week of programming.[5] Later, comparing institution-based local cable program facilities, Jesuale and Smith (1982, p. 74) reported on the following weekly hours of cablecasting:

Facility	Type	Hours/week
Bloomington, IN	Community Access Ch. 3	68
Iowa City, IA	Iowa City Public Library	60
Iowa City, IA	Educational Cable Consortium	8

Knoxville, TN	St. John's Community Video Center	50
Madison, WI	Municipal Video Service	32
Rome, GA	Tri-County Regional Library	30

Fuller (1984d, p. 116) reported on PACTL, the small suburban public access cable television station of Longmeadow, Massachusetts, that produced more than five hundred programs in its first year, not a week going by without a new idea and application for a program. Before the channel even made its debut, it had more than thirty programs already "in the can," ready to go, including: "Antiques Showcase," "Art for Children," "American Field Service," "Careers," "Celebrity," "Conservation," "Cultural Newsletter," "Dog Training," "Fashion and Beauty," "Focus on Fitness," "Just for Fun," "Great Decisions" (a program of the Foreign Policy Association), "Medical Facts," "PET Computer," "Religious Circles," "Sports," "Talk of the Town," and "Who's Who."

Averaging more than nine hours per day, or approximately forty-five hours of programming per week, PACTL had live coverage of the selectmen and school committee meetings, the annual town meeting, budget hearings, candidates' night, Long Meddowe Days [sic], and other special events (see Figure 3.2). Key programs have been archived in case any of the town citizens want to review them at other than airtime.

Every Monday evening on PACTL there was a live broadcast of "Talk of the Town" that allowed telephone call-ins; issues facing the town were discussed by representative sides, moderated by a local resident. Hosted by a high school social sciences teacher, it was the most widely received and reacted to program on the channel. Friday's "On the Air" was another call-in show, featuring entertainment and talk. Other nights typically included various creative or school-oriented programs, and on special occasions, the station also cablecast programs on weekends or holidays.

Five years later, in 1988, Channel 8's program guide, "Access to Access," listed these monthly highlights for June: "Asbestos: The Mineral Menace," "Abalone Rock," "Aerobics with Susan," "Alzheimer's Panel Discussion & Movie," "Book and Author Event," "Book Nook," "Broadway Revue," "Blueberry Hill Father's Day," "Center School Presents Old MacDonald," "Caribbean Connection," "Drug and Alcohol Awareness," "Gospel at Its Best," "Globe Art Awards," "Highlights," "Lady of Larkspur Lotion," "Jewish Nursing Home," "Let's Take a Trip," "Lacrosse State Championship," "M. L. Carr Visits Glenbrook," "Mr. Yuk," "New York Tour," "Ochoa for Fashion," "Travel Shows," "Talk of the Town," "Valley of the Shadows," "Westover Nursing Dept.," "Whispering Giant," and "Zev Blishtein, Russian Refusnik."

A more recent sample program, a weekly, is available in Figure 3.3.[6] Channel highlights are also included in the Pocatello, Idaho, community television guide, including "Access TV Live—Health," a live call-in show

Figure 3.2
PACTL Program Guide—April 1983

Monday	Tuesday	Wednesday	Thursday	Friday
				1 On the Air Just for Fun Music
4 Selectmen's meeting	5 Just for Fun On Stage Dance Horse	6 Highlights Williams School February dates Pelicans	7 Money Think Afro-Am. Railroad	8 On the Air Just for Fun Sports
11 School comm.	12 Just for Fun Selectmen's meeting	13 Highlights Art Basics Glenbrook Sch. Women Careers	14 Talk of the Town On Stage JCC Antiques	15 On the Air Just for Fun Profiles: clergy
18 Just for Fun Regatta Great Decisions	19 Selectmen's meeting	20 Highlights Williams School	21 Afro-Am. Railroad Profiles	22 Music Just for Fun Sports
25 School comm.	26 Just for Fun On Stage (3 parts) Antiques	27 Highlights Art Basics Lacrosse Outdoor survival	28 Talk of the Town Dental dialogue Ch. 8 documen- tary	29 On the Air Just for Fun Music Profiles

Figure 3.3
Pocatello Vision 12—November 15–21, 1992

Sun, 11/15
- 11am Mythical Paths of the World's Religions (Summit U.)
- 12 noon La Radio Mexicana (music)
- 12:30pm Nuestra Familia (information & entertainment for the whole family)
- 1pm La Voz del '92 (Programa de Rosa Ynd)
- 2pm La Voz Latina (Enrique "Hank" Gonzalez and Armanda Martinez)
- 5pm Sound the Alarm (Paul Kaufmann)
- 6pm Incredible String Band

Mon, 11/16
- 11am S.E.L.F.Aerobics (Sr. fitness)
- 12 noon Give 'Em Back (miss. child.)
- 1pm Hillcrest History
- 1:30pm Eric Engerbretson
- 3pm Access TV Live(Pol).
- 4pm Alternative Views
- 5pm Deep Dish TV
- 6pm This Is the Life
- 6:30pm Herald of Truth
- 7pm Search Lord's Way
- 7:30pm Meet the County
- 8:30pm Chamber Talk
- 9pm Groovy Tunes
- 11pm Buffalo Chip Boogie

Tu, 11/17
- 11am Dads Against Discrminiation
- 12 noon Meet the County
- 1pm Poker Party
- 1:30pm Coalition for Fair Free Trade
- 2:30pm Public School Volunteers
- 3pm Campmeet '92
- 5pm Bible Studies
- 6pm Lifestyle Mag.
- 6:30pm Hillcrest History Ft. Hall
- 7:30pm Calvary Rchoes
- 8pm Football Line
- 9pm Knights of Nee
- 11pm Dale's Oldies & Goodies

Wed, 11/18
- 11am S.E.L.F. Aerobics
- 12noon TNT True Ad-venture Trails
- 12:30pm Labor Beat
- 1pm Jean-Luc Ponty
- 3pm Football Line
- 4pm Swingtimes Present: Memories
- 5:30pm Voice of Salvation
- 6pm Summit U. Forum
- 7pm Hillcrest History (Bannock Centen.)
- 7:30pm EcoNews
- 8pm Access TV
- 9pm Live--Health
- 9pm Radio Anarchy
- 11pm Joni Mitchell

Th, 11/19
- 11am Access TV Live--Politics
- 12 noon Take Ch. Life
- 12:30pm This Is the Life
- 1pm P-TV (HS)
- 1:30pm EcoNews
- 2pm 97th Bomb Gr
- 3pm Consumer Access
- 3:30pm Bravo Soundoff
- 4pm County Jukebox
- 5:45pm City Council Ag.
- 6pm Pocatello CC-(L)
- 7pm Given Opportun.
- 7:30pm Coalition Free Tr
- 8:30 Alternative Views
- 10:30 Through Look Glass

Fri, 11/20
- 11am Access TV Live--Health
- 12 noon Modern TV
- 12:30pm Chamber Talk
- 1pm Meet the County
- 2pm Which Way America?
- 2:30pm Access TV Live--Pol
- 3:30pm Lifestyle Magazine
- 4pm Freedom from Smoking
- 5pm Annual World Conf, (religious)
- 6pm Football Firing Line
- 7pm Yes, Jeremy, It's Something Else
- 9pm Album Tracker
- 10:30pm Dukes of Dixieland

Sat, 11/21
- 12 noon On CD Side of Town--Mozart

on food sanitation; live airing of the Pocatello City Council meeting; "Football Firing Line," a discussion of high school, Idaho State University, and Big Sky football; the Greater Pocatello Chamber of Commerce's "Chamber Talk—Buy Locally"; and a new series for the station, a religious revival from Fort Hall called "Campmeet '92." A wide range of religious denominations is represented in worship services, including Lutheran, Church of Christ, Seventh Day Adventist, Church of God of Prophecy, and Church of Jesus Christ of the Latter–day Saints, in addition to religious programs by Summit University, the Lutheran Layman's League, Bible Studies, and the Gates City Christian Church. But consider: Those programs are scheduled side by side with "family" shows; programs broadcast in languages other than English; physical fitness for senior citizens; public service programs like "Give 'Em Back," on missing children, or "Dads Against Discrimination"; music that might appeal to a wide range of tastes; and alternative programming in the form of local political commentary, advocacy for labor unions, "Radio Anarchy," environmental and consumer issues, and the downloading of offerings from Deep Dish TV.

Started in 1977 as part of the Pocatello (Idaho) Public Library, Pocatello Vision became a separate entity from the library, while still remaining part of the city government, in 1989. Offering twelve channels, its staff consists of one full-time, three half-time, and two university work-study persons, in addition to about seventy five regular volunteers. It operates on a $90,000 budget through both its local studio and a remote, producing ten new hours of original programming per week. Each program guide informs viewers that there are many ways to become involved with the station, which offers regularly scheduled workshops teaching how to produce one's own television show, and, for those not interested in learning how to operate the equipment, the guide points out that Pocatello Vision can "introduce you to another person who might work with you to bring your ideas into being." The phone number is included, along with information that these are the only restrictions on program content: (1) Programs must not be commercial in nature, and (2) program content must not be obscene, slanderous, or otherwise unprotected by the First Amendment.

From a major city's community television offerings it is interesting to consider Figure 3.4,[7] one of five such schedules of the Chicago Access Corporation (CAC). An independent, nonprofit overseer of the city of Chicago's five cable access channels since passage of a 1983 ordinance, Chicago Access Network Television (CAN TV) presents programming and information by and for Chicago residents on topics such as local events, ethnic viewpoints, arts, health, social and lifestyle issues. With a staff of nineteen full-time and two part-time persons, and having served over 1,700 nonprofits and 1,800 individuals, CAN TV's offerings are most impressive, considering that more than three hundred original programs are cablecast each week over its channels, including those described below.

Figure 3.4
Chicago Community Access TV—September 1992

	MONDAY Prog. from Sun 5-10pm (repeats)	TUESDAY Prog. from Mon 5-10pm	WEDNESDAY Prog. from Tu 5-10pm	THURSDAY Prog. from Wed 5-10pm	FRIDAY Prog. from Th 5-10pm	SATURDAY Programming for Sat pm:	SUNDAY Prog. from Fri 5-10pm
Noon to 5pm							
5pm	Specials	Wishes & Ideas	Specials	Motorsports Unlimited	Sr. Network	C	Specials
5:30	Hard Cover	Specials				A N	Guest List
6pm	Specials	Word of Faith		Improving Students	Rock Hard Videos	T V	
6:30	Team Chicago Challenge		Miracle Show	Republican House Pub			
7pm	Special	House Party Internat'l		No Matter What	Cinema Talk	S H	You & the Law
7:30	Motosports Unlimited		Team Chicago Challenge	Special	Drag Racing Weekly Special	O W	Orgullo Latino
8pm	On Edge with Razor	Chg Business & Entertainment	The Living Word	Lisa Porter Jazz Show		C	
8:30					HIV Update	A S E	Specials
9	Global Philosophy 2001	Sheridans of Chicago	L-Stop	Spider Show	Jerry Bryant Show		
9:30			Specials	Labor Beat			
10	This Week in Joe's Basement	Mike Kurban Psychic Show					
10:30	Reservations (Bill Fisher)	Here We Are		Deep Dish TV	Feedback		
11	Jerry Bryant Show	Jerry Bryant Show		Specials	Specials		
11:30	Specials			Jack Hubble Jazz Show	Chicago Streett Hits		

CAN TV19—cablecast weekdays from noon to midnight, weekends from noon to 10 P.M., presents a wide variety of programming, including public affairs, entertainment, documentary, and arts and information programs. Just one example is the "All about AARP" program that a group of access-trained Chicago seniors produced recently to tell about the American Association of Retired Persons.[8] From the schedule listed here, it might be noted that the "Here We Are" program on Tuesday at 10 P.M. featured an interview with the consul general of Haiti. Other programs singled out for attention in the program guide include the following: "Creation Station," which exclusively features the work of producers who have developmental challenges, such as Down's syndrome and mental retardation; "Community Alert," in which young artists play to an audience of senior citizens in their first recital; Chocolate Chips Theater's "Rise and Shine," which deals with peer pressure struggles; "Cuba Ya," artists in solidarity with Cubans; "Los Charros," the music of north Texas; "Ne-Ke's Wisemen," a play with women's perspectives on men, drugs, and everyday living; Weird Al Yankovic as the guest on "Cutting Edge Chicago"; Harvard University scholar Dr. E. Issac discussing ancient Ethiopia on "Roots Chicago!"; rap music and dance on "Featured Artist"; and two persons discussing holistic practices on "Psychic Faire."

CAN TV21—offers a variety of educational and informational programs, weekdays from 8:30 A.M. to 11:30 P.M. One special feature is "Hotline 21," a live, interactive television service available for use by Chicago nonprofits. Among many users has been the Public Relations/Publicity Committee of the Chicago chapter of the National Black Nurses' Association, which has used the channel's capabilities to inform its local public about health care. The open television/telephone line format has allowed them to talk about substance abuse, AIDS, stress, hypertension, diabetes, organ transplantation, and other health issues.[9] The Chicago Access Corporation offers an eight-hour training session to nonprofit organizations who want to take advantage of the hotline.

CAN TV27—features "FYI CHICAGO TV27," a continuous graphic magazine which displays "News You Can Use" twenty-four hours a day, seven days a week, from Chicago's nonprofit organizations. Accessible to 700,000 + cable viewers in the city, the service has provided invaluable information to Chicagoans. CAN offers a two-hour orientation workshop for potential participants, the results of which include an attractive handbook, assistance on script writing, final story design by one of the network's graphic artists, and a VHS tape of the organization's completed story. Chicago Access Corporation's 1991 annual report includes rave reviews from the senior project director of the Uptown Center Hull House Association for "FYI CHICAGO TV27" 's promotion of its "Grandma, Please!" story, from the Chicago Children's Choir for helping it recruit singers, and also from the coordinator of the court watch of the Citizens Committee on the Juvenile Court for the channel's use as a recruitment tool.

CAN TV36—presents religious and inspirational programming from diverse denominations, weeknights from 5 to 11 P.M.

CAN TV42—is a twenty-four-hour channel that television viewers can call directly for messages from nonprofit organizations and institutions. Reportedly more than 1,000 viewers use the service each day for free, easy access to news and information about community events, educational activities, employment opportunities, and available resources. Jobs and training agencies have reported to Chicago Access that TV42 is one of their top recruitment mechanisms.

Operating on an annual budget of approximately $1.3 million, CAC has as its mission statement that it "offers Chicagoans a diversity of television viewing choices and the opportunity to exercise their First Amendment right to freedom of speech by providing technical training, equipment, facilities and programming opportunities on Chicago's public access cable television channels." It aims to promote and develop "maximum public awareness of, use of, and involvement in cable television for cultural, educational, health, social service, civic, community and other nonprofit purposes."

CAC has a number of special projects worth mentioning: "Le Journal," a French-language newscast offered daily at 11 A.M., made possible by means of support from French-owned corporations; Senior Project, supported by the Retirement Research Foundation; a media literacy project supported by a grant from City Arts Chicago; Lannan Literary Series, a showcase for major contemporary poets and writers from around the world; Job Connection; and CAN-INFO, a twenty-four-hour telephone service.

According to a personal update from Barbara Popovic, executive director of Chicago Access Corporation, during September 1992 participating agencies reported to CAC that two hundred viewers were placed in training and jobs because of messages on TV42.

Sample Programming

The range of interpretations allowed by cable access will be indicated throughout this book but will be emphasized specifically in this section. As evidenced in the sample schedules cited above, while there are some similarities in the kinds of programs people from different geographic and philosophical perspectives want to produce, actual output varies enormously.

Public Access Programming

Public access programming goes back a long way. As early as 1972, Price and Wicklein (pp. 37–39) cited the case of ECCO, the Experiment in Community Communication project. Established by the Center for Understanding and sponsored by the Ford Foundation, ECCO was affiliated with a public school in Newburgh, New York, but eventually became an independent entity, due to political and economic pressures. Operated by about fifty young people ranging from ages thirteen to twenty, the project was guided by two older supervisors who provided technical advice. It had quite an impact: "ECCO became a kind of club, an object of allegiance . . . for many of the students, (it) provided their first experience of accomplishing something on their own, and the first indication that something constructive and imaginative could be done in Newburgh."

In 1980, Sue Miller Buske, then regional director of the Cable Television Information Center, wrote a descriptive article introducing local community access programming as an innovation, a new way of considering the medium as a community resource.[10] The following responsibilities for facilitators were listed: teaching basic portapak skills classes, studio production classes, and playback engineering classes; scheduling equipment use for these classes and for access users; scheduling programming for the access channel; preparing and delivering all program schedules to the local news media; compiling programming statistics on a monthly basis; advising access users in preparation of their productions; developing programs and program series for the access channel; encouraging local organizations to plan regular or semiregular programs; coordinating volunteers; and contacting and scheduling these volunteers to assist in the various aspects of the access center operations. The key, beyond all the rules and regulations, would be community involvement.

Community involvement is evident in the plethora of programs available, only a smattering of which can be highlighted here. Consider the Alternative Music Television channel in Madison, Wisconsin; Santa Monica's City TV, which programs for seniors, the disabled, Spanish-speaking persons, and children; DIVA-TV, video activists interested in documenting the struggle against AIDS; the Media Coalition for Reproductive Rights, who respond to blockades of abortion clinics; Milwaukee's "Sawed on TV," a series of public access shows on mining, Native American, environmental, and other issues; or Tucson Community Cable's "New Genre Video," "Tucson Panorama," "Kidbits," "Video Warriors," "Barrio Historico: A Walk Through Time," "Be True to Yourself," on gay pride, and "Close Quarter Combat," an instructional videotape on the martial art of ninjutsu, for which the producer was honored in Japan.

Consider arts programming on community television, such as Dallas's "Arts Eye"; Tampa Bay's video show on its performing arts center; Milwaukee's arts series, "Access Alive"; Bowie County, Maryland's, children's dramatic programming; Denver's "Horizon," from its museum of natural history; and any number of channels' participation in various arts weeks.

Consider children's programming on community television, such as Nantucket, Massachusetts's, call-in game show, "Triviosity"; Newton, Pennsylvania's, "General High School," a weekly half-hour soap opera for which teens write the scripts and in which they star; "Time Machine," a look at community life then and now from Fullerton, California; "Jock Rap" from Arlington (Massachusetts), on local sports; Lafayette, Indiana's, "Animal Tracks," featuring zoo animals, wildlife, and pets; the eclectic "Get Moving" from Portland (Oregon); Berkeley, California's, improvisational theater program "Jump In"; "Campfire on the Air" in Reading (Pennsylvania); "Youth Vision" from Cranston (Rhode Island); Cloquet, Minnesota's, "Book Rats"; and any number of newscasts by and for children.

And consider also the many instances in which community television has played a role in social change, such as the coalition of Citizens for Affordable Safe Energy (CASE)[11] airing their nuclear concerns on access channels in Cincinnati, Dayton, and Columbus, Ohio, as well as part of northern Kentucky; the antiracist, antisexist, pro–human rights "Let the People Speak" from Austin, Texas; "Gay Fairfax" on the Fairfax (Virginia) cable access channel; Louisville, Kentucky's, "Know Your Government," which included tapes from conservative organizations like the John Birch Society, the Eagle Forum, the American Security Council, and the Freeman Institute, along with editorial comments; Iowa City's feminist program, "Something's Happening Here"; the National Right to Work Committee's "Sceptre of Violence" documentary on union violence; New Orleans's "Second Line," which analyzes and critiques the news; and several documentaries from Somerville, Massachusetts, that have impacted public housing, preteens, elections, and children's advocacy issues.

Today there is even a national public access program, "Access America," airing on the Comedy Network, which features the "pick of the video litter." It was chosen as "Hot Entertainment" in *Rolling Stone's* annual hot issue (May 16, 1991), which included a photo of the star of "The Man Who Smelt Just a Little Too Much Like Urine." Other sample fare includes segments like "Live Chatter Box," with ridiculous banter; "Sport of Violence," in which a father and son throw themselves off a building; representatives from Self Bludgeoners Anonymous; the "Short Attention Span Theatre"; and other selected shows with topics like cannibalism, debauchery, sex, and sports.

Let's discuss some other programming from around the United States. The Amherst (Massachusetts) Arts Lottery Council has made possible "Primal Time Television," a satire on evening news magazine shows, which can be seen throughout New England. One student at Worcester State College has shared a tape he and some friends had fun making on the Auburn Cable Access, featuring "Big Stupid Butterfly," which had simulations of going to the store and forgetting the milk, the Fat Chance Lottery, a blocked-out person making racist comments, and silly advertisements for items like double-mint tobacco or a cheesy brass necklace.

Cable Access of Dallas is involved in a number of community involvement projects[12]: "Jubilee Dallas," celebrating the city's 150 years of history, diversity, and community spirit; South Dallas Appreciation Day; debates and inauguration of the mayor and city council; summer video camp; "Take Ten," a forum for addressing contemporary issues; an annual awards ceremony; Adopt-a-School, linking businesses with local schools; the State Fair of Texas; Explorer Post 1253, a joint venture with the Boy Scouts; Dallas Video Festival; a cable access conference; and American Deaf Drama Festival, dedicated to advancing deaf awareness by means of promoting scripts dealing with hearing impairment.

"All-Request Community Television" is available on Denver Community Television, "a medium for the exchange of ideas, talents, creativity, and achievements enriching the lives of the entire community." Accessible twenty-four days a day, seven days a week, it features many subjects, including the following: animals, art, authors and books, careers and employment, children, Colorado people and places, community access, consumer issues, cuisine, current issues, environment, film, finances, government, health and fitness, history, how-to, innovative videos, law-related, metaphysics and the supernatural, natural history, parenting, performing arts, personal development, poetry, religion and spirituality, science, seniors, special events, sports and recreation, talk and variety, teen and young adults, and travel. Subscribers choose the programs they want from a monthly catalog, scheduling them at their convenience.

Cambridge (Massachusetts) Community Television has four public access channels, one of which is strictly international, offering Asian, Hispanic, Arabic, Irish, Greek, African, Caribbean, Haitian, and an especially large amount of Portuguese entertainment. Comparing and contrasting Asian and American cultures, "East Meets West" is a cable television series presenting Asian and Asian-American arts, history, social and political issues, and philosophies.[13] Its goal is to move beyond hackneyed media stereotypes of Asians, highlighting instead real people with something to say.

EENET, the Emergency Education NETwork, part of the Federal Emergency Management Agency of the National Emergency Training Center in Emmitsburg, Maryland, provides video training and education via satellite for fire service and emergency management personnel to thousands of receivership sites throughout the continental United States, Alaska, and Puerto Rico. It provides schedules and relays site satellite information to viewers, publishers of satellite programming guides, cable television carriers, professional associations, and others, reaching from the smallest community to the largest metropolitan area.

Kingport, Tennessee, with funding from the Appalachian Regional Commission, sought to provide information about services available from federal, state, and local agencies, especially for the elderly. "Labor Beat," produced in Chicago, has participated in documenting requests from various union locals.[14] The New Orleans Video Access Center counts among its constituency of program producers urban bush women and members of the Louisiana Cajun Music Society. Its French-speaking communities also produce programs like "Voix de la Louisiane" and "Bonjour."

"National Issues Forum" (NIF), a program sponsored by the Kettering Foundation that is modeled after the New England town meeting, is carried on several hundred public access channels. Organizers cite a number of advantages to airing NIF: "First, television exposes a greater number of people to the NIF process than traditional local forums. By lowering the cost of participation (it is easier to turn on a television than to go out to a meeting), cable expands the pool of possible participants. Second, by adding excitement and prestige, television makes it easier to recruit moderators, resource panelists, and forum participants. Third, television creates a permanent record of the forums."[15] Several participants in NIF have won awards in NFLCP's Hometown USA Video Festival. According to one winner, "These open town hall meetings fit perfectly with the concept of community access television. They empower people with a sense of worth by giving them opportunities to talk through the issues with their neighbors, knowing that their thoughts will reach policymakers who can make changes in the system."[16] Another value has been enhancing the image of the sponsoring stations, as reported by Florida Community College at Jacksonville, Lafayette High School in Williamsburg, Virginia, the Boise (Idaho) Public Library, and others.[17]

The Milwaukee Access Telecommunication Authority (MATA) has a long and distinguished history of outstanding programming. When Bob Devine served as MATA's executive director he took very seriously First Amendment notions of public access being a means for citizens to speak and be heard in the utilitarian ideal of a "marketplace of ideas," with access to training, to equipment and facilities, and to channel space. He states, "The promise of access is that it can be what the community *wants it to be.*"[18] Recently, reports Erin O'Meara,[19] MATA's programming has included the following offerings: "Open 24 Hours," "the only show like it in the country"— video art mixed with live audience participation, activism, documentaries, and so on, put together by a national award-winning production team; "Idiot Box Savant," produced for Deep Dish TV; Children's Outing Association (COA)'s "Teen Video Workshop," a multi-award-winning program now in its third season, created by at-risk inner city youths doing high-power, creative programming that challenges mainstream media. Other notable MATA programs include "Tri-cable Tonight," a series on gay and lesbian issues; "Watch This Space," highlighting the arts; "Milwaukee Newsreel," a documentary news series; "Subjects of Survival," on environmental hazards; and regular shows like "Latinos on the Move," "Testimonies of Praise," "Good News," "Teen Talk," "Afro-American Soul," and "Community Speak Out."

From nearby Lake Minnetonka (Minnesota) Cable, producer Carl Borg has explored on video the activities of a local fan club, the "USS Nokomis," which was instrumental in organizing a recent Star Trek convention in the Twin Cities.

Public access has also carved a niche in the lost-and-found department. "America's Children," a service devoted to the recovery of missing, abused, and exploited children, is currently being run on over thirty-two California community television stations. The National Missing Children's Locate Center,[20] a 501(c)3 tax-exempt organization that helps locate lost, missing, or kidnapped children at no cost to the searching families, has had great success with its "Give 'Em Back" series. And in a less somber vein, "Adopt a Dog" has been a successful program for vagrant canines in the Palmer-Monson (Massachusetts) area.[21]

Northampton, Massachusetts, the first city in its region to hold gay and lesbian rights marches, carries "Out & About"[22] on its local public access channel. Guests have included a gay police officer, the founder of the monthly *Lesbian Calendar*, a local poet, a lesbian Buddhist teacher, and members of ACT-UP and Queer Nation. Reaction has been generally positive, but one of the hosts reports running into a woman who said, "I saw you on TV last night," and then ran away.

At the Wainae-Leeward system in Oahu, Hawaii, a private cable system serves a low-income community of people from many backgrounds (Japanese, Filipinos, Portuguese, Hawaiian, and Anglos) with various language programs. There, "Use of the channels aids efforts to increase English literacy, provide job training, improve the quality of education, provide activities for young people so as to combat juvenile delinquency, and solving of its problems."[23] Olelo, the Corporation for Community Television in Honolulu, includes the following on its program sampler: "Elementary Science," "Math Enrichment," "Teach In-Service Training," "Cultural Anthropology 200," "Introduction to Visual Art 101," "Visual Composition," "Preemployment Preparation," "Homework Hotline," "Developmental Approaches to Science and Health (DASH)," "AP Calculus," "Restructuring for Learning in America's Schools," "Analytic Geometry," "Multimedia Applications for the Classroom," "Science/Technology/ Society," "Innovative Uses of Technology in Classrooms," "Homeless Children—the Challenge," "Governor's Task Force on Educational Governance," and "Schools That Work—the Research Advantage." "Video Rodzina," originating from Boston, provides Polish programming that is networked across Massachusetts. A free radio reading service for the print-impaired, "Sun Sounds" has been carried as a service on the Tucson Community Cable system since 1991; teams of volunteers read some 260 publications verbatim, including newspapers, magazines, novels, store ads, poetry, and more, accompanying the station's Community Resource Exchange channel.

Since 1963, when a franchise was granted to Berks TV Cable Company, Reading, Pennsylvania, has had exemplary public access programming. Its promotional brochure, *The Reading Dialogue*, lists some examples:

A famous operatic baritone sings, discusses his career, and chats informally in the same hour with hundreds of people in hundreds of homes.

Three attorneys, together in a small room, answer questions from and talk with people in widely separated parts of the city.

A wood carver, without ever leaving his workbench, demonstrates the art of making fine gunstocks and responds to questions from people all over town.

An expert in emergency psychiatric care talks to the staff of one hospital, while the staffs in two other hospitals participate from their own locations. (p. 10)

Reading also does a great deal for its senior citizen population, including a weekly "Sing Along," the two-way interactive cablecast of "Inside City Hall," the series "Your Social Security," and a program called "Bridging the Generation Gap." The wider community also enjoys "Our Schools," "Your Health and Wealth," "Nutrition Education," "Personal Finances," and arts and cultural, business, religious, and school-related programs.

Another interactive model is the Bronx's "Soul to Soul," a public access teleconferencing network linking three New York City boroughs via microwave signals to "encourage cross-cultural exchange, stimulate new modes of education, and provide a forum for community affairs."[24] The Educational Video Center has developed a program at Bronx Regional High School, an alternative school for dropouts, to empower disadvantaged students.[25]

And public access also makes an ideal communication tool for health professionals. The Springfield (Massachusetts) Cable Channel[26] has produced a number of programs, such as "Women in Trouble: Who Can They Turn To?" "How to Tell Your Mother She's an Alcoholic," "Intensive Care to Home Care," "Handicapped Children: Should They Be in Public Schools?" "Health Care Proxy," "Adult Day Care: What's It All About?" "Teen Age Depression," "AIDS: New Questions, New Answers," and "On-the-Job Wellness." Programs don't just need target audiences to make an impact on health. Project VITAL, for "Video Induced Training and Learning," was created by Little City Foundation of Chicago as a model audiovisual training program to teach persons with mental retardation and other developmental challenges the necessary skills to operate equipment at public access studios. The program offers its participants skills training in producing, directing, editing, and performing in their own videos, later cablecast to the entire community.

Educational Access Programming

Educational access programming, which appears on a specially "dedicated" channel, typically offers school, interschool, and otherwise educationally oriented programs. Library channels are also included here, many of which provide access to encyclopedias, films, and any number of documentary materials. Of particular interest is cable's potential for advances through interactive video, especially telecommunications projects linking various schools and school systems that might help narrow the gap between the information-rich and the information-poor.

Here is how the system might work: Each school is equipped with a microwave tower, two dish antennas, transceivers, and associated hardware components to receive and transmit signals. From a room containing a color camera, live microphone, viewing monitors for students, and two televisions for the instructor to view the classes in other schools, the system provides full two-way visual and audio instructional communication between teacher and students. From the originating point, the teacher can interact with students both near and far on a distant and personal level. The key is the ability to maintain the same spontaneity that the regular classroom allows.

In a 1986 *CTR* issue on "Trends in Access Development," Diana Braiden Radspinner, a specialist in cable communications for the Dallas Independent School District, wrote an article entitled "Educational Access: We've Only Just Begun" (Vol. 9, no. 4, pp. 15+), in which she outlines some of its uses as follows.

To inform—school districts across the country produce programs that tell about board decisions, special projects, community involvement, curriculum, and student activities. They are producing programming designed to bring information about educational issues directly to citizens.

To instruct—both students and staff are using access in a much more sophisticated manner than the "TV teaching" of the 1950s and 1960s. Instructional television now means more than turning on the TV and sitting back. The replay of specific programming to better meet a teacher's schedule has made the television set a useful resource. Teleconferences and live instruction allow students to attend classes that otherwise would not be available. Educational consortia provide services to smaller districts that were not affordable before.

To communicate—both video and data on broadband cable are significantly impacting education. Interactive live programming allows students and staff the opportunity to meet and discuss issues across the city or the nation. Electronic bulletin boards are fast becoming the newsletters of tomorrow.

There are a number of advantages to educational access: decreasing or eliminating the need to consolidate school districts, allowing increased curriculum offerings and greater flexibility in student scheduling, breaking down barriers between neighboring communities, allowing students to work with sophisticated audiovisual equipment, and allowing for teleconferencing among the boards of education and staffs of the school districts, thus eliminating transportation costs. In addition, programs developed by the gifted and talented can be recorded for absent students, satellite educational programs can be shared, in-service training can be held with cooperating institutions, and adult education classes can be expanded.

There are a number of examples (see Appendix 10 for names and addresses). Education Satellite Network[27] (ESN, Columbia, Missouri) was established by the Missouri School Boards Association in 1987 "to provide more equitable access to education for all students in Missouri as well as to expand learning opportunities for students, staff and members of the community." ESN is the only network of its kind in the United States; its satellite delivery system offers enhancement and enriched programming, described in its monthly magazine, *Satlink*.

Executive Communications, Inc. (ECI, Pittsburgh, Pennsylvania), trains professionals through satellite seminars such as its "Empowerment Vision" series, providing techniques and ideas meant to be useful on the job. "Electronic Field Trips," including teacher support materials, an orientation program, events, and computer bulletin boards, is a program of the Fairfax (Virginia) County Public Schools, a leader in distance learning. Other offerings include an elementary science study kit training, multicultural studies, foreign languages, and science seminars.

Instructional Television for Students,[28] billed as a convenient way to take live and interactive courses at California State University at Chico, offers several dozen upper-division courses that are simultaneously broadcast to a variety of sites throughout the northern part of the state. In addition to credit courses in education, finance, geography, health, history, humanities, math, political science, psychology, sociology, social science, and social work, general studies and themes are also available, such as global, environmental, contemporary health, and war and peace issues.

The Kansas Regents sponsor the Educational Communications Center[29] (ECC, Kansas State University, Manhattan). The product of federal, state, and institutional efforts to extend communications technology, ECC has a mission to utilize technology that can deliver "audio, video and data to homes, schools, work places, and learning centers, in both traditional and non-degree formats, including continuing education, professional development and 'lifelong learning' settings." LERN, the Louisiana Education Resource Network (Southern University, Shreveport), a free, live, educational satellite video-teleconference for grades 6–12 and early college-level students, has featured such programs as "Pathway to the Stars: Hawaii's Quest for Space" and "Get Hooked on Aquaculture."

Educational access has become the community television leader in Lubbock, Texas (LISD), although it occasionally works in concert with the government access channel.[30] Started in 1985 in a high school classroom, today the channel has a space at the cable company for its staff of three full-time and three part-time workers, producing 2,115 hours of programs on a budget of $30,000, with $200,000 accrued in fixed assets. Each year forty junior high and senior high students are trained, working to produce programs that air from 4:30 to 7:30 P.M. every afternoon.

Recently named "Most Outstanding Distance Learning Network," Mass LearnPike was developed by the Massachusetts Corporation for Educational Telecommunications as a cost-effective, innovative program utilizing multiple technologies.[31] Working with teachers and students at all levels of interest and achievement in academic modules, the satellite network includes interactive programs in these subjects: science, math, and technology; language arts; social studies; arts and humanities; staff development, parent courses, administrative support, and forums; and foreign languages and culture. Recent specific offerings to enhance existing curriculum have been "The Human Genome," covering historical, scientific, and ethical issues; "Thumbs Up, Thumbs Down," a review of library and media materials; "Artists in Electronic Residence"; "Scientists in Electronic Residence"; cultural enrichment programs for high schoolers in French, German, and Spanish; conversations with the secretary of education; and "Microcosmos," a minicourse in microbiology for teachers. A sample schedule is available in Figure 3.5.

By lease agreement with Storer Communications, Miami–Dade Community College (MDCC) has a cable television channel capable of reaching more than 100,000 subscribers. Broadcasting primarily telecourses for long-distance learning as well as a bulletin board of campus activities and events, the channel provided the catalyst for the South Campus's "Community-Based Television" project, allowing an open forum for chambers of commerce, high schools, and civic clubs to "tell their story in their own words" to members of the community at large.[32] In all, the project has provided access to thousands of potential students and service users, building a foundation for common partnerships with business and industry.

Recognizing that "access to higher education for geographically distant students, those who must travel, and others who cannot attend campus-held classes is becoming a higher priority for the country,"[33] Mind Extension University (Englewood, Colorado) attempts to combine the technology of cable and satellite television with resources from the nation's providers of educational services.[34] Populations served might include full- or part-time employees, homebound parents, physically challenged men and women, shift workers, geographically remote individuals, military personnel, seniors, and prison inmates. Mind Extension University, whose slogan is "Making All America a School," offers a wide range of program choices:

- Live, interactive secondary instruction—Physics, Calculus, German I and II, Japanese I and II, Marine Science, Elementary Spanish, Art History, Anatomy and Physiology
- Staff development—Literacy Plus, In Service of Children with Special Needs,

Figure 3.5
Mass LearnPike Programs—May 1993

Monday	Tuesday	Wednesday	Thursday	Friday
3 8:40 Health Plan 10 Mass Perf. 11 USS Constit. 3 Extra Help	**4** 9:30 Creative Math 11:45 Human Genome 1:15 Vocat'l Ed. 3 Very Special Arts	**5** 8:40 Health Plan 9:30 Writing Workshop 10:30 For. Lang. 1:45 MLP NL Mtg 3 Hands-On Science	**6** 9:30 Order in Chaos 11:45 Creative Physics 3 Stellar Math	**7** 10 Opera for Children 11:45 Arabic Culture 1 My Town
10 8:40 Health Plan 10 AIER 1 Children's Authors 3 Extra help	**11** 9:30 Cr. Math 11:45 Hu. Genome 1 Very Special Arts	**12** 8:40 Health Plan 9:30 Writ. Wrk. 10:30 For. Lang. 3 Extra Help	**13** 8 Espana Diversa 9:30 Order/Chaos 11:45 Creative Physics 3 Stellar Math	**14** 10 Opera for Ch. 11:45 Chinese Cult. 1:15 Tour de France
17 8:40 Health Plan 10 AIER 3 Extra help	**18** 9:30 Elec Field Tr. 11:45 Spec. Event 1 Special Arts	**19** 8:40 Health Plan 10:30 For. Lang.	**20** 8 Komm mit. 11:35 Women in Science 1 Student Forum 3 Stellar Math	**21** 10 Opera for Ch. 11:15 Ancestors
24 8:40 Health Plan 10 AIER 11 USS Constit.	**25** 1 Special Arts	**26** 8:40 Health Plan 10:30 For. Lang. 1 Teachers' Forum 2 TIER 3 Portfolio Assessment	**27** 9 Seasons	**28** 10 Opera for Ch.

Teaching Styles and Strategies, Self Concept and School Achievement, Evaluating and Improving Teacher Performance

- Student enrichment—World Food Day, Coastal Ecology: Managing Man's Impact, Managing Your Stress, Visit with an Artist
- Adult literacy—Learn to Read, Making Literacy Work, GED on TV, Teach an Adult to Read
- Certificate programs—Business Logistics, Industrial Security, Education Technology, Library Science
- Also, graduate and undergraduate degree programs, test preparation (GED, SAT, ACT, CLEP), and education specials.

NASA (National Aeronautics and Space Administration) sponsors an Aerospace Education Services Program for teachers on topics such as space exploration initiatives, life sciences research, aeronautics, and space flight/space station.[35] While most participants receive the videoconference via satellite downlinks at home or off-site, the next most popular means reported is public access television, followed by regional education centers.

The Northern Virginia Youth Services Coalition (NVYSC, Fairfax, Virginia) deserves special attention in this discussion on educational access.[36] From grassroots activity begun during the early 1980s, the coalition was formed from more than two hundred very diverse agencies and individuals to provide services to young people and their families. Its mission statement is as follows:

- To improve the lives of young people and their families in Northern Virginia by: facilitating communication and collaboration among all youth serving professionals (in both public and private agencies) across jurisdictions; offering low or no cost educational opportunities to professional service providers; increasing public awareness of available community services, good parenting skills, and the health and emotional problems faced by local youngsters; keeping the professionals, the public, and the elected officials abreast of youth related issues; and encouraging advocacy on behalf of the youth.
- To increase membership among social service agencies and professionals.
- To foster awareness among members of the benefits derived through the coalition as a networking and referral resource.
- To encourage the use of the NVYSC tape library among the various community groups for peer counseling, parenting, and other social issues.
- To develop quality quarterly programs on Channel 10 *Spotlight on Youth* with a half-hour format on youth related topics.

Obviously, it is that last goal that is most relevant to this book. Airing at different times for the various community television channels in the metropolitan area, its predecessor, "Focus on Youth," had been under the auspices of Joyce Grand as producer and moderator, working within a budget of $16,900. Some of NVYSC's programs since its debut in December 1987 have included the following: "Juvenile Detention Center," "Teen Pregnancy," "Foster Parenting," "Teenage Smoking," "Substance Abuse & Counseling for Children and Teens," "Learning Disabilities," "Alternative Programs for Fairfax Co. Public Schools," "Day Care," "Children of Divorce," "Parenting Skills," "Advocating for Children," "How to Say No," "Eating Disorders," "Children's Toys," "Adoption Practices and Results," "Grieving: Helping Kids Deal with Separation & Loss," "Child Sexual Abuse," "National Bone Registry," "Sibling Rivalry," "Youth in Politics," "Children & Depression," "Youth and AIDS," "Fitness and Handicapped Youth," "Children Raising Children," "Attention Deficient Disorder/Hyperactive Children," "Teen Suicide," "Childhood Incest," "Single Parents Support Options," "Cults & Satanic Worship," "Runaways," "Entrepreneurships," "Dropouts," "Play Therapy," "Music Labeling," "Underachievers," "Youth & the Arts," "Home Schooled Kids," "Bonding," "In Loco Parentis," "Acquaintance Rape," "Street Smart Kids," "Movies, Values & Kids," "Fears in Children," "Domestic Violence," "Kids Out of Control," "Blended Families," "Holiday Blues," "Homeless Kids," "Codependency," "Obsessive Compulsive Behavior," and "Kids from Belfast."

An arts and sciences teleconferencing service, Learning by Satellite emanates from Oklahoma State University as a satellite-delivered instruction service providing live, interactive secondary school instruction in the areas of math, science, foreign language, social studies, and remedial reading.[37] Cablecast in all the time zones of the United States, programs from ASTS (Arts and Science Teleconferencing Service) include German I and II, Russian I and II, Advanced Placement (AP) Physics, AP Chemistry, AP Calculus, Trigonometry/Analytic Geometry, AP American Government, Applied Economics, and Basic English and Reading.

Satellite Scholar (Missoula, Montana) provides a list of a number of groups and institutions that participate in educational access.[38] Satellite Learning (Alvin, Texas), which features live education and training programs, offers a comprehensive program and resource guide with its service.

Talcott Mountain Science Center for Student Involvement (Avon, Connecticut) operates an interactive educational television series called SCISTAR, aimed at alleviating the nation's crisis in science education.[39] In addition to providing three broadcast programs from its television studios, it also runs a coeducational independent day school for grades 4 through 8 and network programming "for anyone from age 3 to 93, including university level sciences, graduate education, and continuing education units for teachers—all with a total staff of less than 40." Since 1967, SCISTAR's "Shoulders of Giants" presenters have included astronauts, inventors/explorers, and experts from all the sciences and technology, including the fields of biology/chemistry, chronobiology/physiology, physics/astronomy/space, archaeology/evolution, environment/weather, and computers/mathematics/magic/ music/education.

And then there is TI-IN (San Antonio), a for-profit distance learning provider since 1984.[40] Direct student instruction consists of the following: Art History and Appreciation, Calculus, Elementary Spanish and Spanish I and II, French I and II, German I and II, Japanese I and II, Latin I and II, Psychology, and Sociology by means of teacher/facilitator training; and Anatomy and Physiology, Astronomy, Marine Science, Physics, and Principles of Technology by facilitator lab. Staff development is an integral part of the TI-IN system, and includes programs like "School Board Member Orientation," "Total Quality Management for Education," "Selling Success and Expecting Excellence," "Hispanic Connection: Making Learning Work," "Science for Every Kid," "Impact of the American Disabilities Act on Schools," "Optimizing Learning for Gifted Students," "What Makes Grand Opera Grand?" "Exploring Global Trends in Education," "Learning Styles of Multi-Culturally Diverse Gifted and Talented Adolescents," and "At Risk: Alternatives to Gang Involvement."

The Agency for Instructional Technology has conducted several national contests searching out the best promotion and utilization ideas that instructional television (ITV) agencies use to increase use of video materials in the educational process. Agatha TeMaat (1986) edited award-winning ideas under six major categories: (1) recognition—a description of a program on nutrition for fourth and fifth graders, and highlights of the media specialist's role in ITV; (2) professional development; (3) curriculum integration—descriptions of the Youth Vote Project, the ASSET Skills Matrix of courses "Media in the Curriculum" for students in grades 4 to 6, NASA Space Shuttle Mission Watch, and a program entitled "Across Cultures"; (4) Promotion—*Sights 'N Sounds* newsletter, Project "On Camera," and PSAs on health issues for young people; (5) video tape library—"Bits and Bytes," a computer awareness videocassette series; and (6) safety—including a poster calling the attention of the educational television community to safety hazards.

Governmental Access Programming

Governmental access programming, the third part of the PEG model, has both internal and external applications, such as between local governmental departments and constituencies and/or the national government and its citizenry.

In a keynote address to the 1985 NFLCP national convention, David Mathews, president of the Kettering Foundation, talked about the notion of community television revitalizing the old town meeting concept, with citizens learning about and participating in important community decision making. He posited a number of theories on how the public learns its business: (1) All issues are interrelated and need to be presented in a way that recognizes that, (2) issues have to be translated from policy language to public language, (3) the most important information that needs to be presented to the public is what their choices are, (4) people need not only an opportunity to hear but also an opportunity to converse or work through issues, (5) there are some things people can know only through other people.[41]

Over the years, more and more cities and towns have been including provisions specific to municipal use of their cable television franchise ordinances, provisions such as dedication specification, equipment requirements, access rights and responsibilities vis-à-vis channel allocation, materials, staffing, training, budgets, and the like. The franchise process becomes pivotal. Merry Sue Smoller, a cable regulatory officer, has pointed out that "the first stage, policy development, is crucial. Perhaps the appointment of a citizen advisory committee will assist city staff in determining and helping perform the needs assessment of institutions and community organizations that can then be reflected in the proposals and ordinance."[42]

Originally "designed to give maximum latitude for use by local governments" by the FCC, the government access channel can be funded directly by the cable operator, as in cities like Boston and Milwaukee, by franchise fees through contracts with city governments, as with Portland Cable Access and Columbus Cable Access, or under the model of a nonprofit corporation management. While each has its advantages and disadvantages, according to Irwin Hipsman, executive director of Cambridge Community Television, individual communities must determine the structure that will be most effective for them: "Community television often delegates access to a basic level of operations, a 'poor little brother' to local origination. Municipal management is prone to major pitfalls and the whims of politics. Non-profit corporations can work very well, provided they are set up properly and funded adequately."[43]

In the early days of governmental access, part of the problem was getting audiences to recognize it on their cable channels. In 1984, the city of Columbus, Ohio, contracted with Ohio State University to determine what people knew about governmental programming and what their attitudes and opinions were regarding it.[44] Under the direction of Dr. Thomas A. McCain, a telephone survey via random digit dialing was performed for a total of 602 responses. Findings included the facts that while only 40 percent of those interviewed could recognize the difference between government and public access programming, that same percentage had seen at least one city council meeting during the year, and 92 percent noted that it was "important that government access coverage of meetings let me see government in action rather than getting second-hand accounts." Some of its local weekly programs included "Columbus City Council"; "Cultural Happenings"; "Connections," a live, hour-long call-in program"; "Consumer Talk"; "Fit"; "Sports Beat"; "Silver Skyline," for those age fifty plus; "Your Health"; and "Missing Children." Monthly programs included "Special Edition," a teen report, "Concerning Equality," "Youth Service Bureau," "Job Show," and also special events, conferences, concerts, theater in the parks, poetry readings, seminars, government meetings, and public hearings.

Andy Beecher's "Government Access Corner" was for many years a regular column in *CTR*. After conducting a needs assessment of the community, surveying local communication patterns, establishing goals, and encouraging wide participation, he cites the following steps to build an effective municipal programming operation[45]:

- Get each department head to appear on a program
- Distribute PSAs to local broadcasters (in addition to cablecasting them)
- Wire the office of each department head, so they can watch "live" proceedings from their offices (if they have to make a presentation, they can work in their office until the appropriate moment)
- Have an occasional open house, featuring departmental liaisons who can encourage other city personnel to get involved
- Send program schedules to all departments, and to the local print media
- Write press releases on individual programs
- Solicit letters and calls about programs from viewers, and produce lively call-in programs on city issues
- Evaluate each program with department liaisons after its completion, and determine how it can be improved (if necessary).

Tulsa, Oklahoma, according to Beecher, was probably the site of the first "full blown" government access programming operation.[46] As early as 1973 the city had a thirty-five-channel system, in addition to a visionary mayor who favored the notion of open government. Deciding to jointly operate the channel with the Tulsa Library, whose enthusiastic director at the time was also president of the American Library Association, it was an ideal setup—especially helped by an annual contribution from the cable operator of $150,000. Its early programming included shows like "Books Sandwiched In," a brown bag lunch discussion, in addition to gavel-to-gavel city commission meetings, programs with the police, fire, park, and health departments, and extensive coverage of local elections and other special events. Yet this case study serves as a warning: By 1979 the channel had ceased operation. A new mayor felt strongly that government should not support media of any type, whether for the Corporation for Public Broadcasting or locally; further, he had his own agenda and was concerned about exposing it. Concurrently, Tulsa's operating budget continued to drop as revenue sharing was cut back, and other local funding never materialized. In hindsight it might be supposed that the operation simply developed too rapidly, or that it had too narrow a constituency; whatever the diagnosis, it stands as an early example of the need for full support.

A government channel that was activated in 1975 in Madison, Wisconsin, eventually developed to produce such programs as "City Dialogue," man-on-the-street questions and comments about city government or city issues; "District Reports," a ten-minute presentation by each of the city's twenty-two aldermen on district and citywide issues; a weekly call-in program; a regular series with the mayor; and regular cablecasting of board, committee, and commission meetings. Another regular feature was the insertion, during intermissions, of the government's business meetings, and of interviews with some of Madison's decision makers. This system is also worth our attention, as it continues to thrive today.

In 1976 the city of Reading, Pennsylvania, began its cablecasting of "Inside City Hall," a project especially effective due to the later introduction of interactive origination points, or neighborhood centers, from the library, a local community college, a public housing project community room, and a senior citizens' center. Some other early models, featured in Jesuale and Smith (1982, pp. 86–89), include the following: Overland Park, Missouri, hooked its traffic control system to cable technology; Brea, California, working in conjunction with its planning department, created videotapes about areas the city wanted to develop, which were "shown to prospective developers, used as visual aids at public hearings, and/or cablecast over the city's dedicated municipal access channel"; and Clinton Township, Michigan, used cable television hardware to monitor the town's water meters.

City 16 in Norman, Oklahoma, has produced these programs on its government access channel[47]: City council and planning commission meetings; "The Public's Business," an issues-oriented series with the city manager; "Norman 2000," focusing on the city's future; "City Sampler," interviews with city department personnel; "Candidates' Forums," with the League of Women Voters; and "Babysitters' Workshop," produced with the police department and the public library. Clark-Vancouver (Washington) Television, with budget monies coming from the general funds of both the county and the city, has produced meetings of the city council, cable commission, and planning commission, Chamber of Commerce Forums, and other meetings; "City Minutes," an issues program hosted by the cable administrator; "Dateline," a monthly in-depth public affairs program; and numerous PSAs.

As a result of a 1981 franchise agreement between the city and its cable company, Southfield, Michigan, contracted for two municipal channels reaching its 18,000 households.[48] Operating on a $240,000 budget, the channels have operated twenty-four hours a day, seven days a week, with five full-time staff members to feature the following:

• An annual program on the current state of property tax assessment. The program is cablecast during the city's property tax assessment process, and it includes information on how to appeal an assessment.

- A show on animal control explaining how the city's animal control unit operates.
- A promotional program on the city's community placement program encouraging interested city residents to use this service.
- Regular programs on fire prevention, produced in conjunction with the fire department.
- Frequent promotion of library services for children, the elderly, and other groups of readers.

Nearby Lansing, Michigan, observed its first National Night Out in August 1992 as part of a crime awareness program. Held outdoors in a city park, captured on the government access channel, the event moved the usual city council meeting from its chambers in City Hall, with citizens addressing council members on various issues. Lansing sponsors a regular "Citizens' Soapbox" on its Channel 28, giving residents access to a mass medium for expression of their opinions.

Governmental Information Channel 29 in Iowa City (Iowa) has recently established a new interactive television service called "Information Services," allowing citizens and staff access to a wide range of community information. Cosponsored by the city's Broadband Telecommunications Commission and cable TV office, the system works this way: Residents tune in the channel, dial a certain telephone number, and "ask for" information by pushing appropriate buttons on their phones. The service has an average of 1,000 calls and over 7,000 screens accessed per week, with the most popular selections being those regarding jobs, "You Tell Us" (an interactive poll), and police information. Some of the other information categories available include voting information, taxes, city budget, income tax information, school matters, PSAs, FBI wanted posters, missing children, a list of cars that have been towed, parking meters, animal shelters, bus routes, entertaining features like jokes, cartoons, and zodiacs, welcoming services, senior center, recycling, housing information, tours of Iowa City, information on safe sex, and a sign language alphabet.[49] Wm. Drew Shaffer, cable TV administrator for the city, has been involved in a wide range of activities relating to community television for some twenty years, having coauthored *Creating Original Programming for Cable TV* in 1984 and more recently having created Iowa City's interactive facilities through his Response Television Corporation (RTC, Technology Innovation Center, #203, Iowa City and Oakdale, Iowa). He says, "I felt it was imperative that access channels do more with their channels; that these channels need to become an integral part of the community and citizen's everyday lives to survive; and that an integration of phone, computer, video, and cable television technology was a way to accomplish these ends."[50] Today, RTC has more than a dozen systems nationwide, invaluable information and entertainment tools for access centers and communities.

LATV is a nonprofit, public benefit corporation in Los Angeles that began as an alternative to cable stations that didn't want to be burdened with their public access responsibilities despite being compelled to maintain them.[51] The idea has been that LATV would administer the facility, comply with its various regulations, and act as a "heat shield" between the cable company and its subscribers, a role that evolved when the Los Angeles City Council mandated that all cable franchises in its political jurisdiction be interconnected. What has happened is that the political prominence of LATV has brought with it a whole new awareness of community television.

Project LEAP (Legal Elections in All Precincts Educational & Research Funds, Chicago) was founded in 1971 in response to a perceived crisis in election integrity.[52] A nonpartisan organization funded by foundations, corporations, and individual contributions that allow it to operate on a budget between $75,000 and $150,000, Project LEAP has used Chicago Access (see Chapter 2, "Civic, Social, Local, and Academic Organizations") facilities to produce a training film for election judges which also serves as public information about vote fraud. It is in the process of trying to produce another such video to meet its current needs.

Since 1981 Lynne Tower Combs has been utilizing the medium of community television to share information about government activities in her locale of Passaic Township, New Jersey (recently renamed Long Hill Township), part of Morris County.[53] One of her first duties as a member of the township committee was choosing a cable company, a prophetic foray into politics, as she was the only woman on the committee and the other members were swayed by the presentation made by a then-famous former Princeton football player for his system. The twenty-five-year franchise made mention of public access, but the township never got its studio, cameras, or anything except the chance to participate at the system's headquarters some distance away, or occasionally to arrange for a mobile unit to visit. When she became mayor in 1983, Lynne began a monthly program called "Mayor's Corner," in which she interviewed key players in the county government. Tapes are held at the local library. Nowadays she continues that dialogue with her constituency in a new position, cablecasting "Administrator's Alley," this time including regular townspeople in the interview process—like the two older gentlemen who had walked the Appalachian Trail, or residents who wanted to get a playground built in town. In addition, she has made an effort to get the cable company to cover major events in the township, like the opening of the senior citizen handicapped complex, the ribbon cutting for a new sewer treatment plant, or sporting events at the regional high school.

Political uses of the government access channel, while expressly forbidden by the FCC, have nevertheless been tested in a number of instances for interpretation. Consider this scenario:

There is a community producer who currently has a show on your access channel. That producer now decides that he or she would like to run for the local board of selectmen or city council. This person, by virtue of the access program, has a decided advantage in terms of exposure before the community who will be voting. Is this an unfair advantage, or do you decide that the program came first so there is no advantage? One could argue that if this producer, who does an access program on home gardening, wants to run for office, then there is no problem because gardening has nothing to do with politics.

The counter-argument is that it is the high visibility, and not necessarily the content, which gives this candidate an advantage. Visual recognition, the counter-argument suggests, is just as important in politics as it is in product advertising.[54]

An actual situation for Arlington (Massachusetts) Cable Access, this example was used for the organization to determine guidelines regarding electioneering. In this instance, it decided to initiate a six-month moratorium on the program just prior to the election and to follow FCC rules applicable to cable television in general.

Andy Boehm, a media consultant to political campaigns, cable companies, and commercial advertisers since 1971, discusses some of the advantages to using cable television: "First, the demographic characteristics of typical cable subscribers more closely approach those of the much desired 'habitual voter' than do those of unwired TV viewers"; further, repetition, spot length, and relative cheapness of advertising and program time are all plusses.[55] A number of politicians attest to the value of local political cablecasting, among them Jeff Bingham (D-New Mexico), Tom Tauke (R-Iowa), Barbara Boxer (D-California), and Tony Coelho (D-California). "I decided to do a show because I think it's very important for those involved with public policy to bridge good communication with the citizenry," said Framingham, Massachusetts's, town manager, moderator of "Discussions for Framingham in the 1990s."[56] From neighboring towns, a former alderman offers "Dateline Newton," Waltham, Massachusetts's, "The Gray Matter" has become a popular political talk show, and Needham has "Live at Town Hall," "Local Environmental News," and "Newton Contact Sports."

Airing on Chicago's public access channel, "Republican Pub Talk" is billed as "a cross between a less adolescent 'The McLaughlin Group' and a League of Women Voters primer on the glories of two-party competition."[57] As the *Chicago Tribune* phrased it, "Public access television is associated, rather unfairly perhaps, with parchment-dry public service announcements, fringe groups, picaresque characters and self-indulgent vanity videos. . . . But Chicago's five access channels bring no small measure of serious politics, especially involving those largely shut out heretofore from mainstream commercial media, including blacks, Hispanics, and, of course, Republicans."

A longtime friend of The Alliance, Michael I. Meyerson of the University of Baltimore Law School penned his opinions on this topic during the most recent presidential campaign, arguing for the allowance of political speech on community television. The letter, reprinted here with permission, appears in its entirety in Figure 3.6.[58]

A recent "Commentary" in *Public Management* (Badeaux, 1991, p. 19) makes this comment about local government cable television:

Cable television has become a significant medium, and the possibility of using this medium to reach a large number of citizens with in-depth information on projects and issues is important for local governments.

Local governments operating a cable channel have enormous capabilities to communicate with citizens at a place where people get most of their daily news—the television set. Information can be presented at the time and in the form and style selected by the government. Each community with a cable company franchise agreement should give serious thought to operating a government channel. Smaller cities may want to explore sharing costs with adjacent cities; larger communities may consider sharing time with their smaller neighbors.

Whether by public, educational, and/or governmental access channels, what obviously is needed by us advocates of community television is informing people of its many different uses.

Finally, since it is oftentimes the most frequent "programming" on PEG access, mention should also be made of community bulletin boards. Ranging in use from full-time to off-time, when other original programming is unavailable, bulletin boards provide an invaluable informational service to their local communities. Of the thousands of running scripts out there, one from the small town of North Brookfield, Massachusetts, provides a good example. Billing itself as "Channel 8, Local PACTV: The First Amendment at Work," it includes information offering telephone devices for the deaf, elections and ballot information, flu vaccine, board of health notices, welfare, water percolator tests, town meeting, overdue sewer bills, emergency phone numbers for police and fire departments, real estate taxes, town government phone numbers and meetings times, hydrant flushing, listings for the American Movie Classics channel, a handcraft and collectible show, hayrides, interviews with senate candidates, theater guild plays, Boy Scout troop events, student activities, recycling, a country/western music festival, foreign student exchanges, church services, a message from the postmaster on packages, ladies auxiliary of the VFW post meetings, and much, much more. The bulletin board also scrolls a solicitation, "Have your message seen 500 times per week," which Brookfield Orchards, a local fruit farm, opted to do. With the continuing decline in local newspapers in the United States, community bulletin boards on PEG access channels undoubtedly provide viable substitutes for finding out about our individual cities and towns.

Controversial Programming

By its very nature the concept of community television is fraught with inherent controversies, implicit in the subtitle of this book. From a wide

Figure 3.6
An Open Letter to the Public Access Community

It has come to my attention that certain access channels around the country have refused to run programming offered by the Jerry Brown for President Campaign. I am worried that such refusal violates not only constitutional and statutory mandates, but violates the principles of public access as well.

Public access was established as an electronic soapbox, to ensure that all could speak. In designing access channels, Congress mandates that they be 'available to all.' Both the Federal Cable Act and First Amendment prohibit governmental censorship of access programming. No governmental entity, including not-for-profit corporations that are licensed or contracted to run public access channels, has the right to censor programming or favor one point of view over another. If someone wishes to use the access channels, they are to be commended, not silenced.

I have heard several reasons given for keeping off the programming. None of these, in my opinion, can withstand legal scrutiny. First, it is illogical (and unconstitutional) to treat political or campaign speech as a lesser form of speech, subject to tighter programming restrictions. Political speech IS speech, and political debate is the heart of a democracy. To limit candidates to scheduled debate in order to ensure 'a level playing field' misses the point of public access. Since all can gain access, without regard to ability to pay, access is, by its very nature, a level playing field for all who *wish* to play. Similarly, to oppose the solicitation of funds misses the distinction between political fund-raising and commercial speech.

The Supreme Court has long recognized that the requesting and contributing of money for religious and political causes is entitled to First Amendment protection, while mere advertisements for commercial products and services do not receive similar solicitude. For the former, the fund-raising is inextricably linked to the communicative values of the endeavors. Finally, people voice concern that if campaigns can solicit money, they will overwhelm access. I have two responses to that. First, I have always argued that, when it comes to access, 'the more the merrier.' I want access used. Second, any and all concerns for monopolization should be treated with content-neutral regulation, designed to permit as many speakers as possible.

In closing, I want it known that I have taken no money for this letter. As a long-time advocate for public access, and one who strongly believes in its promise of free speech and pluralistic communication, I believe that if access can survive the Klan and the Nazis, it can surely survive the Brown campaign.

If you have any questions, please call me at (410)997-6930 or (410) 625-3094.

Michael I. Meyerson, Professor
University of Baltimore Law School

perspective there is even some question about whether or not community television has met its predicted goal of increasing participatory democracy.

In an often-cited article in *The Independent*, "The Promise of Public Access,"[59] Andrew Blau, who serves as a staff associate for telecommunications policy at the Electronic Frontier Foundation and who has chaired The Alliance for Community Media, argues that the medium may in fact have "nothing to do with democracy—nothing, that is, until the people who provide and use access connect the two." Blau cites how, in the two decades during which public access to cable has existed, many new options for access to communication have developed: "conference calls, video conferencing, computer bulletin boards, voice mail, broadcast-fax and fax-newspapers, and other options that are erasing the distinction between traditional mass media and person-to-person telecommunications." Further, he notes, as this book has earlier, the widely increased usage of camcorders and the decreased costs involved in recording, producing, editing, and distributing materials for dissemination. Add to these factors the current regulatory climate and reinterpretations of the First Amendment, adds Blau, and what is needed is a fundamental requestioning of the mission of public access vis-à-vis fostering democracy:

Access centers that are moving in the right direction are those that provide opportunities for producers to develop their communications skills—i.e., to become more effective communicators. They prompt viewers to consider and think critically about the medium; artists to push the medium; users of other electronic media, such as radio or computer networks, to interact with video-based communicators; and all community members to develop access in whatever manner they choose. (p. 25)

Developing broader perspectives on how access centers can be used beyond merely teaching people how to use the technology and/or how to use the channels for communication and outreach, then, shifts the emphasis from production to sociocultural impact.

Then, too, there is the issue of whether, and how, community television might allow disenfranchised groups a means to communicate within and among themselves in an effort to forge consensus. Traditionally that role has occurred through the medium of talk radio, but in recent years the younger generation, having grown up with television, has turned to that format as its medium of choice.

Another potential issue thus arises: Will specific target niches of community television be limited to producing programs merely for themselves? One is reminded of Charles Tate's 1971 fantasy, mentioned in Chapter 1, of blacks programming for blacks, Chicanos for Chicanos, Indians for Indians, Puerto Ricans for Puerto Ricans. Today we have ever more specialized groups that claim the airwaves for their advocacy, ranging from ethnic to gender-choice to issues-oriented groups. Consider: "Indians" is no longer the chosen name for that population, and any number of groups have learned from one another how to access and use the media. Gays and lesbians, for example, have learned some lessons from feminists, just as AIDS activists have borrowed some tactics from blacks.

But then the problem remains: Are these groups talking only to themselves? Insularity not only inhibits the sharing of ideas but also becomes a controversy in and of itself if others are not privy to knowing the agendas of various groups, both manifest and latent. For example, when blacks aired a 1988 access program on Nation of Islam leader Louis Farrakhan, an outspoken black supremacist, they included long excerpts of his speeches, complex analyses about him, and discussions on where he fits in the resurgence of interest among young people in Malcolm X.[60] Think of all the white viewers who could have profited from such a program, but who probably were not considered part of the target audience.

In a study of controversial programming at eighty-one cable access centers in the United States, Aufderheide (1993) found that controversial programming, which she notes is "vulnerable to suppression under some proposed means of implementating the 1992 Cable Act," can frequently not only function as "a valuable service for immediate communities of reference, but (it also) expands the public sphere by expanding public discussion, debate and awareness of community issues and cultural realities." Particularly for special-interest groups, cable access performs a unique function in the civic arena, an "electronic public space" where debates can be aired, regardless of content.

Censorship too remains a continuing issue. While theoretically access programming operates on a first-come, first-served basis, scheduling and selectivity decisions are also at play. According to Baltimore Law School Professor Michael I. Meyerson, "The key is to use content neutral regulations. For example, to prevent monopolization by one group, you can limit the number of times any member from any group can speak."[61] He also makes the argument for preordained standards, saying they help facilitate organizational decision making.

While the Cable Act of 1992 prohibits cable operators from censoring access, and operators are not liable for programming cablecast on their access channels, any number of controversies remain. What happens, for example, when equipment is restricted from certain producers? When a city or town is unhappy about the airing of particular programs? When the old question of what determines obscenity is raised? Throughout, the role of the access center as editor comes into play. Who determines, say, whether one religious denomination should be allowed precedence over others? Fortunately, many individual organizations have legal counsel, and at the national level The Alliance for Community Media has a number of experts at its disposal. Its legal consultant, Jim Horwood, recently reported on its collaboration with other organizations (the Alliance for Communications Democracy, the Amer-

ican Civil Liberties Union, and People for the American Way) in response
to the censorship provisions of the 1992 Cable Act and the Time Warner
lawsuit.[62]

And then there is the issue of how serious any of this discussion on
community television is to academics. While a few media scholars such as
Erik Barnouw, Horace Newcomb, Bob Devine, George Gerbner, Herb
Schiller, Doug Kellner, Pat Aufderheide, and a few others have made reference to it, for the most part cable access has not received either much
attention or much respect. Yet, it has been found that "the presence of local
cable programming on campus is of mutual benefit to the student of information technology and to the Access Center. For the student it offers an
opportunity to create programming that addresses an audience within geographic reach."[63] Novak (1984) proposed that communication departments
use cable television public access channels as a means of providing students
with television production opportunities, claiming they offer a symbiotic
relationship between the channels and college students' firsthand learning
experience of how television works.

Hate Programming

At all levels of PEG access there is potential for controversy. As early as
1972, mainstream newspapers were referring to an incident in Reading (PA)
in which the city's Jewish community raised quite an outcry after the airing
of a documentary on the Ku Klux Klan.[64] Two years later, Somerville (MA)
aroused its aldermen with its first access cablecast, a sample of video shorts
shot by Media Action: "The tape included segments where the camera followed a dog peeing on a hydrant and a SMAP kid getting his hair cut before
enlisting in the Marines saying 'fuck.' "[65] And then there were New York
City's "Ugly George" and "Midnight Blue" of the late 1970s, responsible
for generating much of the negative reputation of public access. While it is
beyond the scope of this book to discuss the many cases and ramifications
of controversial programming on PEG access, an introduction to the topic
should at least spur more interest and research in it, especially in light of
continued concern that access channels are becoming a growing forum for
bigotry (Berger, 1993, p. 29).

Access programmers, according to the Cable Communications Policy Act
of 1984, are liable for any obscene programming that is cablecast over their
channels—and the penalties for violation are quite stiff. Yet, Robert Perry
of New York Law School reminds us, "Public service programming domi-
nates community television, and there is little reason to believe that obscenity will ever be a serious issue for community programmers."[66] Even
the *FCC v. Pacifica* case, which ruled that "indecent" speech could not be
broadcast when it might be heard by children, is not applicable, as cable
involves a contract between private parties in terms of subscription decisions—as determined in *Community Television of Utah v. Roy City*.

Probably the best-known case relating to controversial programming on public access is the "Race and Reason" anti–human rights program produced by Tom Metzger, former grand dragon of the California Ku Klux Klan. First aired on the local access channel in Pocatello, Idaho, in 1985, part of the tape had a guest asserting that the AIDS virus was carried by Jews and black people. Uncensored, the program was delayed until various community groups were afforded an opportunity to review and respond to it. After the actual airing, it was followed first by a lengthy call-in session allowing people to offer their counter viewpoints, then by the film *Bill Cosby on Prejudice*.[67] In Vancouver, Washington, "Race and Reason" was accompanied by a counter-programming tape on racism. More controversial than its cablecasting in Cincinnati was the use of the "community bulletin board" by a neo-Nazi group for recruiting purposes. Results in Austin, Texas, took a positive turn when the interest in counter-programming hate led to the establishment of at least four new programs. The city council of Kansas City, Missouri, responded in yet another way: It essentially gave up the community's right to public access television rather than confront the KKK programming. The Court's decision in *Missouri Knights of the Ku Klux Klan et al. v. Kansas City, Missouri*, #89–0067-CV-W–5, dated June 15, 1989, read as follows:

Group seeking to use public access cable television channel brought action against city and cable television service when city authorized television franchisee to delete public access channel. The District Court, Scott O. Wright, Chief Judge, held that: (1) plaintiffs had adequately alleged that public access channel had become a public forum; (2) complaint stated cause of action under the First Amendment; and (3) there is private right of action under Cable Television Policy Act provision precluding cable operators from exercising editorial control over public access channel.

Motion to dismiss denied.

An editorial in the *Christian Science Monitor*, lauding local access channels as "one of the rare ways that the 'little guy' can have his say on television," nevertheless adds this message: "In some communities they are vigorously used. In many, they lie fallow. The Klan's desire to use these channels for nefarious purposes should waken the rest of us to the possibilities of using them for programming that can knit communities together, rather than divide them."[68]

Graphic sex was an issue that Tucson, Arizona's, public access channel had to deal with; although the program was referred to the local police and county attorney's office, city officials found they were powerless to do anything about "The Great Satan At-Large," a live call-in talk show that involved "exposed genitalia, the fondling of a young woman's breasts by a cast member, masturbation by a cast member, nudity, film clips showing mutilation and real or simulated murder, racial and ethnic slurs, and discussion of bestiality and anal and oral sex by the host, cast and call-in viewers."[69]

Broadcast biweekly on Tucson Community Cable (TCCC) in the fall of 1991, the program featured a basic theme of anti-Christianity, the show's host (Lou Perfidio) claiming the performance was meant to bring attention to societal hypocrisy. The show's cameraman was quoted in the *Tucson Citizen* as saying, "Public access was set up to ensure the right of any individual to come down and express their point of view, uncensored and unimpeded. There's a lot of shows down here that I don't agree with the content, but I'll do everything within my power to make the show come across good technically" (October 14, 1991, p. 4A). A few days later a *Tucson Citizen* editorial read, in part:

It will come as no surprise to viewers who have accidentally stumbled upon Tucson Community Cable Company's televised vandalism that public access programming—also called "Channel 666"—has no standards.

But even the most jaded viewers have been shocked and outraged by the latest piece of public access trash. . . . It's hard to describe the filth in detail without being nearly as offensive. To call [the host] a braying jackass would be an insult to the animal kingdom. His species is more closely related to that perennial Tucson pest, the sewer roach.

And this, ladies and gentlemen—and *children*—is brought to you by city-supported public access. It is sent into the homes of cable subscribers—at their cost—with the City of Tucson's seal of approval . . . shown at 6pm Saturdays, so unsupervised kids can be assaulted along with adults.

The city's rules allow public access to be perverted into a stage for social lepers.[70]

The solution: The TCCC board suspended the show's host and producer for ninety days for "illegal activities" during programming, on the basis of written legal opinions. It also adopted a rule allowing TCCC's management to require programs deemed unsuitable for viewing by children to be aired after midnight.

A local citizen radio/TV columnist, Dan Sorenson, praised the board's actions, particularly those of its executive director, Sam Behrend, who "as befits the leader of a truly open publicly owned public forum, was loath to tamper with Perfidio's freedom of speech."[71] Recognizing the value of the decision in terms of sidestepping a lawsuit, Sorenson added, "And whether you watch it or not, public access is probably more valuable than you think. For every religious fanatic or bathroom humor call-in show, there are informative shows serving small audiences. They may seem dull to many, but that's what public access 'narrowcasting' is all about: serving small audiences who aren't served by the lowest-common-denominator programming of commercial broadcast TV." The other Tucson newspaper, *The Arizona Daily Star*, also praised TCCC's actions: "Rights are at stake in the matter, no matter how appalling the broadcast material may seem. Protecting rights isn't always easy, and it's galling at times to let offensive material parade even briefly under the cloak of the First Amendment."[72] By the next year,

TCCC had produced a document describing its stance, much of which is reprinted in Figure 3.7; since then, it has had no problems. Although the station's no-censorship policy remains, there appears to be no likelihood that any of TCCC's four public access channels will turn into late-night X-rated ones. And you may be interested to know that Perfidio, "The Great Satan," had to plead guilty to one count of contributing to the delinquency of a minor—having allowed a seventeen-year-old female cast member to participate in simulated sex acts on the show.

Responses to Controversial Issues

To deal with PEG programming by extremist fringes, attorneys Joseph Van Eaton and William Earley (1988, p. 4) of Spiegel & McDiarmid make the following comments:

In general the best and most practical approach may be to allow the programming to be shown on the same basis any other program is shown. Any attempt to stop controversial programming by shifting all programming to a "community" channel or a "government" channel controlled by the government or a community board faces substantial obstacles and may endanger the franchise. There are exceptions. An action which is illegal under valid state law does not become legal when it is shown on cable; speakers can be prosecuted for breaking the law. Further, and importantly, access centers can and should encourage more speech in response to controversial programming.

Even topics as seemingly innocuous as religious programming on the access channels also deserve our attention. Van Eaton and Earley (1988, p. 2) posit these scenarios: Can one prevent access channels from becoming the exclusive domain of religious broadcasters? If the community administers a grant program, can grants be given to religious groups in light of the First Amendment prohibition against "establishment" of religion? What is it that determines "community programming"? It may be just as difficult to define as what constitutes obscenity. To protect access operations, they suggest the following:

A. Controversial Programming Becomes A Less Important Issue Where the Community Understands Access and Believes It Important—Make Access Principles Known To the Community Now.

B. Act Affirmatively To Promote Counter-programming (But Do Not Provide Services To Some Groups You Are Not Willing To Provide To Others).

C. Review, Review and Review Your Rules To Eliminate Provisions Which Could Be Read To Allow Unlawful Censorship, and To Establish Clear Guidelines for Operations. (p. 13)

In an introduction to its helpful 1991 resource book on this topic, *Controversial Programming: A Guide for Public, Educational and Government*

Figure 3.7
Tucson Community Cable Corp. Adult Programming Policy

All checkout or cablecast indemnification forms signed by producers or submitters of programs at TCCC will now (6/3/92) have the following language included:

> "You are responsible for your program content. We ask you to be sensitive to protecting children from viewing adult shows.
>
> If in your judgement as the producer or submitter, your program depicts real or simulated sexual acts, representations or descriptions of excretory functions or exhibition of the genitals, or is excessively violent or uses excessive adult language, we ask you to choose a cablecast time of 12:00 midnight or later.
>
> TCCC reserves the right to reschedule such adult programs to a cablecast time of 12:00 midnight or later. If your program is rescheduled and you disagree with the decision, you may present your program to the *Adult Program Review Committee* for review and a determination whether it must be scheduled to an after 12:00 midnight cablecast time.
>
> If there are complaints about your program after it is cablecast, TCCC will review the program and if it is determined that it is adult programming, it will be re-scheduled to an after 12:00 midnight cablecast time. If you disagree with this decision, you may present your program to the *Adult Program Review Committee* for review and a determination.
>
> You may also submit your program or program concept to the *Adult Program Review Committee* before it is scheduled to be cablecast if you are concerned that there is adult language or depictions which are not suitable for viewing by children OR you feel that there is a compelling reason for your adult show to be cablecast before midnight.
>
> The findings of the *Adult Program Review Committee* may be appealed to an *Appeal Board* appointed by the TCCC Board of Directors.
>
> Please read the Time of Cablecast section of the TCCC Rules and Procedures manual for complete information about this policy."

The forms are also being updated to include the following language:

> "Signing this document should not necessarily be understood as an endorsement of these policies, but is rather an agreement to abide by them."

Access Television Advocates, the NFLCP underscores the importance of defining issues and roles, being prepared for the potential of controversial programming, and steps to take in the actual instance of a problem.

First, regarding roles, NFLCP's Controversial Programming Committee offers these role definitions:

- The community makes access programs.
- The access center provides the channels and means of production, plus education of the "speakers" and viewers.
- Government, following the guidance provided by the First Amendment, stays out of free speech issues.
- The courts provide the method for establishing and determining legality.
- The county attorney or district attorney receives complaints that the laws may have been broken, and makes a decision whether to prosecute.

Proactive steps that access centers can take might include the following: Establish content-neutral rules and apply them without respect to content; educate the board, staff, and the community (although the First Amendment is two hundred years old, do not assume a level of knowledge or acceptance); educate local print and electronic media; conduct extensive outreach and form a diverse base of support; and inform the community of the potential for controversy at the start.

If and/or once an actual controversial programming situation occurs, the following suggestions are proffered:

- Seek help from the NFLCP (now, The Alliance) and other access centers.
- Apply your rules and procedures.
- Remain calm and confident that your response is correct; a defensive person is presumed to be guilty.
- Maintain constant communications with local government and media.
- Maintain a log of events.
- Leave your emotions and personal opinions at home.
- Actively listen to anyone making a complaint.
- Provide all feedback, positive and negative, to the producer.

The NFLCP resource book contains a number of other helpful articles, notably Dirk Koning's "Dealing with Controversial Programs," which discusses programming policy, whether or not to cablecast, scheduling imported programs, and dealing positively with other media; Tom Karwin's position paper on controversial programs; Pamela Portwood's "Controversy and Public Access TV," on programming restrictions, offensiveness and indecency, obscenity, unpopular programming, commercial programming, copyright infringement, libel and slander, lottery information, producers' responsibilities, commercialism, and other prohibited content; and numerous helpful case studies, such as how South Portland, Maine, dealt with satanism and punk rock, Albuquerque with nudity, Amherst, Massachusetts, with political candidates, Mankato, Minnesota, with teen suicide, Sacramento, California, and Fort Wayne, Indiana, among several other community television stations already cited here, with hate programming, as well as how Pittsburgh, Pennsylvania, dealt with a locally produced anti-Semitic program.

Another relevant publication is Robert D. Purvis's 1988 *Bigotry and Cable TV: Legal Issues and Community Responses*,[73] published by the National Institute Against Prejudice and Violence (Baltimore), which focuses on implications of the "Race and Reason" series (see above under "Hate Programming") in various communities. His lessons and conclusions for developing effective strategies include the following: (1) Support the First Amendment; (2) become educated about public access; (3) know the cable system; (4) learn about programming options; (5) use controversy as a springboard for action; and (6) consider the option of a low-key response. In 1992 a revised and updated second edition of *When Hate Groups Come to Town: A Handbook of Effective Community Responses* was published by the Center for Democratic Renewal (Atlanta), containing sections on the following: understanding racism and bigotry and how hate crimes begin, the organized white supremacist movement, legal and legislative responses to white supremacists, responses by religious institutions, youth issues in organizing against bigotry, countering the rural radical right, hate group activity at the workplace, responding to anti-Indian activity, responses by government agencies, media strategies, how to monitor and document hate group activity in your community, and more. It also discusses how Klansmen and neo-Nazis discovered that community access cable television is a potential resource to give them more public visibility, but points out that in most cases their programs have been ignored by the larger public.

Or, consider the video response from Deep Dish TV to hate programming "Spigots for Bigots or Channels for Change," a ten-week series produced by Martha Wallner designed to be used as a community resource, particularly against racism. Offered to cable systems around the country, it included the following:

- Parts 1 and 2: "Guess Who's Coming to Public Access?"—discusses the situation in Kansas City, Missouri, mentioned earlier in this chapter regarding the KKK, interviewing activists, constitutional lawyers, and access users and staff.

- Parts 3 and 4: "The Empire Strikes Out!"—looks at white hate organizations in terms of their history, tactics, and ideology. Activists offer information about the tradition of resistance to these organizations and to less overt forms of racism, and lawyer William Kunstler, cultural leader and former political prisoner Dhoruba

Bin-Wahad, and Cornel West of Princeton's Afro-American Studies Department are featured.

- Parts 5 and 6: "Stirring Up the Myth of the Melting Pot"—varying perspectives on multiculturalism and racism in the mainstream media.
- Parts 7 and 8: "Snake Bite Kit for Access"—resources and strategies for combating racism and strengthening public access television, looking at efforts of national organizations like the Anti-Defamation League and the Southern Poverty Law Center.
- Parts 9 and 10: "Chain . . . Chain . . . Change"—youth's resistance to racism and marginalization, especially how music educates and agitates for change, with interviews of anti-Nazi skinheads and musicians active in Rock Against Racism.

Video activism is the subject of Chris Hill and Barbara Lattanzi's article "Media Dialectics and Stages of Access" in the Spring 1992 issue of *Felix*, where they discuss issues like being a KKK viewer/voyeur in the Tennessee tape "Do Y'All Know How to Play Dixie?" or Buffalo, New York's, "Disorderly Concept," a documentation of eighteen artists being arrested at Artpark in Lewiston, New York, by Buffalo Artists Against Repression and Censorship (BAARC). There are any number of examples of meta video programming, or community television televising itself and its activities, for many important purposes.

In response to a report on hate programming on cable television issued by the Anti-Defamation League of B'nai B'rith, Sharon B. Ingraham offered the following important statement:

Along with the thousands of hours of positive, community-oriented programming has come the small, but distinct, voice of hate. In spite of the fact that this programming constitutes significantly less than 1 percent of total access programming, it receives a great deal of attention. . . . While controversial programs undoubtedly cause anxiety and bring out fear, few programs have been found to violate the law. The politics of hate, whether used by members of extremist groups or by our own politicians during election time, are reprehensible, but not illegal. If and when hate programming crosses the line between ideas and actions, and it rarely does, law enforcement authorities can and should take action where laws have been broken.[74]

The most recent FCC ruling, as of February 1993, is a restriction declaring that programming regarded as indecent can no longer be shown on cable television channels open to all viewers; instead, it will be restricted to channels available only to viewers who ask in writing to receive it. Part of the FCC's implementation of the new cable re-regulation law, this rule bears watching.

PROGRAMMING TECHNICALITIES

As is evident in the plethora of examples of programming on community television in the United States mentioned in this chapter, some technicalities also need to be considered.

Structure

Although basic cable television service might look the same no matter where it is or who runs it, "What is different from franchise to franchise is who, how and if community access to the system is provided," suggests Dallas access producer and organizer Jan Sanders.[75] The following questions should be posited:

1. What is the dollar value per year of the franchise commitment? How will the payments be made; in one, two, or more payments? Is the amount set at a flat rate, or is it dependent on the operator's revenues?

2. Will the video production equipment be turned over in good condition? If it needs replacement, will the dollar value be based on the current replacement value of a similar piece of equipment? What about equipment the company wants to repair instead of replacing? Who will own the equipment and be responsible for its insurance, maintenance, and final replacement? What is the reasonable life expectancy of equipment; therefore how many times will each piece have to be replaced during the life of the franchise?

3. How many access channels will be allocated to the nonprofit corporation? On what tier of cable service will they be placed?

4. Who will be responsible for playback and for master control switching? How will the programming be delivered to the cable system headend?

5. Will existing leasehold improvements to buildings become the property of the nonprofit organization? What about the office equipment and furniture?

6. How will the new organization be structured? Who will make up its board of directors and membership? What provisions will be made to ensure diversity on the board and a clear voice to and from the community producers and the community at large?

7. Will the access corporation be clearly held responsible for facilitating access, or will the cable company be the responsible party? What will be the role of the franchising authority in enforcing the provisions of the franchise and the access agreement?

Political activists have long recognized tape exchanges as invaluable tools for sharing information, optimizing resources, and expanding beyond their own operations. Evelyn Pine, a staff person of the Foundation for Community Service Cable Television, lists the following ingredients for successful tape exchanges, which include tape libraries, hard copy directories, local and regional exchanges, and computerized databases[76]:

1. Serves a range of users from individual producers to major institutions
2. Encourages cable users to communicate with one another by eliminating the middleman function between user and provider
3. Emphasizes information sharing rather than the physical archiving of videotapes
4. Provides coordination and outreach to potential users
5. Assists other forms of networking and cooperation
6. Is low cost.

"The localism of access doesn't mean isolation," Pine adds. "Distributing our work allows us to support each other in new ways.... By sharing our programming, our ideas, and expertise, we inspire others within our community of interest to pick up a camera and explore cable's potential to build new networks."

Special-Interest Groups

Although typically considered "problem" cases for many community television channels, special-interest groups rightly can stretch the purpose of what PEG access is all about (Fuller, 1991b).

AARP, as has already been noted, has been trying to encourage retired/older persons to take an active role in local television programming, creating a voice for themselves as a constituency at the community level. The Senior Community Video Project in Portland, Oregon, has been producing "Age Wise," a biweekly program by seniors on topics of interest and concern to them, for about a half dozen years. According to one of its participants, Tom Taylor, "All members are retired, and we volunteer our time. We have demonstrated through our programming and by our very presence with cameras on location that the stereotypes that deaden and limit are UNTRUE."[77]

When the New York State Senate Committee on Investigations and Taxes surveyed its populace in the mid-1980s and found some two million functionally illiterate adult residents, it developed a program using computers and public access cable television to help solve the problem. Figuring that the illiterates cost the state millions of dollars in welfare payments and unrealized tax revenues, the committee believed that since community television was already in place as a resource, it made for an ideal fit.

While public television is developing a service called Descriptive Video Service (DVS) to help the visually impaired watch television, a number of PEG access groups report their work assisting members of that same population to become television producers. Hearing-impaired persons in Sacramento, California, have been aided by the DEAF Cable Project (Deaf Equal Access for Cable), which has "successfully trained deaf community members to script, record, edit, and produce their own series of six television programs dealing with deafness-related themes, and using deaf performers."[78]

"Black Notes," a minority program that first aired in 1972 from the National Cable Company in East Lansing, included a panel discussion about prison systems in Michigan.[79] Over the years the diversified talents and interests of the group have moved from news to variety, from documentary to drama, and to a mixture of news/community, variety, and drama. Its ultimate, ongoing goal is getting blacks and other minorities into the media. In a (Spring 1982, pp. 16–19) *CTR* issue, Jabari Simama provided an important article, "Black Participation in Telecommunications: Guidelines for Right Now!" including information on franchising, ownership, employment, training and community development, black and small business opportunities, programming, and specifics on PEG access and local origination. Another group, women, have also continued to make their mark in the field, as evidenced in numbers alone who are involved in The Alliance (Fuller, 1992).

Gays and lesbians have embraced community television as a valuable means of expression, as has been evidenced in many instances throughout this chapter. Further, it should be noted that subsets of this population, such as gay Asians, have also participated; videomaker Richard Fung, for example, has written about his many goals: "First of all, I wanted Gay Asians to speak for themselves. I wanted to present them as sexual subjects rather than as sexual objects. I wanted to confront controversial topics such as transvestite lifestyles and S&M without glossing over anything. I wanted to point out the variety of opinions and experiences within the Gay Community."[80]

Handicapped access has a whole new meaning when applied to community television. A number of programs have been made by and for developmentally disadvantaged persons—notably, "We All Live Here" in East Lansing, Michigan, "Grab-A-Chair," an exercise program for wheelchair-bound viewers in Manhattan, and the "Handicapped Project" of Oakland, New Jersey. Project VITAL, mentioned earlier in this chapter, is the model for working with the developmentally disabled.

"The demographics of chronic illness in an aging population, and the constraints on the financing of health care, make it important to explore the development of low-cost community interventions to assist the chronically ill to assume greater responsibility for self-care," David Katz has written.[81] A professor of social work at Washington University, he reports on the value of one such program, "Winning over Arthritis Pain: Let Me Show You How," cablecast very successfully over the local origination channel in St. Louis. San Diego began producing "Social Services Gamut" in 1981, funded by a grant from the U.S. Department of Health and Human Services; Madison (WI) offers "Who Cares for the Children?" and Torrance (CA) has developed its own social service program for its "Citicable 22." Media Network has put together a number of workshops on "Seeing Through AIDS," and Adam

Knee of the New School for Social Research has authored a potent document, "AIDS Activism on/through Video."[82]

International and ethnic programs continue to gain in popularity on community television; Cambridge (Massachusetts) Community Television has long been a model for them. Monday through Friday from 5 to 11 P.M., with partial additions on weekends, it has featured ongoing series in Arabic, Haitian Creole, Portuguese, Armenian, Italian, French, and Greek, recently adding more programming in Polish, Spanish, and Gaelic. Throughout New England, these are just a few of the programs available: "RAI Tele-Italia," "Portuguese Entertainment Network," "Voice of the Arab World," "Tele-Kreyol" (a weekly Haitian news show), "Horizon Armenia Hour," "Bonjour," "Tropical Caribbean," "Arabic Hour," and "Grecian Melodies."

Recognizing the wide diversity of religious programming that airs on community television stations, the Reverend Dick Duncan,[83] a media consultant for the United Church of Christ, considers any of the following programming goals in his definition of what determines the genre: provide a means for spreading God's word, reveal the kingdom of God, share the way of the Lord, encourage the viewer to focus on a deity or faith system, communicate a faith message, manifest a Creator, present truth as related to God, ensure the salvation of people's souls, and be ethically, morally, and theologically uplifting.

Access producers in Chicago produced "Welcome Home" as a salute to Vietnam veterans, honoring a parade held twenty years after their return; it was so successful that others followed, like "I Would Never Do That Again." The difference was that the different programs were produced by people on opposite sides of the issue, one mainstream and the other working with Vietnam Veterans Against the War.

Jewell Ryan-White, public relations coordinator for American Cablesystems Midwest, has constructed some outreach strategies for working with minorities and "special human interest users"[84]:

- *Identify* who the minorities and special human interest groups are, including their organizations and leaders—using foundation centers, coalitions, libraries, minority organizations, women's groups, educational institutions, the media, and other local resources.

- *Provide information* by conducting a continuing program designed to cover all aspects of the opportunities offered by your organization.

- *Provide training* through the access center.

- Ensure that your *Board of Directors* reflects all segments of the membership and community served by the organization.

- Give attention to minorities and special human interest groups when locating *consultants and speakers.*

- Set up *programming exchanges* with other organizations.

- Ensure that *recruitment* of minorities and special human interest groups takes place at all levels of your organization.
- Include articles in your organization's *newsletter* on ethnic and special human interest–oriented issues.

Audiences

Johnson and colleagues (1974, pp. 1–15), in the early days of PEG access, recognized that it would be necessary for community television stations to become much more concerned about building and maintaining target audiences in the future, and suggested these steps:

1. Promotional materials for the access center must be prepared and disseminated throughout the community;
2. Program schedules must be published in the newspaper and then adhered to by the access facility;
3. Questionnaires must be administered periodically to measure viewer reaction;
4. Groups utilizing public access television must be encouraged to promote their programs by direct mail, posters, phone calls and announcements at meetings.

Concern for audiences has continued, as narrowcasting has become the modal form of television viewing. In 1987 NFLCP put out a *Cable Programming Resource Directory* as a guide to community television production facilities and programming. Although severely outdated already, it nevertheless is an important resource in terms of listing the wide range of national free and low-cost and international cross-cultural programming sources that are available. Programming is indeed the very crux of community television.

NOTES

1. Editorial, *The Nation* (July 8, 1991), p. 39.
2. Fred Johnson, "Exploring Historical Roots of Access," *CTR* (August 1991), p. 4.
3. Dave Keyes, "N.P.O. Access!" *CTR* 11, no. 5 (December 1988), p. 1.
4. Susan Wallace, "Programming Sources," in Wm. Dean Schaffer and Richard Wheelwright (eds.), *Creating Original Programming for Cable TV* (Washington, DC: Communications Press, 1983), p. 15.
5. New York, NY; Bakersfield, CA; Ann Arbor, MI; East Lansing, MI; Lawrence, KS; Akron, OH; De Kalb, IL; Aspen, CO; Reading, PA; and Casper, WY.
6. Resources from Paul E. Simon, director of Pocatello Vision.
7. Resources from Barbara Popovic, executive director of the Chicago Access Corporation.
8. Mary Gillespie, "Mastering a New Medium: Chicago Seniors Produce Their Own Cable TV Show," *Chicago Sun-Times* (May 6, 1992), p. 43.

9. Patricia A. Williams and Tonya Daughrity, "Cable TV as a Tool for Community Education," *Dialysis & Transplantation* (April 1992), pp. 238+.

10. Sue Miller Buske, "Improving Local Community Access Programming," *Public Management* (June 1980), pp. 12–14.

11. Extracted from Barbara Wolf's article "Cable Access and Social Change: Eight Case Studies," *CTR* 9, no. 1 (1986), pp. 18–21.

12. Letter and resources from James Chefchis, assistant director, Cable Access of Dallas, August 13, 1992.

13. For more information on "East Meets West," contact Ange Hwang at 612/920–8050.

14. "OCAW Jolts Boss with Video," *Labor Beat* (Fall 1991), p. 1.

15. Bruce Adams, "Access Provides a Forum for Discussions on National Issues," *CTR*, 9, no. 1 (1986), p. 23.

16. Ann Sheehan and Randal L. Ammon, "National Issues Forum: The Reading and Pocatello Experiences," *CTR* 9, no. 1 (1986), p. 24.

17. *NIF News*, 1, no. 1 (Spring 1992).

18. Bob Devine, "Protecting the Diversity," *CTR* 9, no. 1 (1986), p. 35.

19. Resources and note from K. Erin O'Meara of the Milwaukee Access Telecommunications Authority.

20. For more information, contact Marilyn S. Mann, president, NMCLC, P.O. Box 1707, Gresham, OR 97030, or the National Center for Missing and Exploited Children in Arlington, VA—written up in *New Media* (April 1993, p. 28).

21. Suzanne Strempek Shea, "Pound Hounds Begging for Homes via Television," (Springfield, Massachusetts) *Union-News* (December 24, 1990), p. 10.

22. Natalia Munoz, "Lesbians Conduct Talk Show on TV," (Springfield, Massachusetts) *Union-News* (January 18, 1992), p. 11.

23. Monroe E. Price and John Wicklein, *Cable Television: A Guide for Citizen Action* (Philadelphia: Pilgrim Press, 1972), p. 39.

24. Wendy Trippe, "Soul to Soul Teleconferencing," *Mediactive* (Summer 1987), p. 8.

25. Liz Grabiner, "Empowering Disadvantaged Students," *CTR*, 8, no. 4 (1985), pp. 10–11.

26. Zedra Jurist Aranow, "Cable TV Show Spotlights Health," (Springfield, Massachusetts) *Union-News* (August 29, 1991), p. 26.

27. Letter and resources from Jeanie Rhoades, ESN support assistant, September 8, 1992.

28. Letter and resources from Ralph F. Meuter, dean for regional and continuing education, California State University, Chico, July 28, 1992.

29. Note and resources from Barbara Newhouse, Ph.D., associate director, academic programs, Educational Communications Center.

30. "Educational Access the Leader in Lubbock," *CTR* (Spring 1991), p. 9.

31. Resources from Beverly Simon, director of communications and membership, Mass LearnPike, January 1992.

32. Reported on in Johnny Mac Allen, "Cable Television: Strategic Marketing through Community Relationships," paper presented at the annual convention of the California Association of Community Colleges, Anaheim, CA, 1986.

33. Glenn R. Jones, *Make All America a School*, 2nd ed. (Englewood, CO: Jones 21st Century, 1991), p. 3.

34. Resources from Andrea Montoni, public relations director, Mind Extension University.

35. Letter and resources from Rick Collin, videoconference coordinator, NASA, Oklahoma State University, August 11, 1992.

36. Letter and resources from Beverly Salera, executive director, NVYSC.

37. Resources from Leigh Beaulieu, manager, ASTS, Oklahoma State University.

38. Telephone conversation with and later resources from Greg Bell of Satellite Scholar.

39. Letter and resources from Ginna Crosby, Development/Public Relations, Talcott Mountain Science Center, September 22, 1992, and February 9, 1993.

40. Letter and resources from Laura Adams, marketing manager, TI-IN.

41. "Access Is Public Power," *NFLCP Newsletter*, 8 (1985), p. 4.

42. Merry Sue Smoller, "Municipal Franchising: A Primer," in Barry Orton (ed.), *Cable Television and the Cities: Local Regulation and Municipal Uses* (University of Wisconsin, 1982), p. 8.

43. Irwin Hipsman, "Access Management Structures—A Primer," *CTR*, 9, no. 4 (1986), p. 8.

44. Reported in Laura B. Greenfield, "Measuring Audiences for Government Access Programming," *CTR* 8, no. 3 (1985), pp. 8–9.

45. Andy Beecher, "Developing a Promotional Plan for a Government Programming Operation," *CTR* 8, no. 3 (1985), p. 7.

46. Andy Beecher, "The Early Days of Government Access," *CTR* 9, no. 2 (1986), p. 15.

47. Andy Beecher, "Government Access Profiles," *CTR*, 8, no. 4 (1985), p. 36.

48. Kathy Sherman, "Information at the Touch of a Button: A Profile of Southfield's Municipal Channel," *CTR*, 8, no. 3 (1985), p. 18.

49. Mark A. Tolstedt and Ronnie Bankston, "Government Information Services and Telecommunication Technology in the Pacific Islands: Using the Iowa City Information Services Model," PTC '92 conference, Honolulu.

50. Letter and resources from Wm. Drew Schaffer, RTC, August 1, 1992.

51. Thanks to Fred Carroll, chair of UPPNET, for information on LATV in his letter of September 10, 1992.

52. Response form and materials from Arlene C. Rubin, executive director of Project LEAP.

53. Personal interview with Lynne Tower Combs, January 15, 1993.

54. Len Tammaro, "Access Restrictions for Candidates Prevent Electioneering," *CTR*, 9, no. 1 (1986), p. 8.

55. Andy Boehm, "Political Campaigning on Cable TV," *CTR* 9, no. 1 (1986), p. 6.

56. Doreen E. Iudica, "Local Access Cable Shows Come of Age," *Boston Sunday Globe* (April 15, 1990), p. W1+.

57. James Warren, "Party On, GOP: 'Pub Talk' Thrives on Cable," *Chicago Tribune* (February 4, 1992), p. 1.

58. Michael I. Meyerson, "An Open Letter to the Public Access Community," *CTR*, 15, no. 2, p. 3.

59. Andrew Blau, "The Promise of Public Access," *The Independent* (April 1992), pp. 22–26.

60. James Warren, "Black Community Finding New Voice through Cable TV," *Chicago Tribune* (February 9, 1992), p. 17.

61. "Censorship: Can You, Should You, Would You," *CTR* 9, no. 1 (1986), p. 31.

62. Jim Horwood, "Community and Collaboration," *CTR* 16, no. 1, p. 7.

63. John Giancola, "The Importance of a Human Values Approach to Telecommunications," *CTR* 9, no. 4 (1985), p. 8.

64. For example, Michael J. Connor, "Controversial Programming on Access," *Wall Street Journal*, 1972.

65. Reported by Bob Matorin in *CTR*, 7, no. 1 (1984).

66. Robert Perry, "Obscenity Law and Cable Communications," *CTR*. 8, no. 2, p. 12.

67. For an in-depth discussion on the comedian's attitudes toward race, see Linda K. Fuller, *The Cosby Show: Audiences, Impact, Implications* (Westport, CT: Greenwood, 1992).

68. "Giving Access to Controversy," *Christian Science Monitor* (December 1, 1988), p. 15.

69. Dan Sorenson, "Graphic Sex on Cable TV Here," *Tucson Citizen* (October 12, 1991), p. 1A. Sam Behrend, executive director of Tucson Community Cable Corporation, told about this issue in depth at the NFLCP 1992 conference.

70. "Public Access Is Twisted into a Public Insult," editorial page, *Tucson Citizen* (October 17, 1991), p. 14A.

71. Dan Sorenson, "TCCC Handled Great Satan Wisely," *Tucson Citizen* (October 21, 1991), p. 1E.

72. "Cable Most Foul: Careful Legal Weapons, Not Censors, Work Best," *The Arizona Daily Star* (October 23, 1992), p. 12A.

73. Letter from Robert D. Purvis, assistant director for administration of the National Institute Against Prejudice and Violence, August 26, 1992.

74. Sharon B. Ingraham, "An NFLCP Editorial Response," *CTR*, 14, no. 4 (September/October 1991), p. 2.

75. Jan Sanders, "Transferring Management of Access," *CTR*, 9, no. 4 (1986), p. 9.

76. Evelyn Pine, "Exchanging Tapes Creates New Communities," *CTR*, 9, no. 1 (1986), p. 29.

77. Tom Taylor, "Seniors Using Public Access Counter Stereotypes on Aging," *CTR*, 15, no. 5 (September/October 1992), p. 11.

78. Dr. Glenn A. Goldberg, "Community Television in the Deaf Community: A Sacramento Experiment," *CTR* 10, no. 2 (1987), p. 33.

79. Marsha Smith and Michael Lewis, "Minority Programming: Breaking the Image," *CTR* (Spring 1982), pp. 4–5.

80. Carol Greenburg, " 'Orientations'—A Profile of Gay Asian Videomaker Richard Fung," *Mediactive* (Winter 1986/87).

81. David Katz, "Building an Audience for Community Health Programming," *CTR* 8, no. 1, p. 24.

82. Adam Knee, "AIDS Activism on/through Video," in Linda K. Fuller and Lilless McPherson Shilling (eds.), *Communicating about Communicable Diseases* (Amherst, MA: HRD Press), 1994.

83. The Reverend Dick Duncan, "Diversity of Religious Access Programming," *CTR*, 10, no. 2 (1987), p. 28.

84. Jewell Ryan-White, "Strategies for Outreach to Minorities and Special Human Interest Users," *CTR* 10, no. 2 (1987), p. 7.

Production and Producers

Public Access Television provides the access-ability to a marvelous medium of communicating, with an unprecedented combination of factors arriving (seemingly) simultaneously on the scene:

1. Virtual removal of all economic barriers, as great equipment is available to use at no cost . . .

2. Free Air Time!

3. Great attitude of technicians available to help (learn and produce).

4. Technical advancement in the Industry.

For any volunteer video producer such as myself, Public Access Television is an extremely viable concept . . . whose time has come![1]

Dick Pirson, Minneapolis

While television production in the commercial arena focuses mainly on audiences in order to attract advertisers, the whole point about community television is that it can concentrate on allowing individual expression. This chapter looks at training in both the technical and nontechnical aspects of production for community television, describes some producers of PEG access, considers some administrative aspects of the process, and cites the importance of volunteers to help it all happen.

TRAINING

While it is beyond the scope and intent of this book to offer in-depth specifics on how to set up and manage community access stations, a number of suggestions are included as to where that information is available (Fuller, 1993a).

In 1986, for example, the Program Department of AARP and the NFLCP collaborated to produce *Community Television: A Handbook for Production,* which includes the following in its table of contents:

1. *Local programming*—some background
2. *Television production: the players*—channel staff, production crew, talent, audience, and a case study from Dallas, Texas
3. *Television production: the tools*—videotape, cameras, players/recorders/editors, switcher, film chain, graphics, set, lighting, audio equipment, portapak, odds and ends
4. *Television production: the process*—getting started/training, the three Ps (preproduction, production, and postproduction), script writing, program formats, legalities, and promoting your program

Recognizing that "video equipment phobia is a common obstacle for potential producers" (p. 19), the contributors to this project suggest not getting hung up on all the gizmos and gadgets, but to remember that community television is about working with people and ideas, too. They then take the future producer by the hand, introducing her/him to the concepts and cautions of working with various pieces of equipment, in much the same way that a formal training session with an access organization would be conducted. There are also a fair number of commonsense suggestions, such as "Don't drop the camera, get it wet, or aim it at any bright light such as the sun or a studio lamp" (p. 21), "The hardest part of editing for most people is deciding what they want the edit to accomplish" (p. 23), "Your program can be more informative, visually interesting, and complete if you use titles and credits that are clear and appealing" (p. 25), or "However marvelous today's video cameras, the human eye remains a more remarkable instrument in terms of light sensitivity" (p. 27).

The production process, it turns out, is actually a three-step one: preproduction, the production itself, and postproduction, no aspect of which is necessarily more important than the other.

Another term for preproduction might be planning, when ideas become organized into scripts, schedules, budgets, and decisions like who is to be involved in what aspects of the program, when, and where. Once the theme is decided upon, the pattern for showing it needs to be determined: interview, lecture, travelogue, story, newsreel, film-poem, cartoon, and the like. Michael H. Adams (1992, pp. 15–16) lists variations of these tasks of preproduction:

1. Select an idea—think about it, write it down, and evaluate.
2. Do research—before an idea is developed into a video production.
3. Develop the treatment or story outline.
4. Write the script—which can be a short screenplay or list, outline, interview questions, or narration.

5. Find locations—scout possible places.

6. Select talent—the on-camera people greatly affect the look of the final show.

7. Select technical crew—camera operator, tape operator, audio person, lighting designer, and set designer.

8. Obtain equipment—and learn how to operate it.

9. Prepare a budget—see what it will cost.

10. Develop a schedule—check locations and activities of the talent, equipment, and crew.

The production itself can be shot live or videotaped for later telecasting; if the latter, allowances for editing can be made, graphics can be inserted, music added, and any number of other technical aspects can be considered. For this phase, whether short or long, Adams (1992, pp. 107–8) suggests these activities: Prepare the set and lighting, rehearse, operate the equipment, set up on location, and direct. Most programming produced by and for community television operations in the United States is "live," with the bulk of the action shot in a studio setting.

It cannot be stressed enough that postproduction is a critical phase, an important time to evaluate the program and promote it for future viewing. Adams (1992, pp. 199–200) considers the following predictable and definable activities making up this final phase:

1. Copy the original—it protects the original from excess wear or damage, and the "work print" can be viewed elsewhere.

2. View and log tape—make notes about shots.

3. Make technical preparations for editing—such as music, narration, and sound effects.

4. Make editing decisions—list the takes, shots, and scenes needed for the final show.

5. Learn to use the editing facility—get orientation, instruction.

6. Schedule the editing facility—for uninterrupted time.

7. Make the edits—your chance to be creative.

8. Create titles and graphics—for a finished, professional look.

9. Complete post-production—you might go into a complete control room with editor, switcher, character generator, and audio mixer.

10. Exhibit and distribute the video—show your finished product, maybe making copies of the master for those involved in the production.

Technical Training

Consisting of skills training like camera work, graphics, editing, lighting, signals and cues, and the like, technical training typically is offered by individual community television stations for their volunteers. The idea of this technical training is to fill in the blanks from the brief introduction recounted above on pre-production, production, and post-production.

Of particular interest is the decisive role of the videotape editor, underscored by John Hewitt (1992, p. 156):

If the raw tape is well shot, then their skills are not quite as crucial. But when the source tape is mediocre or poor or has some holes in it, it's going to take a good editor to make something out of it. Newstape editors, magazine format editors or off-line documentary editors all can have a direct influence.

First, the editor is in a position to encourage either good or bad story design. If an editor previews the tape with a reporter/producer/writer, the editor can emphasize the strengths and lament the shortcomings, assisting the writer with this advice about what's going to be good.

Second, the editor's shot decisions form the basis for the visual aesthetics, while the editor's skill levels can alter the story pacing, the transitions and the cohesion between the narration and the information in the visuals.

Finally, the editor is the last checkpoint for the content. In many cases, editors work alone; and at a lot of broadcast stations, their work goes directly on the air without anyone's reviewing it. For this reason, the editor often serves as both a fact checker and an ethics sounding board.

Consider, for example, condensing eight hours of a regatta down to eighteen minutes! The event took place along the Connecticut River in Springfield, Massachusetts, where a number of college groups gathered to compete. Footage was obtained on the city—the route, some history, a scan of the scenery, inclusion of certain (politically) important people, information on the developing Riverfront project, and so on. In addition, there was documentation on regattas per se—the physical aspects of the sport, rules and regulations, official information and histories, participants, explanations of routes, the shells, finish lines, and more. An "invisible narrator" format was chosen, which allowed the editors to insert scenes ranging from beautiful bodies to avid viewers, in addition to appropriate audio. Also considered were a number of contingencies: rain (the cameras didn't have covers), last-minute program changes, medical and other emergencies. Afterward, the formal evaluation form, a sample of which is presented in Figure 4.1, had to be filled out.

Throughout a number of issues of *CTR*, Dave Bloch, who labeled himself "the Community Videot," provided an invaluable resource for technical tips. For example, he might talk about depth of field and other photographic techniques applied to video, the basics of tape care, portapak comparisons, ideas for portable and mobile productions, even how to make your own portable 300-watt broadlights for about $25 each. One of his more ingenious articles dealt with what to look for in designing an access center.[2] Commenting on how they now exist in very creative accommodations—such as

Figure 4.1
Program Evaluation Form

<u>Data base</u>   Title of program_____

Date(s) aired_____

Producer_____

Length (running time)_____

Videotape _____   Live production _____

Director_____

                             Comments

<u>Criteria</u>   1.Introductory video

2.Introductory audio

3.Lighting

4.Sound

5.Background set

6.Camera work

7.Switching

8.Special effects

9.Graphics

10.Credits

11.Scripting

12.Talent--actors

13.Editing

14.Technical quality

<u>Recommendations</u>:

                             Evaluator:

                             Date:

"service stations, small churches, school classrooms and gymnasiums, store fronts, warehouses and Victorian homes," he first suggests that activists consider a building already serving the community, preferably in an easily accessible location. Bloch encourages variations on looking for these attributes, once space considerations are determined:

- A studio-height ceiling—at least fourteen feet high.
- Lots of ventilation—the key words are "high volume, low velocity," so you want lots of cool air moving through your studio to counterbalance those hot lights.
- A very smooth floor—"Take a marble with you when you inspect a building. If the floor is not carpeted, you can drop the marble and watch how it rolls."
- Isolation from noise—the quieter the location, the less you may have to spend on soundproofing.
- Odd-hour accessibility—as your access center will probably be in use at late hours, weekends, and over holidays.
- Wheelchair accessibility—an important reminder.
- Zoning—check with the appropriate city department.
- Electrical capacity—consider what electrical work needs to be done, and whether the utility company will provide you with adequate power at the location under consideration.

It is instructive to consider training workshops offered by various community television groups. In its 1991 *Report to the Community*, Cable Access of Dallas listed an impressive number of persons who had taken its certification and training classes[3]:

Studio	255
Portable Field Production	187
Editing	126
Amiga/Graphics	77
Mobile Van	56
Total number certified	701

Denver Community Television produces a newsletter entitled *Take 25!* that usually includes a helpful column called "Production Insights." The community outreach manager of DCTV, Carol J. Naff,[4] reported that the organization has a two-chip camera studio, a three-chip camera studio, two edit suites with the control rooms of the studios that are used for editing when not being used for production, three portapak-chip cameras, one Hi–8 camera, and a mobile production van with three cameras—all of which adds up to a wide variety of programming. Working with a current database of over 2,000 volunteers, this was its training last year:

Class	Length	Materials' Fee
Producer	12 hours	$5
Editing	12 hours	$5
Basic lighting	8 hours	$5
Studio	12 hours	$10
Portapak	8 hours	$5
Graphics	8 hours	$5
Audio	8 hours	$5
Directing	8 hours	$5
Mobile van	3 hours	—

Detailed descriptions of workshops offered by DCTV are included in Figure 4.2. According to their schedule listings, classes are offered often and at convenient times for interested citizens. The public access channels have monthly themes for programs, an idea other operations might want to imitate. August, for example, was for children and young adults; September offered programs with Hispanic themes; October featured theater and dance; and November, music.

A *Community Television Production Experience* was prepared by the Workshop Task Force of the Denver Community Video Center, in cooperation with the Department of Technical Journalism of Colorado State University, from materials developed over time. Its theme, "How can media serve you?" stresses a self-evaluation of needs before designing video statements. Other topics include the following: the portapak, audio, microphones, lighting, interviewing, production logistics, video ethics, editing, production design, script realization in terms of both the taping and editing session, evaluation, distribution, and skill sharing.

Suggesting that "a little careful planning before you go out to shoot will be helpful" (p. 24), the manual includes this checklist for production logistics:

1. The camera, camera case, lens cap, zoom lens and specialty lenses.
2. The VTR, two empty take-up reels, head cleaners.
3. An earphone, plus microphone extension cables.
4. Microphones and perhaps a mixer and mike stands.
5. A sufficient number of batteries (charged?) and the AC adaptor.
6. Lights, extension cords, two- to three-prong adaptors, reflectors, cube tapes, fuses.
7. A tripod, monopod, or body brace.
8. Blank videotape—make sure to label each roll as it is shot.

Figure 4.2
Denver Community TV Training Workshops

Basic Lighting: This is an entry level workshop for prospective crew members who will be taking studio or producer classes that want to know about lighting. Basic three-point-subject lighting, set lighting, base lighting, gels, and scrims will be discussed. Participants will practice various studio lighting situations.

Producer: For those who want to produce a program. There is no training on the studio equipment that your volunteer crew will use. Rather, emphasis is on DCTV producer procedures, technical requirements, pre-production planning, crew positions for productions, scripting, script making, and things necessary for a good production.

Studio: Sign up for this workshop if you want to operate studio equipment. The purpose is to introduce studio equipment such as cameras, videotape recorders, switchers, and time base correctors to the beginning crew person. After completing the workshop, you will be able to help producers with their productions.

Portapak: DCTV provides portable video equipment for shooting *film* style or *documentary* style in the field. To use the equipment, take this workshop in basic field lighting, sound recording, site survey, and the setup and operation of a portable camera and videotape recorder.

Editing: When the producer shoots in the field *film style*, a lot of editing is required. When a studio production is shot, some editing may be necessary. Participants will have some hands-on experience to learn about using edit equipment at DCTV including play and record decks, time base correctors, switchers, character generators, audio mixers, wave form monitors, vector scopes, etc. Tape logging, edit decision lists, and both *insert* and *assemble* editing will be discussed.

Graphics: In this workshop, participants will learn more advanced graphics than in edit class. The character generator will be discussed and students will get hands-on practice with it while making titles, credits, rolls, crawls, page sequences, and simple animation. Other graphic options including art cards, superimposing, chronmakey, and video feedback will be demonstrated.

Audio: If you've been through the studio workshop and still are intimidated by all those knobs on the audio mixers, you'll want to take this workshop. Microphone placement, types of microphones available, audio levels, audio mixer, and audio on the record deck are discussed. Participants will have time for some hands-on experience.

Directing: What does the director do anyway? If you feed you need clarification on that question, this workshop will try to answer it. Who the director talks to, what cues the director uses for different crew members, script marking, program segments, and more are discussed. Each participant will have a chance to sit in the director's chair.

(Note: Registration is required, and in some instances, there are prerequisites—workshops or experience, a small nonrefundable, nontransferable materials fee is required, and class size is limited.)

Toward the end, the production manual includes "A Final Word on Community TV Productions" (p. 40):

Community television productions do not have to have large budgets, a lot of equipment, fancy set, etc. They were never intended to compete with the slick productions you see on broadcast TV. But this does not mean that they have to be dull, boring, slow, uninteresting and badly-shot or edited. Because your equipment is lightweight, portable and easy to use, you can make video tapes just about anywhere. There are no commercial considerations to hold you back, so you can make a tape about anything you want. And because you don't need a mass audience, your tape can be shown in a wide variety of places.

Public Access Community Television of Duluth-Superior (PACT 7, Superior, Wisconsin), located in a public library, offers low-cost classes on the basics of television production, "from planning your program and recording the action to putting it all together and getting it on television." They encourage everyone: "Whether you're pretty handy with your own camcorder or have never touched video production equipment before, we'll turn you into a confident, trained producer in just a few sessions." Certified PACT members have free access to all the video equipment, including camcorder packs (VHS and S-VNS camcorders, tripods, monitors, and lighting kits), editing systems, the Amiga computer and video toaster, audio gear, video switcher, and light kits.

The Spring Point Community TV Center (SPTV),[5] located on the oceanside campus of Southern Maine Technical College in South Portland, Maine, is a unique video production facility where "people come together to explore the world of television in a creative, open atmosphere. . . . Emphasis is placed on empowering citizens with the skills needed to communicate freely over this local, non-commercial cable channel." Also a creative media outlet for independent producers, SPTV offers classes that can be applied to college credit in video production, computer graphics, the video toaster, documentary, and editing workshops.

"Making Community TV" was the theme of *CTR*'s Volume 9, no. 3 (1986) issue, including such helpful articles as "Program Formats" by Scott Bartlett, "Doing a Site Survey" by Vicki Cason, "The Truth about Video Sound" by George Stoney, "Getting Together a Set" by John Glaeser, "Unraveling the Editing Process" by Alida Thacher, "Quiet on the Set . . . Live in 30 Seconds!" by Muriel Fleischmann, "How Portland Makes Money in Commercial Production" by Ellen Notbolm, "Where Silicon Meets Vidicon" by Richard Lovett, and an article on electrical circuits by the Community Videot. Andy Beecher's "Government Access: Cablecasting the Council," while specific to a particular kind of programming, is complemented by an article by Penelope Wells[6] in *Cable State*, with advice as follows on establishing a corporation:

- Identify in the license an organization separate from the municipal government to receive the access payments from the operator.
- Insulate the board of directors or other governing body of the access organization from the municipality's control. Set criteria for representation on the board and develop a method for replacing members independent from the mayor or board of selectmen, even if the issuing authority appoints the first board.
- Draft clear and detailed articles of organization and by-laws concerning the purposes and guidelines for operation of the entity, limiting editorial content by the board and municipal government.
- Require that the access organization and by-laws concerning the purposes and guidelines for operation of the entity limit editorial control by the board and municipal government.

Nontechnical Training

Production, direction, promotion, script writing, and other aspects of community television production are just as important as its more technical aspects.

Equipment for community television typically involves a studio, multi-camera setup, and/or a simple portapak/microphone configuration. Depending on franchising agreements, studios can be fancy or basic, consisting of various scenarios of tripod-mounted cameras, microphones, lights, a switcher, video monitors, and a VCR. Studios, as noted earlier, might be housed almost anywhere. They can even be mobile. Cameras can be stationary or hand-held, highly sophisticated or simple. No doubt you get the picture: There are enormous differences in equipment and production facilities.

As the camcorder revolution sweeps the country, and palmable 8mm moviemakers account for half of the more than three million camcorders owned by Americans,[7] consider: There are some seventy-five models from twenty-three brands to choose from, with prices ranging from $700 for point-and-shoot models to $3,000 for "do-everything" imagers. Depending on finances, various stations might also have advanced gadgets like Amiga's video toaster, Adtec's Telecaster 4, which broadcasts programs and displays messages automatically, or any number of different character generators.

Facilitators play a critical role in the success of a community television station. Sue Miller Buske has designated the following responsibilities for them:

- Teaching basic portapak skills classes, studio production classes, and playback engineering classes
- Scheduling equipment use for access users and for these training classes
- Scheduling programming for the access channel
- Preparing and delivering all program schedules to the local news media

- Compiling programming statistics on a monthly basis
- Advising access users in preparation of their productions
- Developing programs and program series for the access channel
- Encouraging local organizations to plan regular or semiregular programs
- Coordinating volunteers
- Contacting and scheduling these volunteers to assist in the various aspects of the access center operations.[8]

Schaffer and Wheelwright's *Creating Original Programming for Cable TV* (1983), although dated, contains several pertinent articles, notably, Susan Wallace's "Programming Sources," which suggests that

the access or community channels may be programmed in a variety of ways, depending on several variables. If there is strong city, company, and community support for these channels, the workshops, equipment, and staff necessary to assist the community producers in producing their programming can result in strong, successful access channels. In many such instances local access channels cablecast only locally produced material a significant portion of the day. (p. 15)

Also, attorney Ernest T. Sanchez provides a valuable article, "Basic Legal Planning for the Producer of Original Programming, or I Wish I Had Thought of That Before We Started Production" (pp. 44–52). He anticipates questions like these: Who will own part or all of the completed production? What source materials will be used in the production? What personnel, talent, and other arrangements need to be considered in a production? What are other uses of the finished production?

Consider a program for the Longmeadow, Massachusetts, public access channel, entitled "Profiles: Women in Careers." Its overall goal was to discuss women in the community as role models, presenting stories of successful women from all walks of life and from a variety of professions, including a good representation of minority women. When interviewers were trained for the series, an attempt was made to choose people who would be familiar with the background of the interviewee in terms of the profession, history of the work experience, philosophy, family situation, schooling, and the like. The structure of the interview was to include the present, the past, the future, and a summary. It took this general form:

- *Present*—Tell about your work: what, where, what type. Where are you in your career at this time? Do you feel fulfilled in your work? In what way(s)? What aspects are most/least satisfying?
- *Past*—Tell about the support you had/didn't have along the way. At what point in your life did you choose your career? Why? What were the influences which affected your career choice? People? Circumstances? Event(s)? What supports did you have initially (family, friends, peers, teachers, counselors)? Later on? What about role

models? What difficulties did you encounter? Did various demographics help/hurt (gender, age, race, religion)? How did your career affect your family life? Social life? What changes have you observed during the time you have been in your present position (company policies, work patterns, colleagues, supervisors)? What are some of the rewards/debts you have accrued? How has your work affected your life as a person? As a professional?

• *Future*—What are some of the directions you note in your career field? What opportunities/differences have you noticed for women/minorities?

• *Summary*—If you were starting out again, how might you/might not you act to gain expertise in your chosen field? How? Why?

After arranging technical requirements so that the interview would flow smoothly, the introduction to one program went like this:

Hello! Welcome to another in the series "Profiles: Women in Careers." I am Linda Fuller, a volunteer for the station, and producer of tonight's program.

"Profiles" is a project under the direction of Maxine Garber and Sue Leary. In it, certain community women are interviewed about their varied careers, sharing with us their experiences: the hard work, the luck, the problems, the achievements. We hope it will be interesting and inspiring—and that you will suggest new candidates for this show. Just call us. Videotapes of this program for schools or civic groups will be available in our tape library. Tonight's program . . .

PRODUCERS

Traditionally, producers of commercial television have been considered alternately as powerful creative sources of programming or as the confounding tools of network policy. Muriel Cantor (1971) found that producers for dramatic television series are influenced by their professional values in addition to their orientations to viewing audiences, the network, and colleagues. She points out that a producer wishing to make commercial television shows must please two audiences: buyers of films and viewers of them. Gaye Tuchman (1974, pp. 119–20) discusses the pattern of economic determination of programming, stating the basic rule: "Plan programs that will attract a large audience (as indexed by rating services) so that the audience may be sold profitably to commercials advertisers."

Yet, Newcomb and Alley (1982, p. 70) contend that producers, "working within the same patterns of organizational restraint, develop varied work patterns, intentions, and styles." As opposed to the other researchers, who found restrictions on creativity within the network systems, these authors discovered producers able to personalize their work, labeling them "self-conscious artistic producers." Bob Shanks (1977, p. 2), a producer, director, and writer of television programs for all the major networks, both commercial and public, declares: "Rule number one for a good producer is that he has the right to the power and the responsibility to use that power."

The question then arises: What happens if that power is virtually unrestricted, as it is in the instance of community television? What is the role of the producer?

Review of the Literature

As part of his 1979 doctoral dissertation, J. Clive Enos III performed telephone interviews with 180 producers of the Manhattan (New York City) cable system out of the 307 possible public access participants—many either unreachable or unwilling to be part of the survey.[9] Pointing out how public access producers are different from Hollywood's, operating as they do in a nonindustrial environment, he found they determined organizational rules and policy decisions with complete freedom, selecting and crafting the content they wanted aired.

Enos constructed these categories for the New York City producers: (1) experimental artists; (2) performers interested in showcasing their talents; and (3) community-minded, public-spirited citizens hopeful of addressing a specific audience. He found these percentages, respectively: 30 percent artists, 45 percent performers, and 25 percent interested citizens. Characteristically, he found the typical Manhattan producer to be a single, white, college-educated twentysomething male who had learned some television production skills either in school or on the job before coming to public access, and who then began producing without any particular audience in mind. Factors of age, race, prior television experience, and television preferences were found to be significant. Enos reported that the urban producers cared preeminently about satisfying themselves; superficially, they were out for fun.

Yet, as Terry Clifford (1982) points out, New York City's community television programming is a phenomenon, "outrageous and lively. . . . Short of actual coitus, pretty much anything can go, as long as it happens after 11 P.M."

PACTL

As part of a study carried out in the mid-1980s (Fuller, 1984a),[10] forty-two out of forty-four producers of a suburban community television station (PACTL) were interviewed in order to determine their motivational interests and experiences for involvement. See Appendix 11, "PACTL Producers Survey." Divided into topics of background to involvement, content of programming, relationship/reaction to audience, personal responses to working with PACTL, and demographics, the completed surveys were coded via SPSS, and frequencies and cross-tabulations were computed. Response errors could have included interviewer, respondent, and/or interaction effects, but caution against bias was maintained throughout. The producer survey methodology had the following characteristics:

Population—PACTL producers (42)

Data collection method—personal interviews

Sample design—non-sampled, tried to interview all

Survey instrument—see Appendix 11

Pretests—none

Data preparation—coded ex post facto, then SPSS terminal

Sampling errors—interviewer effects

Computation—frequencies

Since nearly all the producers were still residing in the area, it was decided not to sample them, but to interview as many as possible. Only two were unavailable—both males, one who was studying for the semester in England, the other a CPA who claimed it was too busy a season for him to be interviewed. While the greatest number (31%) of the interviews took place at the PACTL studio, 26 percent were performed at the producers' homes, 21 percent at their work settings, 12 percent by telephone, 5 percent via mail (two producers who had moved away), and 5 percent by other means (one at a restaurant, one at the researcher's house). No pretests were conducted.

Demographically, here are their main characteristics:

Gender: M 45%, F 56%

Age range: 15–24 7%, 25–34 19%, 35–44 31%, 45–54 21%, 55–64 16%, over age 65 4%

Religion: Catholic 21%, Jewish 33%, Protestant 45%

Marital status: married 69%, widowed 5%, divorced 10%, never married 12%, POSSLQ 4%

Residence: Longmeadow 69%, non-Longmeadow 31%

Employed: yes 74%, no 26%

Income: under $25,000 19%, $25,000–$49,999 48%, $50,000–$74,999 10%, $75,000–$99,999 12%, more than $100,000 4%, don't know 7%

Education: college 71%, graduate school 26%

Few parallels could be drawn between the suburban and urban community television producers (see the discussion of Enos's survey above).

Prior television experience. Whereas the majority (68%) of producers for the New York public access operation had prior experience in television production, nearly the exact opposite was true for the suburban Longmeadow/PACTL group—69% (twenty-nine out of forty-two) had never been involved directly with the medium. Seven of the producers had been performers on but never producers of television programs.

Involvement. Initial involvement motivations and means varied for the PACTL producers: 69 percent came in as individuals, 31 percent as members of a group. While 55 percent started the process in order to make a specific show, 17 percent got involved from an interest in media in general, 14 percent wanted a job, 12 percent just wanted something to do, and 2 percent did it as a course internship. There was also a split as to where the producers had first heard about PACTL: 21 percent from a friend, 19 percent each from school, the newspaper, or a group, and 14 percent knew members of the staff. While 43 percent of them said they did not feel obligated to get involved with the channel, 29 percent did (for example, pressure from a school principal or from a particular club that wanted coverage), and 29 percent felt mixed on this issue, oftentimes blaming themselves for yet another involvement. While 5 percent of the producers had made initial contact by simply walking into the studio, 33 percent had called in advance, 43 percent had attended an announced training meeting, and the remaining 19 percent had different experiences altogether; 76 percent came in alone, 24 percent with a group. Their stated reasons for continued involvement also varied: 36 percent stayed to do a particular program, another 36 percent to simply get involved, and 29 percent for a combination of these factors.

Motivations. Producers' attitudes toward getting involved in new projects in general were queried, and a clear majority (64%) declared they enjoyed getting in on the ground floor. This question, as opposed to the earlier one on obligation, presupposes a sense of risk, and the PACTL producers responded knowingly about their enjoyment of new challenges. Most had come in wanting to make a specific program, then stayed on to do and learn more. Correlations regarding general interest in involvement found statistical significance with employment (p = .01), future career considerations (p = .03), number of programs produced (p = .01), and kind of appeal (p = .01)—particularly for special audiences. Reason for involvement, doing one's original idea, using the experience for a resumé, and having and keeping to an agenda were all highly significant at the p = .01 level. Some of the PACTL producers joined for people reasons, others for personal reasons, and yet others for the training—none of these reasons being mutually exclusive.

Programming: Content of producers' programs for PACTL was mostly of a serious nature: 19 percent public affairs, 29 percent educational, 5 percent instructional, and 21 percent a combination of these; interestingly, only about one quarter of the shows fell into categories of sports (5 percent, typically shown live, then later kept on tape) or entertainment (21 percent). Most of the producers, although they originally came in to do one specific show, ended up making many more of a similar nature; yet, some 14 percent confessed to continuing some of their projects reluctantly. Few shows (12%) were considered "controversial" in nature, but three were negotiated by the

PACTL executive committee during the application process; all were approved. It was rare that the producer had to be concerned with presenting both sides of an issue or offending part of an audience. The type of program was found to be significantly related to the following variables: number of programs ($p = .01$), prior television experience ($p = .02$), reaction to the programs ($p = .05$), and feelings about the show ($p = .02$)—particularly positive for public affairs ($p = .05$), highly significant for program type as standard or out of the ordinary ($p = .001$), and appeal to specific interest group ($p = .001$).

Concern for audience. The truth is, very few of the PACTL producers ever considered the audience for their program(s). The majority (60%) admitted never having thought about a particular target audience but "hoped" for a general response to their shows. Unlike New York City's producers, Longmeadow's were more intent on producing a particular show than experimenting artistically. Some of PACTL's producers, for example, were interested in doing a specific program, such as collecting antiques, horsemanship, a school play, or an issue like the town's dog leash law or a street rezoning—and assumed/hoped there would be viewers interested in these topics. For the most part, Longmeadow's producers were purposeful, not merely "out for fun" like the New York City ones.

Responses to working with public access. Overall reaction to working with PACTL was split. About half the producers (48%) found the experience to have been a positive one, while the other half were negative or mixed in attitude. Reactions were found to be statistically significant only when related to kind of program ($p = .05$) and training ($p = .02$ for technical, $p = .01$ for nontechnical), but not to any specific demographic characteristic or personal variable such as audience concern, prior television experience, feedback, or thinking the experience had increased their status. Since so many producers mentioned learning experiences about themselves, those comments are recorded in Appendix 12, "PACTL Producer Comments on Learning about Self." Ranging from joy in accomplishments and self-discovery to guilt over taking on too much, or not enough, the statements tell volumes about volunteers in community television. Most (84%) mentioned getting some form of feedback, but not too much and not too helpful—mostly personal or mixed reviews, and not too many specifics. So that can't explain why some producers came or why some stayed while others left.

Future plans. Future involvement with the public access station was split in thirds between stopping, continuing and/or taking on more, and not being sure. The only statistical significance for future involvement was related to using the experience for resumé purposes ($p = .001$), which may be both a comment on the times and a message for community television stations to use in their recruiting of production personnel.

Clearly, there is too much diversity in the PACTL sample for a classic bell curve profiling the typical producer of programming for community television (Fuller, 1985b). Although the wide majority (69%) came to the experience having had no previous television experience and are fairly evenly split by gender, they represent a wide range in terms of demographics, interests, and responses. They differed greatly among themselves from the time of their initial involvement to the time of their self-assessments on future participation with the medium.

Motivations for involvement also covered a wide range. Some of the PACTL producers felt obligated to get involved, either from a job or organizational commitment or from their own nagging consciences to produce. For example, there was the art teacher who had always promised herself she would combine artistic media, and the clergyman who wanted to spread the word of his religion to the widest possible audience. Others just fell into the experience, typically by word of mouth. While there was general consensus on their enjoyment of being innovators, the reasons these producers took on this challenge varied according to personality characteristics.

Even programming, while most of it was categorized as educational (10%), civic (38%), and/or informative (22%), varied greatly. As opposed to the New York channels, few shows could be considered controversial, and rarely were the PACTL producers concerned about offending or even jolting an audience. In fact, fewer than half (41%) of the producers in the suburban sample claimed ever to have considered the audience at all; yet, there were exceptions—like the feminist who wanted to interview key women in the town who might serve as role models, the railroad buff who was sure he would unearth fellow hobbyists, or the League of Women Voters meeting on national security defense that was produced to inform people of the kinds of shows they should watch.

In short, there is no prototype here of a program producer for community television—demographically, motivationally, content- or interest-wise, and/or in relation to audience and the general experience of working with the station(s). Obviously it would be fascinating to perform longitudinal studies of a particular group of producers, or of particular stations, and/or of content categorization reports from a variety of programming sources for community television.

SCC

Telephone interviews were conducted with 100 trainees and access producers of Suburban Community Channels (SCC) by N. K. Friedrichs & Associates of Minneapolis in January 1991.[11] A version of the survey instrument appears in Appendix 13, "SCC Public-Access Television User Phone Questionnaire."

Demographically, the only information available is geography (25% from White Bear Lake, 17% Maplewood, 14% St. Paul, 10% Oakdale, 8% Mahtomedi, 5% North St. Paul, 21% from other communities), employment (56% work full-time, 14% part-time, 13% do not work outside the home, and 17% are students), and age (42% are between 35 and 54 and 20% are between 26 and 34). No information was reported on gender, religion, marital status, income, education, prior television experience, amount of involvement with the station, or qualitative attitudes toward motivations, future plans, and/or working at SCC.

Most of the report is quite technical, meant to help the organization in its continuing recruitment and training program. All the interviewees had participated in equipment training within the last three years, only one finding the time and day it was offered to be inconvenient (a weeknight would have served better). A significantly high number of trainees (92%) indicated being able to handle the video equipment after taking a course, only a few wishing they had more hands-on experience or time in training. Satisfaction with instructors was very high, with only one person stating that his/her access instructor was not responsive (he/she needed clarification or something was not understood). Only eighteen of the trainees/producers had not checked out equipment after completing their training, "lack of time" being given as the reason. Of those who did check out equipment, it reportedly was in working condition 90.2 percent of the time, and 89 percent of the tallied responses showed that producers found check-and-return procedures fast and easy. Only 34 percent said they would like additional equipment available—mostly microphones or SuperVHS. Reporting on individual work styles, more than half the producers (58%) indicated a preference for producing their own programs rather than helping someone else produce theirs.

Cross-tabulations of the survey results indicated that those trainees/producers who said they needed more hands-on training in the use of equipment had taken studio equipment training; they also showed that age was not a distinguishing characteristic of those indicating a need for more training. With regard to how the respondents had heard about community television, the survey revealed that residents of a single suburb, White Bear Lake, had been recruited via organizations at a rate of 32 percent, much higher than any other source, and newspapers were found to be the most effective recruitment tool.

The SCC telephone survey conclusions (p. 11) concentrated on marketing efforts, indicating that the committee's prototype for targeting organizations for promotion had proven "correct and effective. The organizational contacts are reaping producers, viewers and referrals." Focusing time and financial resources on that organizational prototype had achieved measurable and consistent success for SCC in the following ways: (1) Trainers and the training program are viewed positively, and (2) time devoted during early training sessions equates to new volunteer involvement. While there was an 8 percent improvement in training satisfaction over the years, specifically with early sequenced training sessions, production van training effectiveness fell 7 percent in the last year; it was determined that new course materials and curriculum development would be focused there. Also, the profile of the access producer was found not to necessarily parallel that of the general cable television subscriber, and more research might help identify future community producers.

As there are so few studies of producers of programming for community television in the United States, it is hoped that readers of this book will undertake a few to add to our understanding of these invaluable volunteers (Fuller, 1990). Then, the next logical step will be to compare American producers and programming with their international counterparts (Fuller, 1993b).[12]

ADMINISTRATION

Organization, "the behind-the-scenes activities that interrelate and co-ordinate the work of our production team,"[13] is but one of the four basic aspects of effective television production—along with the message, the mechanics, and the methods.

Undoubtedly one of the best resources in this area is Oringel and Buske's 1987 *Access Manager's Handbook: A Guide for Managing Community Television*, which deals with the following issues: developing rules and procedures, staff, equipment, training, community outreach, day-to-day management, and audience measurement.

For starters, municipal assistance coordinator Kimberly A. Kyle has formulated the following guidelines for creating a facility[14]:

1. The rules should be available for all users in the form of an organized, easy-to-read manual.

2. If the organization is run on a membership basis, the membership form should accompany the rules manual. Membership criteria should be stated clearly. Fees, if any, should be mentioned in the membership information.

3. The philosophy and description of the access corporation should be included in the introduction to the rules manual.

4. Penalties for abuse of equipment or violation of the facility's rules and procedures should be indicated in the manual or on the membership form, as should any appeals process.

5. Training, production procedures, equipment resources and equipment certification steps should be spelled out. All forms involving equipment responsibilities should accompany the rules.

6. Guidelines for program production, including airing schedules, should be detailed in the rules.

7. Information regarding program content and rights of the producers should be explained thoroughly. This section should include guidelines regarding obscenity, libel, copyright, commercial advertising, invasion of privacy, production liability, sponsorship, credits, and political campaigning rules.

8. A statement of compliance to be signed by the producer should accompany the

rules package. The statement should outline all responsibilities individuals assume when they become involved in access productions. The access facility should maintain a list of all users and compliance statements for a period of time. Often facilities will keep these records for two years or more.

One of the most important administrative jobs is working on franchises and their renewals, the subject of an issue of *CTR* (Volume 15, no. 2) that was guest-edited by Sharon B. Ingraham. Ingraham and Peter J. Epstein (p. 4) provide some valuable overview information:

- *Preparing for the process*—keeping the municipality up-to-date regarding the cable operator's performance; allowing municipalities to build a complete compliance history; and collecting data on provisions that were poorly or unclearly stated in the present franchise or are needed in the future franchise document.

- *Community responsibilities in the franchise process*—collect all relevant documents including the current franchise or ordinance, state and federal regulations, copies of all prior performance reviews, subscriber satisfaction documents and financial reports; conduct consumer and community needs ascertainment; assess the legal, technical and financial ability of the operator; and carefully consider the community's cable-related needs, including but not limited to PEG access provisions such as operating funds, equipment, facilities, channel capacity and management models.

- *The cable television renewal process*—identify future cable-related needs; and review the performance of the cable operator under the current franchise.

Also included in this issue are several helpful articles. "Access Negotiation and Renegotiation: The Whats and the Hows," by Genya Gail Copen (pp. 5–6), suggests being educated, informed, questioning, and articulate, identifying future access needs and interests of your community, building a strong community base, creating a strong position from which negotiations can take place, preparing presentations for public hearings, and developing a record of needs and uses. Sue Miller Buske's "Ascertainment: Key to a Successful Franchise Renewal Process" discusses workshops providing information about how the franchise renewal process works, how a cable system works, the nature of modern cable service in critical areas, and PEG access. "Engineering and Technical Concerns in the Renewal Process," by Alan S. Hahn (p. 9), outlines what a typical engineering review of the cable system might include:

1. Reviewing the existing system, including the coaxial cable system, headend equipment, satellite and broadcast receiving equipment, microwave equipment, and subscriber terminal devices

2. Conducting field inspections of the operational cable system

3. Reviewing the geographic coverage areas of the cable system's subscriber and institutional networks to ensure that these conform to franchise commitments

4. Preparing a detailed engineering report describing the theoretical capabilities of the present cable system; its operational condition compared to those capabilities; significant discrepancies found during inspections; and recommendations for corrective action.

In addition, editor-in-chief Ingraham interviews four professionals on the front lines of the renegotiation process (pp. 10–13): James Horwood, an attorney with Spiegel & McDiarmid of Washington, D.C.; attorney Adrian Herbst of Moss & Barnett in Minneapolis; Paul Proctor, a consultant of the Proctor Group in Raleigh, North Carolina; and Neil Lehto, an attorney with O'Reilly, Ranchilio, Nitz of Sterling Heights, Michigan. The various experts answer these questions: How is access faring in recent renewals, or renewals that are now under way? How can municipalities build flexibility and enforceability into a franchise? What are the consequences of denying a renewal? When is municipal ownership a viable option? How good an option is overbuilding? What effects do you think that proposals such as video dial tone will have on the renewal process? What's your best piece of advice—perhaps the best or the worst thing a municipality can do in the renewal process? To that last question, it would seem that the answer is being informed—which is what this book intends to facilitate.

Another good reference source is Pringle and colleagues' *Electronic Media Management* (1991), which, although it mainly focuses on broadcast stations, also includes information on managing cable television systems and public broadcast stations, and how to gain entry into the electronic media business. Special attention is devoted to programming, economics, and promotion, with a warning to management to be "vigilant" about PEG access: "The courts have ruled that users are protected by the First Amendment and that neither the franchise authority nor the cable operator may engage in editing or censorship. Problems may arise if sensitive subject matter is covered or if participants engage in verbal attacks on others" (p. 253).

As part of a packet on general information on SCC (Suburban Community Channels of Maplewood, Minnesota, mentioned above) came some materials that might be administratively helpful to other operations, including a "Proposal for Providing Access Training for Municipalities"; "Advertising/Underwriting Guidelines" (editorial control, commercialism, credits and procedures, and various personnel roles); SCC's "Long Range Plan"; "Tactical Marketing Plan"; "Identity Standards Document," including information on the station's logo; and sample newsletters (general articles, volunteer profiles, class schedules, program highlights, and "Connections" on the back page, listing items such as availability of volunteers for various purposes, help wanted for others, courses and conferences, tapes wanted, and equipment for sale). SCC's "Membership Promo for Suburban Community Channels" (Figure 4.3) is a clever self-marketing idea; in addition, a keen suggestion the operation uses for public relations is placing a noticeable

Figure 4.3
Membership Promo for Suburban Community Channels

*A 50-percent discount on course fees. During course registration, you will be asked if you are a member, and will receive the discount.

*The monthly SCC newsletter, which will be mailed to your address.

*Access to SCC library materials. Printed reference materials and copyright-free music are available at White Bear Lake community TV studio.

*Eligibility for community television production and crew grants. Call SCC offices for information or an application form.

*Voting privileges at SCC's annual meeting, during which board members are elected. Members can express their opinions and increase their say in community television.

*A membership directory, included in your welcome kit, that allows you to network with other volunteers and find others interested in working on video productions with you.

*A program to match members with groups and individuals that seek video production help or are willing to provide it. Forms are available from SCC on which you can identify your production needs and abilities.

*A members' production club, which allows you to socialize and share production experience with other volunteers. Quarterly meetings will include production projects and opportunities, tape critiques, guest speakers and presentations, and tours and field trips. Contact SCC for information on upcoming meetings.

*Assistance with the promotion of your video production, to increase viewership of your program. Call SCC to explore options available to you.

*Quarterly member events, including an annual member/volunteer recognition program, to which you will be invited.

*Sponsorship of your production tapes in video contests. Call SCC for information on available competitions and sponsorship information.

*Access to the production equipment available at the community TV studio, and the means to cablecast your program throughout the area.

*The satisfaction of knowing you support quality television programming within your community!

(2 1/4" × 4 1/2") ad in the telephone yellow pages under "Radio/TV/Cable"; including the logo for about one third of the space, the ad reads as follows:

Promote yourself to
23,000 cable TV viewers
FREE!

Produce a TV show about
YOUR business!

- Free airtime on cable TV
- Free use of cameras, studios
  and other equipment
- Low-cost training sessions
- Help in recruiting crew members

Call us today at 779–7145!

Another valuable checklist for promotion is the one offered by Margie Nicholson, included in Figure 4.4. The idea is developing and being aware of a "promotion quotient" for each program you produce.

Winthrop Community Access Television (Winthrop, Massachusetts) bills itself a "non-profit group which trains people in the community—*people just like you*—how to produce their own programs. The model for this is called *Public Access*. Not only does WCAT offer video production and computer graphics training for people of any age and ability, we offer the video equipment for you to borrow—*at no charge to members*—to make your community show happen." The basic course covers everything from camcorders to directing; after that, "The rest depends on your imagination and effort!" Some of WCAT's recent workshops, many of which are funded by the Winthrop Arts Lottery Council, have included the following:

- Painting with Light—computer art with the Amiga 2000
- Basic Production—cameras, VCRs, mikes, lights, audio, editing, graphics, directing, multicamera studio production
- KidVid—video for twelve-to-fifteen-year-olds
- Scriptwriting for TV—the ins and outs of the professional screenplay format, plotting, dialogue, and more
- Feature/Dramatic Screenplay Writing Workshop—a hands-on experiential writers' workshop, in which writers have the opportunity to direct their finished scenes as a studio shoot with actors

WHBC Community Television (Willowbrook, Illinois), representing the communities of Willowbrook, Hinsdale, Burr Ridge, and Clarendon Hills, is a cable television consortium providing public access cable programming produced by and for the general public. Its equipment, paid for through a

Figure 4.4
What's Your PQ? (Promotion Quotient)

THE "A" LIST: <u>Your show should include</u>: 1.Famous or appealing talent; 2.Interesting, controversial or timely topic; 3.Memorable title and logo; 4.Hummable or know-their-socks-off music; 5.Special set or location; 6.Unique angle or viewpoint; 7.Date and time set well in advance; 8.Viewer involvement or participation; 9.Studio audience or on-location crowd; 10.Several cablecasts.

<u>Your word-of-mouth promotion should include</u>: 11.Tell everyone you know or meet; 12.Have your guests tell everyone; 13.Have your crew tell everyone; 14.Alert access and cable company staff; 15.Pan the crowd at all studio audience and on-location shoots. Tell them to watch and spread the word; 16.Ask experts and opinion leaders to act as your advisory board or focus group. Tell them to watch and spread the word; 17.Contact educators and have them tell students to watch as a class assignment; 18. Tell viewers to watch with their kids, parents, neighbors, or to call and alert their neighbors; 19.Organize viewing parties. Have 10 people each invite 10 people to their homes to watch; 20.Throw a party at some public place with a cable outlet and watch with the group; 21.Set up a Speakers Bureau or launch a public speaking campaign; 22.Call and ask a public relations pro for help; 23.Call and ask a critic to attend taping or review the show; 24.Call a reporter who covers your target area (health, city government. . .) and invite them to attend the taping, or appear as a guest, or review the show; 25.Ask your minister, priest or rabbi to spread the word.

<u>Your cable-related promotion should include</u>: 26.Create 30- and 60-second promos to run on the access channel; 27.See if you can also run them on other cable channels; 28.Appear as a guest on other shows to plug yours; 29.Run a message on the bulletin board channel; 30.Get a listing into the cable program; 31.Ask for, or buy, an ad in the guide; 32.Get together with other access producers and do a joint promotional campaign; 33.Put a sign in the cable office lobby; 34.Ask the sales staff to tell potential subscribers about the show; 35.Ask the installers to tell new subscribers; 36.Put a flyer in the new subscriber packet; 37.Put an announcement in or on the cable bill; 38.Put a sign or a bumper sticker on the cable trucks.

THE "B" LIST: <u>Your print and press promotion should include</u>: 39.Announcements or ads to corporate and organization newsletters and church bulletins; 40.Targeted distribution of posters; 41.Flyers; 42.Bill stuffers; 43.Postcards; 44.or Brochures; 45.A complete press kit; 46.Business cards with your logo; 47.Stationery with your logo; 48.Press releases at every step, from planning; 49.to Grant received; 50.to Shooting on location; 51.to premiere showing coming up; 52.to Host Profile; 53.to Premiere coverage; 54.to Response to show; 55.to Awards won!; 56.Have photos available for press.

Figure 4.4, continued

THE "C" LIST: Your traditional media promotion should include: 57.
Radio PSAs; 58.News coverage; 59.Editorials (write and submit); 60.Ad-
vertising (buy your own or ask a local business to let you piggyback on
theirs); 61.Talk show appearance; 62.Reviews; 63.Television PSAs; 64.
News coverage; 65.Editorials; 66.Advertising; 67.Talk show appearances;
68.Reviews; 69.Newspapers (daily, weekly, special interest, shoppers'
guides) display or classifieds ads; 70.Mention in a column; 71.Editorial;
72.Review; 73.Feature; 74.News coverage; 75.TV listings; 76.TV highlights
list; 77.Direct Mail to target groups; 78.Zip code areas; 79.Organizational
mailing lists; 80.Access members, users, and supporters; 81.Cable subscribers; 82.Billboards (your own or run on a business' board).

THE "D" LIST: Your premium promotion should include: 83.T shirts;
84.Buttons; 85.Bumper stickers; 86.Pins; 87.Pens; 88.Notepads; 89.Book-
marks; 90.Calendars (with day and time of your show written in); 91.
Balloons; 92.Paper visors; 93.Keychains.

Your miscellaneous promotion should include: 94.Signs in or on bus
stops and buses; 95.Supermarket bulletin boards, sacks, receipts; 96.
Library bulletin boards; 97.Your answering machine; 98.A neighborhood festival booth; 99.A parade float; 100.Banner on the access center
building; 101.Logo on the back of a white balance card; 102.Tape played
in store windows; 103.Notice on the local computer hacker bulletin
board; 104.A sign on your car; 105.A sandwich board when you shoot.

Source. Margie Nicholson, *CTR* 9, no. 3 (1986), pp. 30–31.

grant from Continental Cablevision as part of its franchise agreement, is
available at no charge to residents of the member communities. Occupying
approximately 1,250 square feet of space, the WHBC studio contains a fully
equipped television studio, control room, editing suites, two offices, and
storage facilities for portable equipment. Its promotional brochure suggests
that producing a program is "as easy as 1–2–3": (1) Take a class—available
for interested persons; (2) plan a program—a wide range, including political
programming, fund-raising by nonprofit organizations, airing of board meetings, sports and theater events, and opinion programming; and (3) produce
a show—for airing 6–9 P.M., Monday through Thursday.

Joe Windish, executive director and access coordinator of LMC-TV, serving the villages of Larchmont and Mamaroneck in suburban New York, makes
a strong argument for studio control rooms going mobile.[15] While the nonprofit organization had happily shared studio space in the Mamaroneck High
School for a number of years, there were problems operating in other than
daytime hours, and due to custodial union contracts, weekend hours were
prohibitively expensive. Add to that the matter of the organization's institutional identity, which was very unclear, as most people thought LMC-TV
was a project of the high school. So, they moved to a new site: the

Mamaroneck Free Library. A boon came from a conversation with George Stoney, encouraging Windish to consider putting the control room at the new facility inside the studio space. When the board of directors didn't agree with his original idea, the technician came up with another one: Put the control room on wheels, so it could be rolled to appropriate shoots. The rest of his article attests to the unqualified success of this solution.

Beginning on page 42, the NFLCP *Yellow Pages* (Cardona, 1992) includes a number of valuable administrative resource suggestions, such as a listing of access management firms, reference sources on access television history and philosophy, cable system engineering, community needs assessments, community politics, computer information systems, computers and video, controversial programming, copyright, A/V equipment, financial analysis, franchise negotiation, fund development, management consulting, marketing and promotion, nonprofits, training, video production engineering, and video programming development. Further, it has information for networking, both nationally and internationally, and includes addresses of media producers and distributors, NFLCP members and public policy platform, related organizations, and the complete text of the Cable Communications Policy Act of 1984.

Other helpful resources for the administration of PEG access centers are available from the Benton Foundation (Washington, D.C.), which publishes a series of occasional papers called *Benton Bulletins*, providing information and advice to nonprofit organizations on media strategies and resources for issue advocacy. One such contribution is Margie Nicholson's "Cable Access," summarized in *CTR* (Spring 1990, p. 10+) as "An Access Primer for Non-Profits." Evelyn Pine's article on tape exchanges is also helpful, suggesting these key ingredients for successful ones[16]:

1. Serves a range of users from individual producers to major institutions
2. Encourages cable users to communicate with one another by eliminating the middleman function between user and provider
3. Emphasizes information sharing rather than the physical archiving of videotapes
4. Provides coordination and outreach to potential users
5. Assists other forms of networking and cooperation
6. Is low-cost

Yet another important issue for administrators of community television organizations is fund-raising. That ever-present battle of the budget remains. Thomas J. Karwin, chair of the Santa Cruz City-County Cable Television Commission, offers some suggestions for strategies, abbreviated here[17]:

• *Clarify your mission*—be explicit about whom you serve, and how.
• *Organize your financial records*—have them audited annually.
• *Offer your center's services as in-kind grants*—by these steps:

1. Identify the value of all assets.
2. Assign those assets to each area of your center's services.
3. Allocate your overhead costs to each service area.
4. Identify your "service units."
5. Estimate the number of each service unit you provide each year.
6. Divide the number of service units into the total cost of the appropriate service area. This yields the cost of each service unit.
7. Then, award in-kind grants equal to the costs of those services.

- *Document your results*—in your annual report, press releases, and correspondence with prospective donors, grantors, and corporate underwriters.
- *Seek support from those you serve*—the "marketplace model."
- *Seek support from those who share your mission*—other people and groups who are also committed to service.
- *Commit resources to raising more resources*—pay someone to serve as your "resource development officer."
- *Prepare for the long haul*—use patience, persistence, consistency, imagination, skill, and donor development.
- *Address your needs through service projects*—identify local needs.
- *Research the need or problem*—learn all you can.
- *Plan your response to the need*—define objectives, outline how you would pursue them, and determine evaluation criteria.
- *Determine the cost of your project*—your budget.
- *Study the full range of fund-raising possibilities*—consider possibilities for gifts, grants, corporate underwriting, special events, and earned income.
- *Study the fund-raising strategy you choose*—check it all out.
- *Identify matching funds early*—be prepared to identify in-cash and in-kind resources.

Karwin also includes information on the role of The Alliance in the fund-raising process, such as its grant-writing packet and many other supportive endeavors. A number of fund-raising books, periodicals, and grants publications resources are also listed.

Should your center be interested in finding out about your audiences, Vassoler, Reino, and Vizzone's handbook *Cable Television Sample Surveys: Ascertaining Your Community on Cable Television Matters* contains a number of survey instruments from New Jersey.

VOLUNTEERS

At the crux of any successful community television operation are its ranks of volunteers. Ranging from technical to support personnel, they are a vital ingredient not only for production but also for morale. Yet, as is evident in the paucity of reportage on producers for PEG access, very little research has been done in this area.

The Corporation for Public Broadcasting puts out a booklet entitled *Instructions for Valuing the Personal Services of Volunteers*, first issued in 1980 and revised in 1988. While it may seem amazing that we need to be instructed in the art of appreciation for their services, we can learn a lesson from what public broadcasting does. The booklet lists three advantages of valuing volunteer services:

1. Inclusion of the value of volunteer services in NFFS (nonfederal financial support) will increase the amount of NFFS reported by all elements of the public broadcasting system. Since federal appropriations for public broadcasting cannot exceed 50 percent of total NFFS, increases in NFFS permit increases in the amount appropriated.
2. Since a station's Community Service Grant (CSG) depends in part on its NFFS, valuing and reporting personal services of volunteers in calculating NFFS would likely result in a high CSG.
3. Stations may benefit in other ways from recording and valuing the services of volunteers. Although the process may incur costs, the information obtained should allow a station to use and manage volunteers in more effective and productive ways.[18]

For reasons other than monetary or image concerns, cable access has traditionally encouraged volunteer involvement as a mainstay of its operation. Consider, for example, the blind volunteer who operates a camera on voice command at Kalamazoo's Community Access Center; according to Kanti Sandhu (Western Michigan University Media Services Department), she is one of their best ever. Volunteer and personnel management, virtually the same thing, typically involve recruitment, training, placement, evaluation, and recognition. Of all the aspects, that last is probably the most important for feedback, so volunteers know how important they are to the whole. It is strongly urged that one consider scheduling a volunteer recognition night, at a minimum of once a year.

Referring to league members' training in community service, Kirsten Beck wrote an appealing article about access in the Junior League's newsletter:

Cable offers League members a variety of opportunities to influence, shape and exploit a communications system rooted in their communities. Some may choose to become cable program producers, some to represent community interests as board members overseeing the local cable company. Others may set up partnerships with cable companies to produce local programs or engage in other mutually beneficial activities.[19]

Wisely, Beck has done her homework on the capabilities of this potential womanpower base. She cites cases in which the League has already been involved—notably, the Junior League of Akron's twenty half-hour segments of "Community Collage: In Focus with Community Agencies," the Junior League of Portland, Oregon's liaison with the Portland Cable Access Corporation to provide video training, and the appointment of a League member to the Pasadena Community Access Corporation.

Peggy M. Gilbertson, general manager of Community Television of Knoxville, Tennessee, claims there is a hassle-free, adaptable way to assist a producer in forming a volunteer crew. Wanting to recruit more volunteers and produce more programs, she and her colleagues redesigned their basic workshop for in-studio production, "to attract a group of like-minded volunteers with good ideas and to effectively use the limited time they could spare to make a television program on a regular basis."[20] The key: a leader who could bring the group together, plus workshops tailored to the production needs of the crew. To begin developing a volunteer crew, she suggests mini-workshops as a good way to have a quick product but mainly as a means of teaching the concept of program unity. The result: "a wealth of community programming produced by committed, excited volunteers" (p. 7).

Don't forget the independent producers. Abigail Norman,[21] access coordinator at Shrewsbury (Massachusetts) Cable Access Television (SCAT), points out that when their various producers receive outside recognition for their work, the whole access center shares in their glory. Citing accomplishments ranging from grants receipts to overhearing compliments about one's program, she claims, "I believe producers will strive for quality. I believe producers are the heart and soul, the flesh and blood, the raison d'être of access. When they feel a little bit glorified, we do, too." And so we all should, no matter what our involvement in community television.

NOTES

1. Cited in "Access Makes a Difference," *CTR* 15, no. 5 (September/October 1992), p. 10.

2. Dave Bloch, "A Resource of Technical Tips," *CTR* 6, no. 4 (Winter, 1984), p. 25.

3. Letter and resources from James Chefchis, Assistant Director, Cable Access of Dallas, August 13, 1992.

4. Response form and materials from Carol J. Naff, community outreach manager, Denver Community Television.

5. Response form and materials from Randy Visser, director of Spring Point Community TV Center.

6. Penelope Wells, "Access Advice: Establishing a Corporation," *Cable State* (Summer 1989), p. 3.

7. Stephen A. Booth and Frank C. Barr, "Pieces of 8," *Popular Mechanics* (October 1992), p. 65.

8. Sue Miller Buske, "Improving Local Community Access Programming," *Public Management* (June 1980), p. 13.

9. J. Clive Enos III, "Public Access Cable Television in New York City: 1971–5," unpublished doctoral dissertation, University of Wisconsin-Madison, 1979.

10. Variations on this study were presented to the Popular Culture Association in 1985 and published in *Medien Psychologie* in 1990.

11. N. K. Friedrichs & Associates, Inc., "Ramsey/Washington Counties 1991 Survey."

12. Nick Jankowski, Ole Prehn, and James Stappers (eds.), *The People's Voice: Local Radio and Television in Europe* (London: John Libbey, 1992) is a wonderful resource, but it does not contain any information about producers.

13. Gerald Millerson, *Effective TV Production* (Focal, 1976), p. 9.

14. Kimberly A. Kyle, "Access Advice: Creating Guidelines for Your Facility," *Cable State* (Summer 1988), p. 7.

15. Joe Windish, "A Studio Control Room Goes Mobile," *CTR*, 13, no. 1 (Spring 1990), pp. 12–14.

16. Evelyn Pine, "Exchanging Tapes Creates New Communities," *CTR* 9, no. 1 (1986), pp. 28–29.

17. Thomas J. Karwin, "Fund-Raising and Community Access," *CTR*, 15, no. 1 (January/February 1992), pp. 5–6.

18. Corporation for Public Broadcasting, *Instructions for Valuing the Personal Services of Volunteers* (May, 1988), p. 1.

19. Kirsten Beck, "Connecting with Cable," *Junior League Review* (Fall 1984), p. 18.

20. Peggy M. Gilbertson, "Building a Volunteer Crew," *CTR*, 9, no. 3 (1986), p. 6.

21. Abigail Norman, "Quality: At What Price?" *CTR* 13, no. 2 (Summer 1990), pp. 14–15.

Examples of Community Television

> Access at its best is a vehicle for pure communication. It's real people
> talking about real things. No glitz and no commercials.[1]
>
> Karen Haselmann, Minneapolis

The first experiment in community television in the United States took place
in 1968 in Dale City, Virginia, about twenty-five miles south of Washington,
D.C., through a system called Cable TV, Inc. Run by the Chamber of
Commerce as the first community-operated, closed-circuit television channel, the experiment went unnoticed nationally and was unable to draw
enough local support to last more than two years. But the times certainly
have changed.

The Alliance for Community Television, as an advocate of community
television, has been the best and most consistent documenter of various
groups and their efforts, particularly through its quarterly newsletter, *Community TV Review*. Among the many, many examples are cooperation between Bay Area Community College in Oakland, California, and local
programmers for television documentaries relating to courses, registration,
and counseling information, telecourses for credit, and community billboard
news; the St. Paul, Minnesota, experience with the cable cooperative idea;
development of the public access plan in Boston—an amazing case study in
politics; Atlanta's negative franchising experience; and Madison, Wisconsin's, programming, including "Jobline" (employment information and opportunities), "City Scope" reports by its aldermen, local election coverage,
cultural programming, fire department training, and legal workshops for the
hearing-impaired.

Another important collection of case studies is contained in Margie Nicholson's *Cable Access* (1990):

1. Wrightwood Improvement Association—reports on how a grassroots Chicago neighborhood organization used its local public access channel to publicize information about an impending referendum on home equity.

2. Milwaukee Audubon Society—how it used access to reach its 3,300 members and other interested citizens on environmental issues.

3. Roger B. Chaffee Planetarium, Grand Rapids, Michigan—a cooperative airing of a program about the Voyager 2 spacecraft.

4. Foxborough (Massachusetts) Council for Human Services—an annual auction.

5. Good Samaritan Hospital and Medical Center, Portland, Oregon—a successful series called "Health Visions."

6. Los Angeles Jazz Society—using public access for public relations.

7. United Way of San Luis Obispo (California) County/Neighbors Helping Neighbors, Inc.—community outreach program highlighting different community agencies.

8. American Association of Retired Persons, Area VII, Dallas—special video training class for members, "Senior Speak Out" being the result.

9. Northern Virginia Youth Services—successful weekly Fairfax "Focus on Youth" program.

10. Animal Rights Kinship—a spay/neuter service made possible by Austin (Texas) Community Television.

11. Little City Foundation, Palatine, Illinois—a demonstration that people with mental retardation and other developmental challenges can participate in public access training and operation.

12. League of Women Voters of Bucks County (Pennsylvania)—"At Issue," an ongoing weekly documentary series on local issues.

Notwithstanding the fact that this book is already replete with examples of programming and production, what this chapter aims to do is give a wider structural approach to the topic of community television. As case studies often provide insight into one's own comparable situation(s), I hope that this section also will be helpful both for learning about what other operations have faced and for anticipating what parts of the process work best (Fuller, 1988). (See Appendix 14 for names and addresses of organizations discussed in the case studies.)

CASE STUDIES

Allen County Public Library—A Library Liaison[2]

Rick Hayes, station manager of the public access center located in the Allen County Public Library (ACPL, Fort Wayne, Indiana), makes a good case for the many commonalities between access and libraries: "They both exist to inform, educate, entertain, and enlighten the public. They are both 'narrowcasters' of information."[3] Extending his argument at the NFLCP 1992 conference, Hayes chaired a session designated "The Library and the Communication Revolution" in the Future of Access track, including cases from a program librarian in Minnetonka, Minnesota, and a media librarian in Forest Lake, Minnesota. Of his own center, he recalled that the Fort Wayne library began using video production in 1977 for oral histories, book talks, and recording special events, incorporating the cable system in 1980. Ever since, the library has operated the access center as one of its full departments, paying for all operating costs beyond the franchise-purchased production equipment on a budget of around $355,000. There are six full-time staff, who share equally many of the duties involved in training volunteers and helping producers develop their programs.

In its first year alone, 291 programs were produced from 1,325 hours of facility usage to create 791 total hours of community programming. In 1988, the library was chosen by the city of Fort Wayne to be the management entity for an educational access channel—another productive venture. Each year, usage of the access center has increased steadily, peaking in 1986 when 1,164 programs were produced as a response to an influx of new equipment. More rapid growth occurred in 1990 (1,168 programs) and 1991 (1,560 programs), due in part to the addition of more portable equipment and the continued growth of the educational access channel.

To ascertain whether it is truly serving its viewing audience, ACPL began conducting telephone surveys in 1986, repeated every two years, finding it has a high visibility factor among the 63,000 cable subscribers. When asked if they were "aware of public access," 87 percent responded they were, while a total of 43 percent reported watching it regularly. Program preferences were mainly arts and entertainment (40 percent), local sports (34 percent), public information (30 percent), health and wellness (24 percent), and religious programs (18 percent). The top programs listed in statistical order were "Speak Out," "Komet Hockey," "The Uncle Ducky Show," "Situation Number Nine," "Highway Videos," "YWCA Body Shop," and "Raiders of Access." Further, the effect of access programming on subscribership showed some 27 percent of the respondents saying its presence was important to their decision to have cable service.

ACPL's Public Access Channel 10 is on the air Monday through Saturday from 10 A.M. to midnight, Sunday from 2 to 7 P.M., translating to an average of eighty-nine hours per week, over 4,100 per year, most (78 percent) of which is original programming. Its Education Access Channel 20 averages twenty-five hours per week. The access center's impact cannot be measured just by programs produced and hours of programming; it also trains about two thousand volunteers each year in entry level positions, stating, "If you can hold a camera we can teach you to operate it!" The youngest volunteer is eight years old, the oldest, seventy-five, and the center has also trained several physically challenged people in video production. One way it has ensured accessibility is that the studio camera and audio manuals are printed in Braille, and the studio control room equipment is also so labeled. Diversity comes from working with over 150 community groups—yet another key to this library model of access.

Austin, Texas—"Alternative Views"[4]

One of the first cities in Texas and in the United States to recognize the benefits of community-produced media, Austin Community Television (ACTV) has, since its start in 1972, wanted to produce programs reflecting the personality of its city as no form of television had before. Emanating from an initiative by a group of University of Texas students who wanted to bring public access to the city, and encouraged by a group of progressive Austin residents who shared the 1970s vision of grassroots communication, ACTV incorporated in 1973 as a nonprofit corporation. Its goals were as follows[5]:

1. To gather and disseminate information about cable.
2. To provide community members with a way to videotape their own programs.
3. To provide a video equipment library to the community whereby a person could check out portable equipment.
4. To provide production advice and assistance.

Encouraging programming by the people rather than for the people from the start, it has distinguished itself as innovative, many of its programs having enviable longevity, such as "Alternative Views," "American Atheist News Forum," "David Chapel Worship Service," "El Evangelio en Marcha," "Everlasting Gospel," "His Love Alive," "Let the People Speak," "St. James Baptist Church," "Stone of Help," "Sunday Morning Mass," "That Which Is," "Videot's Choice," and "World of Pentecost." What is striking is the contrast between approaches, the sacred juxtaposed with the profane; in 1985 the NFLCP rewarded this diversity of programming by recognizing ACTV as a model for access operations across the country.

The first program mentioned on this list, "Alternative Views," warrants highlighting. It is one of the oldest social-issue programs on public access television; since 1978 more than five hundred hour-long programs on a variety of topics have been produced. One of its founders, Douglas Kellner (1992, pp. 102–32), tells about the early days:

On our first program, in October 1978, our guest was an Iranian student who discussed opposition to the Shah and the possibility of his overthrow; we also had a detailed discussion of how the Sandinista movement was struggling to overthrow Somoza. This was weeks before the national broadcast media discovered these movements. We then had two programs on nuclear energy and energy alternatives. Among the guests was Ray Reece of Austin, whose book *The Sun Betrayed* later became a definitive text on corporate control and suppression of solar energy. On early shows we had long interviews with former Senator Ralph Yarborough, a Texas progressive responsible for legislation like the National Defense Education Act, and we learned that he had never before been interviewed in depth for television. We had an electrifying two-hour, two-part interview with former CIA official John Stockwell, who told how we had been recruited into the CIA at the University of Texas. Stockwell discussed CIA recruitment, indoctrination and other activities, and his own experiences in Africa, Vietnam, and Angola, experiences that led him to quit the CIA and write his book *In Search of Enemies*, which exposed the Angola operation he had been in charge of. Stockwell presented a thorough history of CIA abuses and provided arguments as to why he thought the CIA should be shut down and a new intelligence service developed.

Other exciting interviews included discussions with U.S. Atheist founder Madalyn Murray O'Hair, who gave her views on religion and told how she had successfully produced lawsuits to eliminate prayer from schools, thus preserving the constitutional separation between church and state; with Benjamin Spock, who discussed the evolution of his theories of childrearing, his political radicalization, and his adventures in the 1960s as an anti-war activist; with the former Stokeley Carmichael (now Kwame Ture), who discussed his 1960s militancy and theories of black power, his experiences in Africa, and his perspectives on world revolution; and with Nobel Prize winner George Wald, former Attorney General Ramsey Clark, anti-nuclear activist Helen Caldicott, and many other well-known intellectuals, activists, and social critics.

Frank Morrow, an "Alternative Views" producer, claims that the program is shown in approximately thirty-five cities, reaching over 2,500,000 households.[6] He adds that some of their lesser-known guests have shared "their poignant—and sometimes painful—personal experiences, includ(ing) a *Texas Monthly* reporter who spent several months in the mountains with Mexican guerrillas; former political prisoners from Chile, Iran, and Argentina who were arrested and tortured; survivors of the Nagasaki bombing; travellers returning (with pictures) from Cuba, Vietnam, El Salvador, Jamaica, Grenada, Nicaragua, Iran, and South Africa." Response to the program has been overwhelming:

- A nutritionist received fifty phone calls over a three-week period in response to her appearance on the program.
- An alternative political newspaper received new subscriptions after the editors were interviewed.
- A presentation on urban problems in Austin and the county was recorded by city officials and circulated among staff.
- One guest commented that he had been besieged with phone calls and stopped frequently on the streets by total strangers who complimented him on his appearance on "Alternative Views."

As Kellner (1992, pp. 103–4) has noted, most of the material on this program "would not have been shown on network television, or if shown would have been severely cut and censored. Consequently, at present it seems that the best existing possibility for producing alternative television is through public-access/cable television." He delineates the implications: "Obviously, progressive groups who want to carry through access projects need to develop a sustained commitment to radical media politics and explore local possibilities for intervention." "Alternative Views," meanwhile, has accrued much special recognition as winner of the 1983 Austin Community TV Achievement Award; recipient of a commendatory resolution from the Texas State Senate; and winner of the 1984 American Atheists' First Amendment Award, 1985 Home Town USA Video Award, and the George Stoney Award from the NFLCP in 1989.

With an annual budget of about $600,000, ACTV works with about one thousand producers each year, aiming to reach an audience of around 350,000. When Christopher Francis White chose the station as the topic of his dissertation in philosophy at the University of Texas-Austin in 1988, which he called "Eye on the Sparrow: Community Access Television in Austin, Texas," he discovered that 71.8 percent of the sampled public was aware of the channels, 43 percent saying they watched at least once a month. The reasons they watched were given as "uniqueness or alternative nature" (24.5%), local character (23.2%), and educational or informative value (19.2%). Of producers for the channels, although their numbers were not available, the greatest proportion (28 percent) said they did public access programs because of a general interest in video, while other responses given were opportunity for expression (25 percent), desire for social change (23 percent), availability of equipment (19 percent), and other reasons (5 percent).

By the time of ACTV's groundbreaking for a new facility in 1992, 93 percent of the station's programming was being produced locally. Nearly two thousand Austinites are certified as producers, five hundred of that number currently producing. During the 1990–91 season, for example, some 35,317 programs were cablecast. Through all its years, ACTV has not been without its controversies, its arts contributions, and its (mostly) fond memories.[7]

Brooklyn Park, Minnesota—100 Percent Local Community Programming[8]

Featured on the six channels of Northwest Community Television (NWCT), "The Local Station," are twenty-four hours a day of community programming. Serving Minnesota's communities of Brooklyn Park, Brooklyn Center, Crystal, Golden Valley, Maple Grove, New Hope, Osseo, Plymouth, and Robbinsdale on a budget of $1.2 million, with the goal of "subscriber satisfaction," are the following channels:

- Channel 32—program guide/local weather, with commercial-free forecasts by the National Weather Service
- Channel 33—community programming, featuring "live" call-ins, talk shows, and concerts
- Channel 34—community programming, featuring church programming, community events, sports
- Channel 35—twenty-four-hour local community news and information, Northwest Edition/Northwest Cities
- Channel 36—community programming of sports, school events
- Channel 37—"City Network," for city council meetings, local government

While a number of Minnesota's neighbors could also be cited for access activity, Hudson Community Access Television in Hudson, Wisconsin, is worth mentioning here.[9] Formed in 1983, it operates Community Channel 10, supported by two thousand subscribers and a budget of approximately $36,000. In addition to city council and village board meetings, documentaries, and church, school, elderly, and military programming, it also has talk shows, entertainment, and kids' programming.

Also, Cynthia Shearer, an assistant professor of English at Mankato State University, has documented her local public access television station in both a fifty-five minute documentary and a paper entitled "Who Do We Think We Are? Images of Ourselves in Public Access Television" (1986). From interviews with ten people who had been trained to use the station equipment and facilities, she had an opportunity to test her theory that while commercial television provides us with images of who it thinks we should be, public access television tells us something about who we really are.

Calaveras Community Television—"Sponsor-System"[10]

Calaveras County, situated in the Sierra Nevada with about 35,000 residents, began its community television with a "deal" from the cable company around 1983 for two two-hour slots: 6–8 P.M. Tuesdays and 10–12 Saturday mornings. Basically, the volunteers were given a key for the headend and shown two RCA jacks to plug in their own equipment. Advocates for a more advanced system held a video workshop for the public, formed an organization, and although they had absolutely no equipment and no funding, today run a system with sixteen hours of Calaveras-generated programming, some of it reruns from former events.

From the start, they decided to establish a "sponsor-system" to defray costs, a policy that holds up still: They do programs only after a sponsor is found who is willing to pay for a simple, one-camera production for $65 for a day or less, or a more involved one for $125. In 1983 one of the founding members purchased an RCA VHS camera and recorder, so nothing could hold them back. Soon they were able to rent, then build, studio space from membership fees ("production cost participation"). Contribution levels are designated "active" ($12), "contributing" ($25), and "supporting" ($50); membership numbers about forty. These funds are used only for equipment purchases, losses, maintenance, overhead, and the station newsletter, which is sent to more than one hundred U.S. and state senators along with other interested persons. All work is performed on a 100 percent volunteer basis, with no payments for mileage or other expenses.

On the second Wednesday of each month, Calaveras Community Television has a "video party" in one of the members' homes, a social gathering with potluck and viewing of recent productions. Working with local service organizations (like the American Association of University Women [AAUW], Rotary, Lions, and many others) and the local Department of Education has proven extremely valuable. At one time the station won a grant, for "Rural Renaissance," for three shows to stimulate tourism and to encourage business and industry to settle in Calaveras County. However, the elaborate accounting required for the shows took as long as the research and production efforts.

Although it still has no budget, Calaveras Community Television spends about $18,000 per year, taking in the same amount. With the exception of the studio construction loan, it has no debts. It does have great community support, and it receives praises from both The Alliance and its nearby association with Access Sacramento.

Columbus, Ohio—Anticipating PEG Access Mergers

According to ACTV executive director Carl Kucharski, Columbus, Ohio, "has always had a unique cable television situation—the home of the Warner Amex interactive Qube system, four systems operating in the city, the first Black-owned system in the country and a franchise fee dedicated to cable related services including access since 1979."[11] When the city considered merging the existing PEG access operations in 1987, it established a task force to make recommendations. Although to date Columbus Community Access remains intact, Kucharski suggests some key lessons from the experience:

1. Educate decision makers about PEG access so that if and when this type of situation arises they will have some idea of the complexity of the issues involved.
2. Create an apolitical and inclusive process for the review.
3. Stay focused on the purpose of the potential merger—that is, the improvement of PEG access for long-term community benefit.
4. Create deadlines and adhere to them—keep the process moving.

In view of the possibility that mergers of PEG operations might become a national trend, his warning should be carefully considered.

Grand Rapids, Michigan—"Empowering the Community"[12]

With a stated purpose of "empowering the community with non-discriminatory access to television," the Grand Rapids Cable Access Center (GRTV), along with the Radio and Middleton Film Society, is committed to combining its efforts with those of related institutions and individuals. Considered a medium-sized center, serving a population of about 190,000 on cable, about 400,000 on radio in the metropolitan community, by its tenth anniversary in 1990 GRTV had cablecast its 25,000th hour of community television. "It's television by, for and of the people, the realization of democratic communications in a nation driven by commercialism in the media,"[13] announced a local newspaper on that occasion. "Programming," it added, "runs the range from the controversial to the comedic, from issues with a message to sometimes madness; in short, whatever strikes a producer's fancy."

Structurally, the operational model for GRTV's philosophy is included in Appendix 15, "Community Access to Dominant Media: A Model," by Dirk Koning, executive director of GRTV. An important element of that process is demystifying the media. According to Koning, "One of the best things that's happened to community television is that it's so simple today. The fact that it's user-friendly allows virtually anyone to convert their ideas to television." Recent examples are GRTV's productions "Without a Net" and "Festival '92," demonstrations of how like-minded arts and media institutions can work together, the first commemorating the fifteenth birthday of the Urban Institute for Contemporary Art, the latter the largest all-volunteer arts festival in the nation. In addition, there is regular programming like "The Job Show," "Healing the Ancient Arts," "Yo! Grand Rapids," monthly call-ins to the mayor, the local UAW's "Images of Labor," "Now Is the Time for Real Estate," twelve hours of back-to-back religious programming on Sundays, "Video Voters Guide," "Going Critical," "Middletown Movie," and many more. As Koning wrote in *Grand Rapids Magazine*:

The words "community" and "communication" share the identical Latin sub-root, meaning "to share." Information is its own commodity. Grand Rapids must peer into a crystal ball and determine how it intends to establish, manage and allocate its community of communication infrastructure. Hundreds of communities around the world are "light years" beyond us in the process and implementation. But they also have myriad models worthy of study, and many are willing to share. We must look and listen, see and hear, then act.

A revolution is under way; let's televise it commercial-free.[14]

International Mobile Video—Associated with "The Smallest Community Television Anywhere"

So far, no community cable programming operation has been found to be smaller than Sierra Buttes Cable Television (SCTV) in California, of which

David Bloch (*CTR*'s "Community Videot" and owner of International Mobile Video) is a board member. According to Bloch, this tiny town of 225 people has a system owned and operated by Tim Smith, who lives in a mobile home up the side of the mountain. Smith has the system headend in his living room, which also serves as the studio and editing suite. The whole thing runs off a small hydroelectric system he built on a stream that runs down the mountain through his property. Consider, comments Bloch: "This is the way cable television once was—no multi-national corporations, no home office; just an entrepreneur building an independent business and having fun with it."[15]

A twelve-channel system run solely by Tim and his son Paul, SCTV consists mostly of character-generated ads and community announcements, with audio from KABL-FM in San Francisco. It will also play community- and self-submitted programming, none of which to date has been commercially sponsored. There's no particular budget and no particular schedule, although special programs usually get an article in the local weekly paper; but each year SCTV does a telethon to help a local school raise money for its yearbook. Also, during a period of major forest fires throughout California in 1989, Tim spent every day behind the fire lines of Sierra County's Indian Valley Fire, talking with firefighters and getting specific information about where the fire was going; he would then play the unedited tape for interested residents.

While there are only about 160 cable subscribers, Bloch continues, the only other local news source is "the old guys who sit on the bench every day at the Sierra Country Store. Sooner or later, they'll know everything being said by everybody to everybody else. After all, we all go down to the Post Office every day."

Kalamazoo, Michigan—"Best Access Center in the USA"[16]

Winner of the coveted NFLCP Community Communications Award in 1990, the Community Access Center of Kalamazoo has been in operation only since 1983. Its mission statement, "To invite, encourage and enable a diversity of local voices to exercise their first amendment rights through the medium of cable access television," is probably best exemplified in its "Open Studio" program, encouraging nonprofit organizations to produce free videos about their services.

As part of its application for the NFLCP award, Kalamazoo Community Access Center reviewed how it reflected the interconnectedness of the community and its institutions, having trained 3,594 people to use its facility and equipment since opening its doors. Averaging thirty-six workshops annually, it has provided instruction in basic and advanced studio, remote/edit, and special courses in animation/paintbrush, lighting/special effects, directing, interviewing, scripting, introduction to video, and programs like "Television for Teachers" and "Community Meetings." To help meet the budget of approximately $300,000, a "Telefest" is held annually, a ten-hour live cablecast that brings in about $30,000.

Volunteers, involved in over 90 percent of Kalamazoo's programming, donate some 30,000 hours of their time each year so that more than two hundred organizations can share their messages with the wider public over the system's four channels. Volunteer recognition is an integral part of the process, some thirty persons receiving "Anni" awards at an annual ceremony recognizing excellence in local productions, and a "Volunteer of the Month" being featured in each newsletter. Various volunteers share their sentiments about the access center:

- Curly Stricklin—"I'd love to do more volunteer work, especially live shows in the studio. I love meeting people, and it amazes me what all can be done with the equipment. You really can't comprehend what goes into a television program until you get involved with it yourself."

- Jeremy Young—"I love the access center because it doesn't cost me anything to use really cool equipment, and I'm able to get a lot of practice because the equipment is so easy to book and it's available so often."

- Karen Augustine—"What impresses me most about this facility is the quality of both the staff and volunteers. This access center has been a lot further ahead than others because nobody ever reaches a plateau of success and says, 'that's enough.' "

- Steve Leuty—"Community Access is an important source for connecting Kalamazoo citizens with all of the good programs and events happening in the community."

Longmeadow, Massachusetts—Lost Leader

Public Access Cable Television of Longmeadow, Massachusetts (PACTL) began in 1981 as a unique example of a "pure" community television station organized non-hierarchically, volunteer-dependent for both decision making and operation. An affluent suburb of Springfield, with a high percentage of professionals and a number of civic- and city-minded residents, it had a 74 percent cable penetration in a population of approximately 8,000. Geographically located in a Top 100 television market, Longmeadow had such knowledge of and enthusiasm for access that the station had over 150 volunteers before its debut. Training for volunteers was offered in both technical and nontechnical areas of television production year-round in weekly meetings at the studio. Roles were allocated on the basis of interest, skills, and availability rather than on positional power, and activities were arranged to meet the constantly changing time commitments of most volunteers. Positive reinforcement for work efforts was a basic tenet in daily operations of the channel, teamwork was encouraged, and recognition for individual contributions was offered on a regular basis. The station's motto was "We're Channel 8 and We're All Yours!"

The historical development of community television in Longmeadow began in 1975 with considerations on whether the town wanted or needed cable. At that time a core group held a public hearing on its own initiative to discuss the many aspects of the technology. At that time, a demonstrable need was not indicated, but an ad hoc committee was formed to study cable technology and report whether the service might be advantageous. In June 1980 the same group was responsible for drawing up governing guidelines for public access and choosing Times-Mirror as the cable operator. With 28,000 cable subscribers in Massachusetts, 500,000 nationwide, a promise of 100 percent equity financing, the lowest subscription rates, and a full-time staff member dedicated to local and access programming, Times-Mirror was thrilled to get the bid—mainly because it really wanted the plum of nearby Springfield. Prior to commencing service, Times-Mirror commissioned a customer attitude survey of the town, which indicated, among other findings, that two thirds of the seventy respondents wanted more news and information programming available.

PACTL had its debut on December 1, 1981, with wide and enthusiastic coverage of the event in the local newspapers, one reporter phrasing it this way: "More than 150 volunteers, with ages ranging from 16 to 70 and with backgrounds from law to farming, have been learning to handle a color TV camera and computerized editing machines."[17] The station aired information about itself, some crime watch tips, and a task force meeting on declining school enrollments. The next day a woman who had lost her dog came on the screen to make an appeal—and she got him back within hours, so someone must have been watching! Yet that first night was not without its problems, as when the school meeting tape broke and the station had to show its logo for fifteen minutes because it had not yet prepared a "Please Stand By" graphic.

Once the station was up and running, the ad hoc Cable Advisory Committee drafted a statement on guidelines for community access, reproduced here in Figure 5.1. Bylaws were also constructed, including information on name, purpose, location, corporate seal, and fiscal year; voting members; nonvoting members; board of directors; officers and agents; execution of papers; personal liability; indemnification; and miscellaneous items.

Organizationally, PACTL's ad hoc Cable Advisory Committee decided that "law and logic leave the business end of the cable operation with the selectmen, who have the power to license and the contracts to sign." Technical and functional aspects were assigned to the local high school, where facilities and personnel were already available through the A/V department. The executive director was, in fact, head of the town's A/V program[18]; only he, a technician, and a secretary—all part-time positions—were paid, from a budget of $15,000. Since expenses for equipment and salaries were always a concern, various fund-raising attempts were held, such as art auctions of original oils, lithographs, serigraphs, sculptures, woodcuts, and other works. The executive director made a big point about shared responsibility among

Figure 5.1
Guidelines Governing Community Access to PACTL

a.Policy and definition: the goal of Public Access Cable Television of Longmeadow, Inc. is to provide community access in order to increase opportunities for community expression on issues and topics that affect the lives of community members.

b.Community goals: community access is a community service which makes cable television channel time, studio facilities, video equipment, and production personnel available to the community franchise area members.

c.Eligible users: any individual or group preparing material for display on PACTL may be eligible for application to community access privileges.

d.Program content: PACTL will neither arbitrarily censor any qualified user, nor exercise any control of program subject matter of community access programs. . .within law and community standards.

e.Videotape preview: community access users wishing to have pre-recorded videotapes cablecast must submit the tapes to PACTL for preview prior to the cablecast.

f.Videotape playback: any community member or group may submit videotapes for playback through the cable television company or its designated agent.

g. Videotape technical: all community access taped programs must meet technical standards prior to cablecasting.

h.Time restrictions and scheduling: program scheduling is within the discretion of PACTL. Criteria: 1.timeliness; 2.series scheduling; 3. selective programming; 4.audience demographics; 5.target audience; 6.spontaneity; 7.blocking/flow

i.Production assistance

j.Equipment use and rental

k.Special service and charges

l.Copyrights and liabilities

m.Application procedure

all the volunteers, and he established early on an atmosphere for emphasis on cooperation; at the same time, his personality was such that everyone enjoyed working with him and turned to him constantly for approval and advice. Figure 5.2 depicts the organizational structure of PACTL.

Content categorization was performed on PACTL's programming for the first year of operation, with program formats found to be of three basic types: (1) creative (designed by local citizens), (2) static (town selectmen meetings, school committee meetings, etc.), and (3) ad hoc (special, one-time meetings or events).

Figure 3.1 in this book lists categorical breakdowns for PACTL's first year of operation. While informative shows predominated, they still commanded less than one quarter of the total; for the most part, there was a pretty fair mix proportionally among programming types and times.

In an attempt to understand audience attitudes and opinions, prior to the town's being wired for cable, an all-town survey was conducted. Once the system had been in operation for a year, a second survey was performed. With a 100 percent penetration of cable available in the town, and with 74 percent of the residents being hooked up to it at the time the survey was taken, a goal of 10 percent of the 3,700 subscribers was adopted; in fact, 11 percent, or 428 households, participated because of an exceedingly low refusal rate in the telephone survey.[19] It was found that an impressive 94 percent of the sample were familiar with the town's public access channel, with 45 percent being considered "regular viewers," tuning in at least three times per week. It was also discovered that 40 percent felt the channel had increased a sense of community (see Figure 5.3).

With forty-five hours per week of programming, PACTL after one year of operation had both an audience and a good supply of producers, hardly a week going by without a new idea and application for a program. The following describes the audience survey methodology:

Population—Longmeadow, Massachusetts, cable TV subscribers (428)

Data collection method—telephone survey

Sample design—systematic sampling with a random start

Survey instrument—see Appendix 1

Pretests—six

Data preparation—SPSS terminal (precoded)

Sampling errors—response effects

Computation—frequencies, correlations

Recognizing the importance of promoting itself, PACTL produced a self-descriptive brochure for distribution to local businesses and media, sent newsletters home with the elementary school children, prepared a fifteen-minute composite tape about its progress, and displayed posters and video-

Figure 5.2
Organizational Structure of PACTL

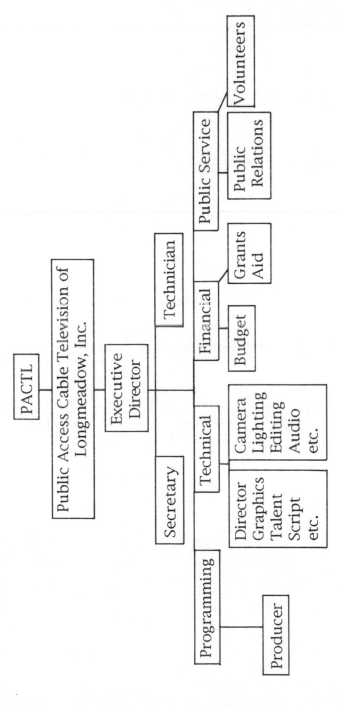

Figure 5.3
Regular Viewing of PACTL and Thinking It Has Increased a Sense of Community

Increased sense of community

Regular PACTL viewing

	No	Yes	Don't know	Total
None	28	54	79	161
	17.4	33.5	49.1	45.5
	51.9	31.4	61.7	
3+ programs/week	2	30	10	42
	4.8	71.4	23.8	11.9
	3.7	17.4	7.8	
1-2 programs/week	3	24	10	37
	8.1	64.9	27.0	10.5
	5.6	14.0	7.8	
Every 2 weeks	8	36	12	56
	14.3	64.3	21.4	15.8
	14.8	20.9	9.4	
Once/month	13	28	17	58
	22.4	48.3	29.3	16.4
	24.1	16.3	13.3	
Column	54	172	128	354
	15.3	48.6	36.2	100.0

p=.00 with 8df
gamma=+.36

tapes at town events. To maintain strong internal communication, it instituted an annual Recognition Night to honor individuals and groups who participated in the channel's work, sent Christmas cards to all volunteers and supporters, and gave each producer an individual certificate of appreciation designed by an in-house graphic artist.

Yet, all was not rosy. From nearly the start, there were problems with the cable company: where the antenna was to be installed, failure to meet contractual obligations for extra channels and provisions for two-way communications, and of course the ever-growing rate issue. Then when the executive director left in 1988, so did most of the other movers and shakers.[20] The only continuing representative on the board today is from the cable company, and he basically wants PACTL to dissolve; the fifteen-year franchise is almost up, and the company undoubtedly wants to take it over. Programming is minuscule, and according to the current executive director, there are no workshops, only a few producers, no quorum for the board, hardly any student involvement, and worst of all, no sense of what public access is all about.[21] There is no question about it: A good executive is a prize.

Executive directors play critical roles in a number of other PEG access centers in Massachusetts, and many of them could have been highlighted here for both their everyday work and their contributions to this book—notably, Myra Lenburg of Amherst Community TV, Paul DeMaria of Access Bellingham, Curtis Henderson of the Boston Community Access and Programming Foundation, Irwin Hipsman of Cambridge Community TV, Chuck Sherwood of Cape Cod Community Television (C3TV), Jon Gianetti of Fitchburg Access TV, Debbie Almeida of Greenfield, Rika Welsh of Malden Access TV, Garrett McCarey of Pittsfield Community Television,[22] Lisa Berg of the Shrewsbury Access Connection, Abigail Norman and Gerry Field (formerly) of Somerville Community Access TV, and Mauro DePasquale of Worcester Community Cable Access.[23]

Middlebury, Vermont—"Community is Our Middle Name"[24]

A narrative history of the development of Middlebury Community Television (MCTV), which was conceived as an independent, nonprofit organization dedicated to developing and operating public access, is entitled *The Little Station That Grew*. Grew, that is, from January 1986, when the only reverse feed was located in the town's municipal building, when the station had only four or five producer volunteers, the cablecasting equipment had to be carried back and forth from the high school, there was no editing deck, no staff, a budget of $1,000, and programming consisted of approximately one show per week, repeated on a second evening.

Soon, cablecasting began regularly, featuring especially live coverage of sports, the community news shows "Front Page" and "In View," and coverage of events expanded, like the Breadloaf Citizens Race, Festival on the Green, the Governor's Hearings on Vermont's Future, the League of Women Voters' "Meet the Candidates" program, and various community hearings. In 1989, after a renegotiated contract ($27,000 or 5 percent of gross revenue, whichever was greater), the first staff members were hired, start-up equipment was purchased, and the next year MCTV moved its studio into third-floor attic space in the public library—"a funky system," comments executive director Nelda Holder, as studio controls are in the office space and studio shoots are held in the library's secondary meeting room, so cameras are moved in and out depending on schedules. Programming is now regularly produced from 10 A.M. to 10 P.M. Monday through Friday, trainees number over two hundred, live coverage keeps increasing (select-men, school board, "Community Dialogue"), and phone-in availability has been added for viewers. Servicing some 2,100 households, informal surveys have found viewership to be high and the programs to be popular, on at least a sporadic basis, a finding confirmed by a larger survey performed by the selectmen.

Operating exclusively as a PEG access station, with emphasis on live coverage and community projects, MCTV imports three outside shows: Austin's "Alternative Views," "Bonjour," a French-Canadian program from Manchester, New Hampshire, and "Journey" from Burlington, Vermont, produced by the Roman Catholic Diocese. Under the category of "unique" programs are the live series produced by volunteers that focus on mental health professionals and another one by high school students; in addition, "Art and the Rosenbergs" and "The Artist Joseph Hahn in Middlebury" both focus on the political impact of art.

Speaking at a regional NFLCP conference in 1991 on public policy and advocacy, Nelda Holder outlined the grassroots philosophy of Middlebury's model, one that has been helpful to a number of start-up stations; still, she wondered, "How do we preserve the function of access?" Toward that end she completed some personal research for a master's project, titled "Grass-roots Visions: Environmental Advocacy and Public Access Television."[25] A study of the horizontally democratic concepts of cable public access and how their technical manifestation can be utilized as tools for environmental advocacy, the report introduces the activist history of public access, details various forms of programming available, explains the potential of ad hoc networking, and provides a dozen profiles of environmental producers from a perspective of "ecofeminism," briefly extracted here:

1. Zed Zabski, Middlebury, Vermont—Initially getting involved in access "almost by accident," the now-prolific producer has done shows including the environmental poetry of Gary Snyder, information on the search for a landfill, a "Spirit and Nature" environmental art exhibit at Middlebury College, and other shows

"to orient people who would otherwise not have been exposed . . . to right sharing and global stewardship of resources."

2. Gail Moretti, Londonderry, New Hampshire—A local recycling activist and volunteer environmental educator in the schools, she has produced "Backyard Composting" on her local public access station.

3. Bob d'Ancona, Bearsville, New York—Host of a weekly environmental show, he has moved from professional television and film work to "personal" video to document alternative architecture and energy resource projects of his own.

4. Jeff Orchard, Windham, New Hampshire—A professional wetlands scientist and one of the rescue workers in the aftermath of the infamous Exxon Alaskan oil spill, he aired footage from that experience. Since then, he has remained involved in public access, an advocate of tying environmental issues to local, individual responsibility.

5. Joel Odum, Washington, D.C.—Involved in saving a park in his neighborhood, which led to associations with the Sierra Club and Audubon, he has since set up the nonprofit Environmental Network, which highlights groups like the Natural Resources Defense Council, the Wilderness Society, Greenpeace, Scenic America, American Rivers, American Forestry Association, Zero Population Growth, Animal Rights, National Parks and Recreations, and many more.

6. Thomas Mealor/Frederica Russell, Tampa, Florida—Operators of the nonprofit Save Our Earth Productions, a program that began by tackling the water issue of Sulphur Springs, they now cablecast regularly on any topics relating to the environment.

7. Paul Ryan, Staten Island, New York—Working with a small nonprofit organization called Earth Environmental Group in New York City, he has been working to get a dedicated environmental channel up and running.

8. George Mokray, Cambridge, Massachusetts—Involved for nearly two decades in environmental issues, food co-ops, and sustainable agriculture, he has been interested in documentaries of solutions, like ones on worms, waste treatment, the Cambridge water system, the Boston Area Solar Energy Association's monthly lectures, leaf composting, and the Boston Harbor project.

9. Kevin Duggan, New York City—Working with Media Network, he has been involved in its periodically produced "Guide to Media and Environment," has coordinated a "Green Screen" project for Deep Dish TV, and works to get environmental groups networking.

10. Roger Bailey/Paul Connett, Canton, New York—Teachers at St. Lawrence University, they also work as partner-activists on the hazardous waste and incineration front and are known for their "W.O.W." (Work on Waste) videotape series on the solid waste crisis. The two have traveled beyond their backyards, too, documenting geothermal concerns in Hawaii, activist groups in Germany, Dutch farmers concerned about dioxin levels in their milk fat, and groups in Canada who want to produce French-language versions of the "W.O.W." tapes.

11. Wally Ames, Brattleboro, Vermont—Coordinator of the first tape for AMUSE (Artists and Musicians United to Save the Earth), released in time for Earth Day of 1990, he has helped sustain its interest.

12. Francene Amari, Somerville, Massachusetts—Member/supporter of many different environmental groups, from Sierra to PETA (People for the Ethical Treatment of Animals), she decided to form her own organization: Environmental Alert Report, producing videos in the areas of global issues, water, waste, animals, and health. Using local people like the Union of Concerned Scientists at Cambridge for global warming, and a local private consulting firm as well as the EPA on household hazardous waste, she has found public access the ideal medium to get out her message.

Missoula, Montana—Creating a Community Dialogue[26]

A fairly new access center (since 1989), fairly small (the office is open only Tuesday through Friday, 1–5 P.M.), but highly successful (having trained over one thousand community members in twenty-eight months), Missoula Community Access Television (MCAT) is based on providing an opportunity for residents to "create a community dialogue in which they communicate their interests and concerns as producers and receivers of television programs." Having negotiated franchise fees of $500,000 from the city of Missoula, which maintains a neutral position regarding the content of programming, the station provides these PEG access services:

• *Public access*—Offers diverse programming, covering the arts, entertainment, public affairs, religion, education and information.
• *Educational access*—Works with School District One, Missoula County High Schools, the City-County Library, the Missoula Vocational and Technical Center, and the University of Montana.
• *Governmental access*—Links the local jurisdictions and the community, including Missoula City Council meetings, important public hearings, civic services, and a listing of municipal events on the community message board.

Missoulians represent a wide range of cultural, artistic, and intellectual diversity, and have heartily embraced the notion of community access television as both a valuable outlet for local talent and an avenue for civic dialogue. Producers are required to warrant that their programs abide by the center's policies, including notions of first-come, first-served along with nondiscrimination, eligibility, and various programming policies, including abstinence from the following: any advertising or material that promotes any commercial product or service or lottery; any unlawful use of copyrighted material; any material that is libelous, slanderous, or defamatory of character; any material that is an unlawful invasion of privacy; any material that violates state or federal law relating to obscenity; any solicitation or appeal for funds; and any material that violates local, state, or federal laws.

Overwhelmingly, according to assistant director Mary Canty, Missoula loves access; testament to that is available in Figure 5.4. Yet, continues Canty, the center is of course not without its political and fiscal battles.

Figure 5.4
Missoula Community Access TV (MCAT)

	July	Year to Date	MCAT Total to Date (4/22/90-7/31/92)
Cablecasting			
Total Video Hours	195 hrs 15 min.	1400:05	3755:30
Weekly average	44:05	46:01	31:36
Daily average	6:18	6:34	4:31
Locally produced hrs.	104:35	769:10	(New statistic)
Imported hours	90:40	630:55	
Local/total hours ratio	53.56%	54.94%	
Live	10:05	101:25	364:24
Videotape	185:10	1298:40	3391:05
Premiere (1st run)	71:00	531:55	1602:05
Replay	123:15	867:10	2152:25
Premiere/total ratio	36.36%	37.99%	42.66%
Video/total available time	26.24%	27.39%	18.81%
Message board	548:45	3681:50	4591:05

New Programs	90 (71 hrs. 00min.)	626 (531:55)	1993 (1602:05)
Locally produced	44 (33:25)	288 (254:25)	999 (818:00)
Live	6 (10:05)	41 (101:25)	207 (364:25)
Imported programs	46 (37:35)	388 (277:30)	988 (784:05)
Local/total radio	44/90=48.89%	288/626=46.01%	999/1993=50.13%

Training

Orientation/basic portapak	18 people	159 people	188 people
Advanced portapak			
Edit #1 (Basic)			
Edit #2 (Advanced)			
Cablecasting			
2 camera remotes			
Studio cameras			
Control room			
Total new individuals trained			

Portapak Use	29 people (20 Basic, 13 Adv)	106 (89B, 48A)	248 people

Edit Suite Use	41 people (19B, 27A)	111 (98B, 53A)	211 people

Studio Use	11 people	70 people (new statistic)	
	14 studio blocks	106 blocks	2367 blocks
	34 hours	319 hours	

Total Active producers   398 people
Active Producers/Workshop Participants Radio=398/987=   40.32%

Community dialogue comes with a price; as the *Missoula Community Access Television Handbook* states, "The success of MCAT is in your hands!!!"

Multnomah County, Oregon—Sharing Resources

A nonprofit corporation established in 1983, Multnomah Community Television (MCTV, Gresham, Oregon) services parts of Portland, the suburban community of Gresham, three smaller cities, and unincorporated parts of the county on an operating budget of about $700,000. Beginning with a philosophy of providing a mix of community programming produced by both staff and the public, MCTV offers more than two hundred workshops each year free to the public on all aspects of creating television. It also tries to keep its goal of "equitable scheduling of shared resources. Approximately 60% of all locally produced programming is public access. The remaining 40% is a combination of staff-produced programming. This ratio has remained fairly constant as production has increased."[27] A number of volunteers from the center have gone on to become prolific public access producers, according to general manager Alexander Quinn: "The combination of staff and public access productions contributes to a climate of creativity, diversity, learning and professionalism whereby everyone benefits."

One particular Oregon access center deserves special note here as a model in community programming. Portland Cable Access[28] operates five channels, funded by franchise fees paid to the city of Portland by local cable operators. Its report on the 1992 fiscal year showed 206 volunteer hours for outreach, 74 for training, 5,285 for production, plus nearly three thousand hours of new programming, including the following: "From Broadway to Rock" (Cascade AIDS Project), "Food Gram from the Oregon Food Bank," "Gathering of the Guilds," "Model Democratic Convention," "Sabin Neighborhood Festival," "Metropolitan Youth Symphony," "The Last Empire," and "Yom Hashoah—Holocaust Remembrance Day." The station is continually inundated with praise and appreciation from the community.

New York City—Nothing Like It

New York City's public access channels have been in existence since 1971; it was the first urban area in the country to require the establishment and operation of such a system. Early on, Gillespie (1975, p. 36) cited it as an example: "Although beset with numerous difficulties, such as those evolving from defective technology and unmanageable geographic disbursement of citizens with common ethnic interests, the experiment continues at this writing with at least moderate success."

One of the biggest problems, at least in the beginning, was underutilization, despite the large number of people in entertainment and service industries in New York City. Training became available to nonprofessional groups from organizations such as the Alternate Media Center,[29] Open Channel,[30] Global Village/Survival Arts Media, and the Center for Understanding Media; they have all been helpful in encouraging people to use the access available to them. In addition, the Fund for the City of New York, part of the Center for Analysis of Public Issues, financed informational materials about the potential of public access channels and disseminated them to various groups.

The New York experience is best described as narrowcasting, geared to specialized groups. In its 1971 report *On the Cable—The Television of Abundance*, the Sloan Commission on Cable Communications reported that programming to date had included the following: "Theatre for the Deaf," a report on their homeland by Friends of Haiti, Hebrew-language instruction, various ethnic art and dance performances, readings of Shakespeare, black poetry, "Metropolitan Almanac" of community events, and much more.

Much academic research has focused on the Manhattan cable system. Anshien and colleagues (1973) and David Othmer (1973) both give background information on franchising, wiring patterns, usage, funding, cable operators, and studio equipment after two years of public access, the latter going on to document problems inherent in the system: censorship, liability, labor unions, technical quality, production costs, equipment, and audience responsiveness. That negative tone is shared by Richard Calhoun in his 1972 six-month report on the channels for the Center for Policy Research; he found the general public unaware of the channels and how to use them, no available model program formats, two few skilled production assistants, too little equipment, and financing difficulties. The general impression was that access shows are boring and don't satisfy audiences' needs.

Yet, Alan H. Wurtzel's 1974 dissertation[31] disputed the pessimism, concluding that the New York channels had enjoyed an initial measure of success, for the following reasons: (1) They attracted a large and diversified number of producers to supply the programming; (2) program content was often community- or neighborhood-oriented and was generally communication unavailable via traditional broadcast media; the channels experienced a consistent upward growth in terms of the number of programs and airtime cablecast.

Another dissertation on the New York channels, performed by Patricia Bellamy Goss in 1978,[32] found that the FCC's original objectives for public access were being met in terms of citizen participation in community dialogue through a mass medium, promotion of diversity in television programming, the advancement of educational and instructional television, increasing informational services of local government, and increasing access to media. Morris and colleagues (1972) contend that broadly based usage would occur with greater audience penetration and an interactive rather than passive attitude toward cable, plus better technical equipment and means for funding.

Alexis Greene (1982, p. H1) reported that a dozen years after its inception public access in New York City had served numerous individuals and organizations in terms of channel usage, that the predominant program categories were public affairs, religion, and variety/entertainment, but that there were still problems with the technical quality and with financial support from cable companies.

Public access is very much alive and well in Manhattan today, even vital and growing, according to artist/critic Douglas Davis:

As viewers zap through the spectrum, they are likely to be stunned most any night by a full-breasted male or female stripper on Channel J, the commercially leased channel, or assailed by a full-throated Mayor or Comptroller haranguing the citizenry on Channel L, the city government's municipal-access window.

But out beyond J and L, lie Channel C and D, those rarely patronized citadels of electronic democracy. Rather than strippers and pols, C and D offer on shoestring budgets high-minded seminars on topics ranging from urban decay to sexist mythology, video-art experiments featuring frisky computerized graphics and earnest documentary studies of often neglected subjects. . . . Manhattan's facilities for access production will undoubtedly improve. In recent negotiations with cable franchisers for the outer boroughs, the city has obtained services far superior to those it got in 1970.[33]

According to a franchise agreement between the city of New York and the cable operators of Queens, four channels are reserved for public access via Queens Public Access Television (QPTV),[34] cablecast into the homes of 315,000 subscribers. With the motto "Queens has a lot to say," the station has an impressive list of programming, plus lots of media attention.

The Participate Report: A Case Study of Public Access Cable Television in New York State (Agosta, Rogoff, and Norman, 1990) profiles a number of centers other than New York City, answering these questions: How available are access channels? Who actually uses them? What programs get shown? What helps access thrive? Published with support from the New York State Council on the Arts, *Participate* is a comprehensive snapshot, based on responses from 141 cable systems, of the workings of access, discussing the following: programming, forms of access management, equipment and training, hours and channel time, outreach, funding, colleges and universities, public schools, libraries, arts and art organizations using access, profiles of access centers, and some background on federal legislation and state regulation.

Pennsylvania—A State Filled with Community Television

As a whole, Pennsylvania is probably the state with the oldest success stories of community television. David Hoke[35] has reported on York Community Access Television (YCAT), which worked with the local community college to produce twenty hours of programming per week: "Users range from artists to neighborhood organizations to religious groups to local schools. Feedback from the community has been good, and participation has been growing." He lists these combined factors as important for success: (1) education, (2) positive relations with operator, (3) low-cost means, (4) support structure, and (5) regulation.

Berks Community Television in Reading, a nonprofit, community-based producer of interactive cable programming, has often been "show-cased" as a success story in terms of governmental interaction with its citizenry via the cable technology. The Berks Cable Company has put out an impressive amount of PR material, such as a color brochure entitled *The Reading Dialogue*, and a whole history of its venture called "A Story about People" from the Community Video Workshop. Some examples of its programming: A famous operatic baritone sings, and talks about his career; attorneys answer legal questions; emergency psychiatric care is discussed, senior citizens enjoy a weekly "Sing Along"; schools and hospitals participate in programming; religious services are performed; business issues are explained; and governmental concerns are addressed to a wide constituency.

The Philadelphia story is something else again. While the city *should* be an ideal place for community television, having as it does not only the needs and volunteers to help serve them that any major city might, politics has caused actual implementation of public access to drag. One of the persons who has been in on this process from the start is Keith Brand,[36] spokesperson for Philadelphia's Citizens for Public Access Cable Coalition and now a graduate student at Temple University. He has documented the fact that although the first cable franchise was awarded in 1966, by 1973, when the Philadelphia Community Cable Coalition was formed, construction still had not begun. In 1980, when William Green became mayor after Frank Rizzo's regime, he summarily dismissed franchise boundaries approved by the previous administration. When Wilson Goode became mayor in 1983, things got rolling: In 1984 the city made some franchise awards, a bill allowing structure of a public access corporation was filed, a budget was drawn up, and plans were in place for all the possibilities—yet, to date, Philadelphia still does not have public access. No one, it appears, is willing to give up the sizable amounts the city receives (nearly $6 million annually) in franchise fees from cable. Brand blames lack of consistent grassroots lobbying efforts for Philadelphia's inaction, along with concerns over controversial programming and insufficient funding; one hopes that his work will speed the process.

Wilbraham, Massachusetts—An Emerging Community Television System[37]

In December 1991 cable television residents of Wilbraham,[38] who might have been grazing along on their remote controls for something to watch, found this bulletin board notice on Channel 46: "Welcome to WTV–46, your community television." Unfortunately, the producers had forgotten to include the name "Wilbraham" in the computer generator making the announcement. But in a way, that's what this is all about: WTV is, indeed, Wilbraham's own television channel—and it is an all-volunteer project.

The background to this activity began several years ago, when interested citizens came forward to say they wanted to support an electronic medium for the town. Members of that early Public Access Cable Television Committee, headed by the director of media services at the high school, held nearly weekly meetings until the committee was able to hash out a policy manual defining and describing access principles, user and program qualifications, and operating rules and schedules. As part of the negotiation with the cable company, the town was granted $22,500.

Wilbraham was late entering this exciting activity. Consider: its only print "news" sources had been the *Union-News* (a Springfield, Massachusetts-centered newspaper with a daily circulation of 128,000, 172,000 Sundays) and *The Reminder* (a free, weekly, house-delivered "shopper" with a circulation of 32,000), neither of them Wilbraham-specific. There were two local television network affiliates that occasionally included news of the town, but in typical fashion only if it was sensational and/or if photos were available. Most communicative of all, however, was Greg the Barber's storefront window in the center of town.[39]

Then, in January 1992, the Wilbraham Public Access Committee was able to acquire a room in the (regional) high school, buy some equipment, and offer its first training course, which consisted of the following: a brief introduction to cable television technology, including the vast possibilities of programming that it allows; learning about cameras, lighting, and audio- and videotape script writing. There were in-class and out-of-class production exercises ("remotes"), training for editing, production of a short video program, and, in the end, certification that the trainee was now a full-fledged producer, able to borrow the WTV–46 equipment and produce a show for the channel.

Sign-ups for the first training course, which was advertised on the Channel 46 Bulletin Board and limited to the first seventeen people, had an immediate waiting list. Interests and areas of expertise among members of this first training course were widely diverse. Many had never held a camera before, while others were professionals in the electronics field. Reasons for wanting to get involved with Wilbraham's community channel ranged from just wanting to do something for the town, to wanting to educate people (about solid waste, disabled citizens, and/or issues like fair housing, the Wilbraham orchestra, or ambulances), to sheer curiosity about this new medium. Contrary to Hollander and Stappers's[40] typology of research approaches, the eclecticism of this first group was duplicated in the second training session of volunteers.

While the Bulletin Board has continued to be produced, and commented upon, it deals mostly with simple civic events like concerts, activities at the Senior Center, school events, Town Hall business like dump stickers and dog licenses, club activities, and, that first summer, information about fund-raisers (an "ice cream social" and a dinner dance) for a local young mother who was about to have expensive, experimental cancer treatments. After five months, the first whole show aired—a compilation of works from the various volunteers. In December 1992, a group of volunteers met with the selectmen to fill them in on what had transpired to date and what some of their future plans might involve—a very politically smart move.

Volunteers have begun to take turns on Monday nights as room coordinators, so trained and certified producers know when they can come check out equipment and/or do some editing. Efforts so far, in other words, are quite modest—but enthusiasm remains high, and courses keep filling up. Still, the director has decided to cut back on his involvement with the station, so volunteers have regrouped responsibilities. There was a positive article about the station in a free shopper,[41] and lots of people have commented on it, many becoming volunteers themselves.

Even though many of the other community television stations cited here undoubtedly have more sophisticated documents for their operations, some of the forms Wilbraham's public access channel uses are shown in Appendixes 16–23.

Yakima, Washington—Celebrating the Uniqueness of Life

When a community television plan was drawn up for the Yakima City Council in 1982, the underlying philosophy was "to celebrate the uniqueness of life in Yakima. Through the limitless communication qualities of television, we want to examine ourselves as a community—our joys, our fears, our needs, our conflicts, our successes, our failures, our history, our expectations and our hopes for the future."[42] A recent telephone call to the station was answered by a person having "severe technical difficulties," with a live show airing as the conversation took place. Each station, each community, each producer, each show, and each transmission is unique; cheers to Yakima for celebrating that uniqueness.

CONCLUSION

Knowing that community television in the United States derives from the First Amendment, that the strength of our democracy depends on the provision that our citizenry be "heard," and that this provision is grounded in the utilitarian ideal of the "marketplace of ideas," Bob Devine is particularly concerned about protecting the diversity of those voices: "In an era in which the 'marketplace' is dominated by electronic communications, the social invention of cable protects this marketplace notion by providing fair access for all to an arena of electronic discourse."[43] The many case studies here, only a fraction of the thousands that could have been highlighted, are a clear demonstration that diversity flourishes.

NOTES

1. Quotation from "Access Makes a Difference," *CTR*, 15, no. 5 (September/October 1992), p. 11.

2. Letter and resources from Rick Hayes, station manager of the Public Access Center, Allen County Public Library, Fort Wayne, Indiana, August 13, 1992.

3. Rick Hayes, "Libraries and Access: Building Partnerships," *CTR*, 10 (November/December 1991).

4. This section on Austin owes a debt of gratitude to Rosalind Brinkley, community services officer, for many resources and also lots of fun at the NFLCP conference in St. Paul, Minnesota.

5. "The First Ten Years of Austin Community Television, 1973–1983," *ACTV Grand Opening* (April 12, 1992), p. 3.

6. Frank Morrow, "*Alternative Views* Has an Impact," *CTR* 9, no. 1 (1986), p. 26.

7. See "Controversy in Austin," *CTR* 8, no. 2, p. 14; Anita Brenda Stech, "I Remember When . . . Memories of Austin," *CTR* 9, no. 3, p. 26; Frank Morrow, "Sustaining a Series," *NFLCP Newsletter* 9, (1986), p. 5; Lynda Suzanne Lieberman, "Community Television and the Arts: Austin Style," *CTR*, 10, no. 1, p. 8; and the *ACTV Information Guide*.

8. Tour of the Northwest Community Television's facilities with Mike Johnson, assistant executive director, July 15, 1992.

9. Response form from Kathleen Greenwood, of Hudson (Wisconsin) Community Access TV.

10. Letter and resources from Paul A. E. Moeller, director of operations and training, Calaveras Community Television, July 14, 1992.

11. Carl Kucharski, "The Long and Winding Road to Columbus," *CTR* (Spring 1991), p. 6.

12. Resources and enthusiastic support from Dirk Koning, executive director of the Grand Rapids Cable Access Center.

13. Tim Goodwin, "GRTV, 23/J," *On-The-Town* (September 1990).

14. Dirk W. Koning, "The Currency of Democracy," *Grand Rapids Magazine* (May 1992), p. 48.

15. Fax from Dave Bloch of International Mobile Video, August 1992. He adds, in a later fax (July 20, 1993): "SCTV also operates the local channels in Downieville, the county seat, with a population of 325. Tim programs via the phone line, and runs tapes by playing them back in an old garage in Downieville where the only upstream cable drop is located. When we do the annual telethon, we do it LIVE simultaneously from both locations—one show from Tim's living room, the other from that garage."

16. Response and resources from Joan Burke, executive director of Kalamazoo's Community Access Center.

17. John Appleton, "Public Access TV Cameras Focus on Longmeadow," *The Morning Union* (November 18, 1981), p. 13.

18. Merrill Oltchick.

19. Don A. Dillman discusses the advantages of telephone surveys for obtaining a representative sample and accurate answers in *Mail and Telephone Surveys: The Total Design Method* (New York: Wiley, 1978), pp. 74–75. On a qualitative note, I might add that many of the participants wanted to make it clear that they had never participated in surveys before, adding comments to the effect that the researcher sounded "so nice," or "so honest," or that they had sons or daughters who had gone or were going to the University of Massachusetts. Whereas interviews were billed as probably lasting five to ten minutes, the majority went longer than that—not because of the instrument, but because most people wanted to talk about a subject near and dear to them: television. Television viewing, consuming as it does such a chunk of our time, can become a very intimate subject.

20. Telephone conversation with Merrill Oltchick, now executive director of MPACT (Municipal Public Access Cable Television, Monson-Palmer, Massachusetts), February 11, 1993.

21. Telephone conversation with Emily Bent, executive director of PACTL, January 8, 1993.

22. In a letter to me of August 14, 1992, Garrett McCarey of Pittsfield Community Television wrote, "I am very pleased that someone is going to be examining the 'other side' of community programming. It's about time 'Ugly George' and 'Midnight Blue' aren't the public's only frame of reference when it comes to Access."

23. I am indebted to Rika Welsh, chair of the northeast region of The Alliance, for reviewing this list.

24. Letter and resources from Nelda Holder, executive director of Middlebury Community TV, August 12, 1992.

25. Nelda Frances Holder, "Grassroots Visions: Environmental Advocacy and Public Access Television," unpublished master's project submitted to Antioch New England Graduate School, 1991.

26. Response form and resources from Mary Canty, assistant director of Missoula Community Access Television; also, more information was provided by Temi Rose/Perceptions.

27. Alexander Quinn, "Creativity, Diversity & Professionalism in East Multnomah," *CTR* (Spring 1991), p. 8.

28. Response form and resources from Deborah M. Luppold, general manager of Portland Cable Access. See Paul Steele, "Portland Cable Access: A Model for Community Programming," *CTR* (Summer 1984), p. 25; and Adam Haas, "Local Origination in Portland: A Lesson to Be Learned," *CTR* (Winter 1984), p. 16.

29. Kletter (1973, p. 25) made note of AMC's goals as a resource center going beyond the notion of public access to use "television, or more accurately, video, to enable people to take charge of the information that directs their lives and to open up neighborhoods and towns to the vibrant, new patterns of communication."

30. See Theodora Sklover, "The Open Door Policy on Television," in George Gerbner, Larry P. Gross, and William H. Melody (eds.), *Communication Technology and Social Policy: Understanding the New Cultural Revolution* (New York: Wiley, 1973), pp. 327–37.

31. Alan H. Wurtzel, "The Electronic Neighbor: A Source and Content Analysis

of Public Access Channel Programming on a New York City Cable Television System," unpublished doctoral dissertation, New York University, 1974.

32. Patricia Bellamy Goss, "A Policy Analysis of Subscriber Reaction to Cable Television Access Programming in New York City," unpublished doctoral dissertation, New York University, 1978.

33. Douglas Davis, "Public-Access TV Is Heard in the Land," *New York Times* (June 11, 1989), p. H31+.

34. Response form and resources from Liz Bartucci, community outreach assistant for Queens Public Access Television.

35. "Cable Access: Myth or Reality?" in Morton I. Hamburg, *All about Cable: Legal and Business Aspects of Cable and Pay Television* (New York: Law Journals Seminars-Press, 1979), pp. 551–53.

36. Letter and resources from Keith Brand, with whom I have spoken about the Philadelphia problem at meetings of the Cultural Environment Movement, June 21, 1993.

37. A version of this write-up was delivered for the Working Group on Local Radio and TV of the International Association of Mass Communication Researchers, Guaruja, Brazil, August 1992.

38. According to 1990 census: 4,474 households, 12,635 residents.

39. Linda K. Fuller, "The Media of Wilbraham and McKnight." Paper submitted to the "Sense of Place" Study Group—Connecticut Valley Region, Massachusetts Foundation for the Humanities, 1991.

40. Ed Hollander and James Stappers cite three basic approaches: localism-cosmopolitan, integration or community ties, and community structure. See their "Community Media and Community Communication," in Nick Jankowski, Ole Prehn, and James Stappers (eds.), *The People's Voice: Local Radio and Television in Europe* (London: John Libbey, 1992), p. 23.

41. Linda M. Rowland, "The Camera's Rolling at Minnechaug High School and All Over Wilbraham," *The Reminder* (September 15, 1992), p. 4.

42. Community Television Plan, presented to the Yakima City Council by the Community Programming Advisory Committee, 1982. Thanks early on to Bruce Crest, Cable Communications Coordinator.

43. Bob Devine, "Protecting the Diversity," *CTR*, 9, no. 3 (1986), p. 34.

Implications and Predictions

Genuine democracy requires the participation of individuals in matters
of concern to their common social and political life.[1]

Douglas Kellner, 1992

As the twentieth century draws to a close, the re-regulatory climate in
Washington will undoubtedly have a substantial impact on the future of
community television.[2] While cable programming continues to threaten traditional broadcasting audience ratings, competition also looms from a number
of other sources, in particular video rentals and sales, but video games like
those produced by Nintendo and Genesis are also fighting for the same
niches.

Meanwhile, cable has its own concerns—mainly, the threat of telephone
companies ("telcos") entering the business of video delivery, offering "video
dial tone" via fiber-optic cable. Potentially allowing anywhere from 500 to
5,000 channels in a true common carrier environment, telco video dial tone
could easily inflict on cablecasters the same economic worries that cable has
dealt broadcasters. The economics of fiber-optic cable demand our attention:
"Fiber is cheaper to install, easier to maintain, more durable, and can carry
many times more data than conventional coaxial cable" (Belsie, 1993).

Another delivery source might be by conventional copper wire, utilizing
digital compression technology. Competition is also expected from "wireless
cable" technologies such as cellular television and, as will be discussed later,
multiple channel microwave services (MMDS) and direct broadcast satellites
(DBS). The wider potential is for the creation of "virtual television" in addition to information systems; that is, the "Information Highway" that has
received recent attention in the press. For proponents of public access to
information delivery systems, concern focuses on economic constraints of
who will sponsor and who will be able to pay for these added services.

There are also a number of other considerations regarding the future of community television.

AN ASSESSMENT TO DATE

As of this writing, community television efforts under way in the United States are growing exponentially, and, although there are exceptions, like the Philadelphia case study cited in the previous chapter, there are promises of many more groups to follow. The most important element, we are learning, is political will. Barry Orton wrote the following about planning and utilization of access channels back in 1982 (p. 23):

The experience with access-type programming has varied widely from city to city, with some notable successes and at least as many failures . . . [they] can be important sources of local entertainment and information. At a relatively low cost, the government channel *can* be used to allow home viewing of all public meetings from city council to school board. The educational access channel *can* become a means of linking schools with subscribers. The public access *can* combine the best of the political soapbox and the local theater. The library *can* televise story hours for children. All that is necessary is planning, funds, and the time of talented and dedicated people.

Community television, as has been outlined here, especially in the form of PEG access, offers invaluable resources both by and for the localities it serves. Echoing some of the early cries for the medium as offering grassroots democratic dialogue, public access allows individuals and groups to program according to their own interests, while educational access allows whole target niches to develop learning skills otherwise unavailable, and governmental access keeps the citizenry in touch with their locally elected officials. Emphasis is on the word "access," which, except for community television, is practically a media nonentity.

Broadcasting has reported on a survey of 145 general managers and program directors at commercial television stations on where their programming dollar would go in the foreseeable future, with more than half of the sample citing local programming.[3] With the growing popularity of magazine-style infotainment shows—not news or informational programming but sheer entertainment, run by network entertainment divisions[4]—in addition to more emphasis on conservative provincialism in general, "local" and "regional" seem to be emerging as the media buzzwords of the 1990s for both traditional and alternative programmers. As programming becomes more expansive and more expensive, local programming may, in fact, be the only way to go.

Add the fact that the image of access programming seems to be changing. Media critic Ron Powers recognizes it as no longer "an arcane refuge for the disaffected political left wing. Right-to-lifers are busily spinning out their programs now. . . . In fact, the most beguiling aspect . . . might not lie so much in any given show as in the straightforward, can-do, utterly *American* approach to it that is being demonstrated by ordinary people."[5]

Still, Pat Sparks of the Community Council of Greater New York is concerned that not enough service organizations recognize community television as a cost-effective way to effect the following[6]:

- Educate the community about concerns the agency is addressing
- Sensitize the community to the circumstances and needs of the population the agency serves
- Acquaint potential clients with the agency's services
- Raise issues and stimulate discussion
- Influence the public, public officials, and potential funding sources
- Create videotapes which do double duty for specialized purposes such as training and fund-raising
- Recruit volunteers and offer public acknowledgment for their contributions.

As community television efforts continue to move toward third party, nonprofit operation of their channels, separating out from the control of the local government, cable operator, or other institutions, it is important to assess what the role of other competing technologies might be. Dirk Koning has warned, "In this electronic age of information trafficking, communities have to decide if they are going to be an information mint, bank or panhandler."[7]

EFFECTS OF COMPETING TECHNOLOGIES

New communications technologies undoubtedly will continue to change the picture of community television as we know it (Fuller, 1991a). As Pringle and colleagues (1991, p. 355) have predicted, "Four important influences will shape the operation of the electronic media in the 1990s. They are social, technological, economic, and public policy forces."

Drawing on data from the Electronic Industries Association, John Carey (1993, p. 36) has constructed this chart on the penetration of selected media in terms of households in the United States:

Technology/service	Penetration percentage
All television	98
Color television	97
Telephone service	93
VCR	77
Basic cable	61

Answering machine	46
Compact disc player	35
Home computer	33
Video game player	31
Stereo television	31
Camcorder	17
Projection television	8
Backyard satellite dish	3
Cellular telephone	3
Home fax machine	1

While television is clearly the most universal of all media, it is surprising that Carey left radio out of the picture, as it is the most ubiquitous and pervasive medium in the world. Also, take a minute to consider his chart and question who is not included here: Who, for example, does not have telephone service or access to cable technology, and how many people who have them actually use their home computers? For our purposes, one wonders, hopefully, how many persons with camcorders might want to air their shows over PEG channels.

For those of us involved in community television, the future of the industry will undoubtedly respond to innovations in communications technology. Knowing that it will cost the American public somewhere in the area of $40 billion to upgrade the telco infrastructure to optical fiber capable of delivering those 500 plus channels, plus another $100 billion to upgrade to high definition television (HDTV), we need to ask: Who will pay, how, and when, and who will benefit? In terms of pure practicality, Koning extends his model on "Community Access to Dominant Media" that appears in Appendix 15 to consider "Diversity for Survival" in Figure 6.1. While there are a number of uncertainties in the goal for diverse ideas in the marketplace, he outlines several potential areas of diversification and offers some potential models for administration and sources of income.

Certainly the VCR revolution has played a substantial role. Many people report that their first introduction to community television was inadvertent—that they discovered their local channels while grazing along the dials, then tuned in from then on to see what it had to offer. With A. C. Nielsen reporting that some 87 percent of American television households have videocassette recorders,[8] it is also important to note that VCRs are about to undergo a conversion from analog to digital technology—meaning clearer, static-free pictures (Pollack, 1993, p. F9), a development that many industry officials are carefully monitoring. VCRs will be required to accommodate HDTV by the year 2008, when current television sets and videocassette players will become obsolete and will not be able to play anything except

Figure 6.1
Community Access to Dominant Media: Diversity for Survival

This is an outline for the growth and survival of community access to dominant media based on the model of public access television and the premise of broad-band and base diversity of service for ultimate survival in an emerging telecommunication spectrum. . .or. . .how to turn your cable access center into a media access center.

Need for diversity:
   *Uncertainty of city subsidy post Cable Act scenario
   *Uncertainty of cable industry dominance of delivery
   *Uncertainty of community tolerance of free speech
   *Avoidance of too many eggs in one basket, especially if you don't
    even own the basket
   *Uncertainty of government backing of independent thought
   *Financial and philosophical independence

Potential areas of diversification:
   *Low power television
   *Cable and broadcast radio
   *Film and video archives
   *Film training, equipment check-out and production centers
   *Desktop publication opportunities
   *Printing capabilities: laser, mechanical, etc.
   *Computer graphics generation, computer literacy training
   *Telecommunication access--i.e., BBS systems, data base access, FAX
   *Institutional Networks
   *National and international exchanges, uplink, downlink
   *Institutes for study

Potential models for administration:
   *Library, communication department, cable office
   *Multiple divisions of a single non-profit organization with steering
    committees
   *Multiple non-profit organizations with independent boards with
    representation on a shared management 'super' board

Potential sources of income:
   *Cable, telco, city subsidy
   *Nominal charge back for services or access rights
   *'On-air' fundraising
   *Training fees
   *Foundation, grant support
   *Membership fees, archive fees
   *Distribution rights

Source: Dirk Koning, *CTR* 13, no. 1 (Spring 1990), p. 7.

old, low definition videos and video games. One wonders: Why has there been no public debate on these issues?

School plays and sporting events on community television have become fund-raisers for participating groups, council and committee meetings have been taped and requisitioned for legal purposes, and cooperative networking between access centers has allowed for diverse and challenging programming. Yet, let us be ever aware of the nonparticipants in this process, questioning who is left out and why. Although this book is laden with examples of active people and programming, we realize that there is no incentive for local governments to participate in the process.

The camcorders that oftentimes accompany VCR usage have been noted often in this book, permitting what ABC news analyst Jeff Greenfield (1992, p. 17) has called "The Videotaping of Darn Near Everything." While he argues that camcorder users are changing the face of racial politics, in light of cases like the Rodney King incident, Bob Devine (1991, p. 8) is more concerned that "the proliferation of home video in recent years has contributed to a general de-legitimization of access as valid public discourse." Also, *Newsweek* recently has reported on the proliferation of video diaries on American television (Talbot, 1993), a genre of self-chronicling semidocumentaries that have also enjoyed popularity in Great Britain.

High-definition television (HDTV) is right around the corner. While our current television signal consists of 525 lines of resolution, the new technology will more than double that capability, providing superior picture quality and a visual clarity unmatched by our conventional televisions. While HDTV has been delayed mostly for political rather than for technical reasons (the FCC has already allocated the HDTV channel in the UHF band, 470–890 MHz), its eventual introduction can enhance community television aesthetically. Public television stations, however, are another story: How can they be expected to afford upgrades costing anywhere from $12 to $20 million each? From where would monies come for new cameras, transmitters, recorders, and the like? And where, in this discussion, is the notion of promoting diversity?

Television as we know it is changing rapidly due to new technologies. Michael Morgan of the University of Massachusetts, who envisions a day in the not too far future when we will be able to choose endings to television shows, even place ourselves in the action, predicts: "You'll be able to freeze it, play it backwards, turn it inside out. You can turn on your own camera and put yourself in a movie, play with it. It'll be the video equivalent of karaoke."[9] Now is a good time for us to judge our media literacy, assessing skills and desires in addition to considering what additional equipment we might need and what we might be able to afford.

Designed not for retransmission, but to go directly into viewers' homes, direct broadcast satellites (DBS) offer great potential for sharing community television not only nationally but internationally as well. The idea is that from a satellite in a stationary orbit 22,300 miles above the equator, the DBS operator can broadcast multiple programming services to homes equipped with small, inexpensive rooftop satellite receivers. While to date the system has not been economically feasible enough to impact community television, that possibility in the future is worth monitoring. In light of an economy burdened with a $4 to $5 trillion deficit and more video competition, one wonders what is economically feasible. How much can and will the public be willing to spend on its beloved television? Also, what should the role of the U.S. government be in terms of allowing propagandistic transmission, such as might filter in from countries like Libya, North Korea, Iraq, Cuba, and others that force us to take a stance on the free flow of information? The topic of DBS also makes us come to terms with attitudes toward how much we are committed to notions of local origination, as opposed to national satellite distribution.

The modified final judgment (MFJ) of 1984 determined specifications for the breakup of AT&T, prohibiting the seven regional telephone companies (Ameritech, Bell Atlantic, Bell South, NYNEX, Pacific Telesis, Southwestern Bell, and U.S. West) from engaging in information services such as video program services, newspapers, and classified advertisements outside their regions. Then, in July 1992, the FCC decided to relax its ban on cable-telco cross-ownership,[10] allowing telephone companies to distribute programming through what became known as the "video dial tone" plan.

While the telcos could acquire up to 5 percent equity interest in and provide financing for program services they might offer in their entry into the $25-billion-a-year cable business and the $8-billion-a-year video-rental business,[11] they would be under no restrictions against obtaining municipal franchises, as cable systems have had to do. Still, the telcos at this point are not able to set prices, own, or exercise editorial control over programming; further, according to the Cable Act of 1984, they cannot own colocated cable systems and are limited to a common carrier relationship with program producers. The Cable Act of 1992, allowing the FCC to promulgate rules for cable operators regarding censorship of PEG channels, goes against the grain of everything community television activists have fought for all these years.

Tom Hargadon, editor of *The Green Sheet*, a San Francisco–based newsletter focusing on the convergence of multimedia computing and high-bandwidth communications, strongly recommends that the regional Bell operating companies (RBOCs) abandon thoughts of providing broadcast video services, "a business they know little about and do not have the technical means to deliver. . . . The RBOCs will only be able to deliver one or two channels of video programming over the existing twisted-pair copper wiring even with the newest compression technologies. By contrast, the cable industry already serves 90% of the homes in America with coaxial cable."[12] AT&T may soon be in competition with RBOCs for local service regarding cellular transmissions, and RBOCs may soon compete with AT&T for long distance services.

The FCC has recommended congressional repeal of the telco-cable cross-ownership ban, and in the meantime advocates for community television are collectively holding their breath to see what transpires next. "Much more is at stake than ordinary telephone service or cable television," notes the *New York Times*.[13] "The real fight is over who controls the next generation of communications services into the home." The Electronic Frontier Foundation has been at the forefront in the debate about the future of our communications infrastructure:

At stake is the future of the web of information links organically evolving from computer and telephone systems. By the end of the next decade, these links will connect nearly all homes and businesses in the U.S. They will serve as the main channels for commerce, learning, education, and entertainment in our society . . . the national, public broadband digital network will emerge from the "convergence" of the public telephone network, the cable television distribution system, and other networks such as the Internet.[14]

Although telcos have been successful since January 1993 in lobbying Congress not to upgrade Internet as *the* public information network, telcos would not be profitable if the government were the provider of such services. One wonders again about what really is in the best public "interest, convenience, and necessity."

CD-ROMs, laser discs capable of storing and retrieving video information, provide innumerable possibilities for combining thousands of programs on a single disc. Rather than having to keep an enormous reference library, individuals and organizations can use this advanced technology to perform complex categorical searches in a matter of seconds—accessing, for example, historical local film footage, documents relating to town government, program time fillers of specific lengths, profiles of prominent citizens, highlights of athletic events, works by particular producers, and endless other choices.

Wireless cable, known as multichannel, multipoint distribution services (MMDS), has transmitters sending microwaves to special antennas and receivers for paid programming in dense locations like apartments and hotels. As the signals can travel up to twenty-five miles to distribute programming and information services to high-population spots, MMDS is mostly of interest in areas where complete cable systems remain underdeveloped, but as a delivery service to a specific area it offers potential for community television fare.

Interactive, two-way television, where the subscriber can send signals back to the central computer located at the headend of the cable company, has already been part of community television's history. Predicted in E. M. Forster's 1909 story *The Machine Stops*, in which humans were isolated from one another and forced to communicate through a two-way television device, the notion of interactivity has long fascinated us. The premier two-way system in the United States was Warner Amex's Qube experiment in Columbus, Ohio, in the 1970s, which demonstrated state-of-the-art interactive technology in terms of home shopping, game and talk shows, home security, voting, and other services. Hailed in its day as the prototype of lifestyle changes for the information age, the Qube system eventually proved unable to sustain itself; still, the thinking is that as television viewers become ever more active, interactive television will be the norm even locally. The issue of paying for something that has traditionally been free still concerns many people; however, the final word has not yet been heard on this.

"Telecomputers," a term popularized by James H. Clark, chair of Silicon Graphics, Incorporated, are also part of our developing electronic data highway. Harnessing the same computer power that has been used for special effects in movies like *Terminator 2* and *Jurassic Park*, telecomputers will allow the television viewer "to order and process digital data, including movies, search through electronic libraries and catalogues and be operated by a remote-control pad" (Tierney, 1993, p. 24). Interactivity promises the world at the fingertips of the information rich, media as a "computer smorgasbord" (Powell, 1993), added "information appliances" (Rogers, 1993), and, predominantly, big bucks for the privileged players. We learn that two of the giants, "Time Warner, the nation's second largest cable operator, and U.S. West, the fifth largest telephone company" (Elmer DeWitt, 1993, p. 52), have decided to become digital partners,[15] and we ponder Microsoft Corporation's interest in alliances with cable and entertainment companies (McCoy, 1993).

Recently, the FCC proclaimed a Notice of Proposed Rules Making to establish Interactive Video Data Service (IVDS) as a personal broadcast service allowing viewer interaction and access to over-the-air television, cable, pay-per-view, and direct broadcast satellite services.[16] Representing the tip of the iceberg for interactive services that the FCC supports, IVDS undoubtedly will find favor with the growing numbers of remote-control aficionados in this country. The catch for community television programmers will be to harness this capability within their own franchise agreements, staging access shows where viewers can vote on zoning issues, participate in auctions to benefit the station, simulate sporting events, and engage in any number of interactive activities. In the first instance, however, unless the technology for voting is universally available, this system would certainly be inconsistent with our "one person–one vote" principle.

Now that we can "morph" on the Mac—computer-creating seamless transitions from what had traditionally been complicated special effects, like transforming an image of a tiger into a cat, or a man into a motor vehicle—we need to come to terms with whether we will control the technology or be controlled by it. Richard Zoglin (1993, p. 56) offers his version of the television revolution: "The final destination is a post-channel universe of essentially unlimited choice: virtually everything produced for the medium, past or present, plus a wealth of other information and entertainment options, stored in computer banks and available instantly at the touch of a button."

New technologies need to be recognized and understood, then evaluated for applicability not only as technical tools but also as means of opening doors for new participants in the process of community television. Underlying this whole study has been a continuing concern for the information gap between rich and poor, and what the roles of the government, the private sector, and the citizenry should and could be.

FUTURE CONSIDERATIONS

Keeping in mind that both the power and the potential of cable television rest in the fact that it has dual facilities of importing and boosting existing over-the-air broadcasts in addition to originating its own programming, one might think that the "wired nation" would dominate without competition. However, community television in the future may not necessarily exist via cable technology. Right now telco's video dial tone looms on the landscape as a potential threat to replace cable television as our programming resource, and no doubt other technologies are in line to cash in on our seemingly bottomless search for infotainment. At this point there is no promise from any sources of continued support for PEG access.

Should we care? Is there anything we can do? Perhaps one point to begin with would be recodification of the Fairness Doctrine, a sentiment that has been reactivated yearly since 1987. Another consideration would be educating Congress about our ideas, ranging from concerns about censorship to the virtual elimination of PEG access if Time Warner has its way. If we are serious about promoting participatory democracy and advancing the "marketplace of ideas," we need to protect the one means we have of allowing broadcasts that are free of underlying economic interests.

Cable television predictions, according to Clift and Garay (1986, p. 2), can be placed in two general categories: the economic/technological growth of the cable industry (predictions about such things as its growth, system channel capacity, and income-generating methods), about which most people from within the industry are concerned, and the public service role of cable (predictions about cable program channel content and consumer services), typically by those from outside the industry. The value of the participatory action research approach comes from straddling several sides of the study; in the words of Mao Tse-tung, "If you want knowledge, you must take part in the practice of changing reality."

This is a good time to recall National Community Network, which premiered in the spring of 1993, bringing a promising perspective to community television in its own right. Depending on its success both financially for its creators and socioculturally for the population at large in terms of spreading the word of media access, its role could be pivotal to the future of community television. Still, we need to remember Devine's (1991, p. 9) scary scenario, in which "the development and sanctioning of public access could be seen as an attempt to co-opt the fringes of the disaffected, to consolidate the hegemony and to diminish disorder." Until we have a comprehensive national policy for telecommunications, anything is possible—maybe even a world federation of community television. The First Amendment, although in place to handle these issues, needs to be reconsidered and reconceptualized.

Kellner (1992, p. 105) reports on discussions at a Union for Democratic Communications (UDC) conference in 1984, where various access groups explored the possibility of leasing weekly satellite time, to pool their efforts so that progressive programming could be beamed throughout the United States. Costs were surprisingly determined not to be prohibitive, at around $100,000 to $150,000 per year; Deep Dish Television was the result. He offers his own proposal, for a national political channel (p. 109):

In an age of cable and satellite television, with over 60 percent of the nation wired for cable and over two and a half million homes with satellite dishes, why not make a satellite transponder available to various groups that want to broadcast political views and information. There could be a public-interest satellite channel—provided to representative groups free of charge—so Democrats, Republicans, labour, blacks, hispanics, women, gays, and any number of other groups could present their political views and programs every day. . . .

There are a number of steps needed to transform our broadcast system:

1. expand and democratize the current public broadcasting system;
2. expand and strengthen the public-access system;
3. use cable and satellite television to produce new public-broadcasting channels open to groups currently excluded from national communication; and
4. develop an entire satellite and cable system of broadcasting that will allow every group, alternative voice, and political opinion to be broadcast.

While the goals and objectives of Kellner's mission must be clearly defined and delineated, it is at least a beginning. As the next step, we need to consider the economics of it all: What will be the sources of funding, both initially and ongoing? Politically, what topics might or might not be included that would be considered appropriate for the viewing public?

If cable television is the "now" scenario for community television and video dial tone is positioning itself as the future one, yet another possibility to consider is that the phenomenon might cease to exist at all, squeezed out either legally if new regulations don't require it and/or popularly if it lacks enough attention and support. Certainly New York and Hollywood have a stake in any competition these days.

Yet, while hopes for community television have been high since its inception nearly a quarter century ago, and while this book certainly has demonstrated its viability in fulfilling many of its promises, its key problems remain politics, a lack of its recognition, misunderstanding of its potentiality, underfunding, and not as many people involved as the promises warrant. Andrew Blau (1992, p. 25) suggests having access centers teach people to use new technologies:

Access centers that are moving in the right direction are those that provide opportunities for producers to develop their communications skills—i.e., to become more *effective* communicators. They prompt viewers to consider and think critically about the medium; artists to push the medium; users of other electronic media, such as radio or computer networks, to interact with video-based communicators; and all community members to develop access in whatever manner they choose.

In a White Paper subtitled "The Musings of an Access Codger," Carl Kucharski (1990, p. 7) sees the existence of access as a political statement that "must evolve into true community communications and learning centers for video, data, computer networks, community publishing, and national and international communications." He suggests these steps:

1. Formation of a free speech political action committee in cooperation with affinity groups throughout the country.
2. Increased support for the Alliance for Communications Democracy to enhance litigation efforts supporting and promoting access.
3. Create organizational and economic partnerships with affinity groups whether they are community media–related or not.
4. Insist on community operation of all access channels without government control.
5. Redefine educational and government access channels.
6. Develop working relationships with our counterparts in Europe, Africa, Asia, and Latin America.
7. Create with affinity groups, at research and development sites, nationally and internationally, to test, adapt, and implement communications hardware; establish international exchanges of people and their works; develop new, appropriate training/education approaches; act as "think tanks" and meeting sites for community media; and develop additional resources and networks.

But keep in mind the operative word here: access. Access as discussed here is synonymous with fairness. As fewer and fewer resources are available for us as audience members of both print and electronic media to give feedback, let alone get involved, community television emerges as our only hope. It is the last bastion of media access, and we had better do all we can to preserve both our rights and our responsibilities regarding it. True, we have the First Amendment, unique in all the world, with its provisions of free speech and free press, but it is now mainly the preserve of press owners. What we need is effective political organization for access, something that currently is sorely lacking. Consider: The media are not apt to cover the access movement from the perspective of citizen/consumer rights; rather, they opt for *Wayne's World* depictions. In an ideal situation, all political parties and points of view would be respected, even hate groups, the KKK, devil worshippers, and pornographers, allowing opportunities for all intended audiences to be reached. Think back to the many creative ways controversy has been handled in the case studies cited here. In the ideal situation, the economics would also be equitable.

In Kellner's words, "To be revitalized and even survive, democracy requires the development of an open-access communications system" (p. 110). Recognizing that "public-access television is not a substitute for political organization and struggle, but is rather a vehicle for participants and local political groups to provide information about their activities and to involve people in their efforts" (p. 107), he proposes a national political channel, as noted above. These are the steps to transform our broadcast system: (1) Expand and democratize the current public broadcasting system, (2) expand and strengthen the public access system, (3) use cable and satellite television to produce new public broadcasting channels open to groups currently excluded from national communication, and (4) develop an entire satellite system of broadcasting that will allow every group, alternative voice, and political opinion to be broadcast.

Concerned with cable policy in the public interest, Aufderheide (1992, pp. 60–61) suggests the implementation of PEG access as a medium for electronic public space:

A percentage of channel capacity—in a fixed, low range of numbers—could be reserved for public use on all cable systems, (guaranteeing) universal, local, and multiple access channels, and as well provide for nontraditional services as technology evolves. Access centers would also need to be funded adequately—for facilities, professional production assistance, local public production funds, and promotion— through the franchise and through annual franchise fees.

Centers should universally have funding for professional staff, which would not mitigate access' value as a public space.

National public cable channel capacity, with protected funds to avoid both censorship and the distortions of corporate underwriting, could further broaden the public forum.

Such national channel capacity would boldly raise the perennial problem of who should broker information and how.

Another resource for such a reinvigorated public interest could be a national video production fund, with its products available for distribution through all televisual vehicles, including cable, broadcast television, and videocassette.

Knowing that universal access to programs such as are outlined here comes only with universal access to the appropriate technology, we need to be reminded that the Cable Acts of 1984 and 1992 say that access *may* be allowed for PEG channels, not *must* be allowed. Except for media ownership, access as such is often a moot issue. Information in the United States today is brokered by owners, publishers, and people who can afford to pay for production and distribution. Congress can subsidize some information for us when markets fail or when it is overwhelmingly considered to be in the public interest, but Congress also takes a strong hand in censorship of what information it will allow.

Fred Johnson of the Media Working Group has proposed a "Modest Manifesto" on access in the 1990s, which appears in Appendix 24. Elsewhere calling on access center managers and producers to identify their points of conflict,[17] he suggests grounding a dialogue based on their values and conditions, which are typically "extremely democratic and geared toward empowerment, community development and diverse participation." His philosophy: "If one combines sincere discussion with an attempt to conceptualize cable channels as dynamic communication spaces that go far beyond anything called television, or mass media for that matter, then a framework for growth emerges." But let's dissect some of Johnson's propositions: Whose values and what conditions does he mean? And what is his vision of democracy?

This study has contained a persistent theme of the promise of community television, with producers' rights to construct and audiences' rights to receive programming. Those audiences, it is argued, need to decide whether they are ready and willing to pay for the services the PEG access offers, or whether a whole new system can and should be developed. This book presents a clarion call to interested individuals and groups to be informed of the process and the means for gaining entry into a system that has generally been considered closed.

On a wider scale, it has been argued here that the key value for studying participants and organizations of this movement is to monitor their attitudes and behavior toward new communications technologies. Cable television, through its access capability, offers potential for a reconceptualization of television as a tool for the public, although now only just about two thirds of the public, the ones who can afford it, literally, in addition to media conglomerates. Keep in mind Time Warner's pending lawsuit challenging the constitutionality of federal legislation designed to protect children from indecent programming, a law that places liability with the cable operator for even the content of its public access programming. Consider, also, the impact of Warner Bros., the only major studio without a broadcast or cable outlet for its television programming, in its deliberations toward creating a fifth network.

As individuals and community groups begin to consider television not just passively but also as an outlet for their artistic and/or informational interests, they need to develop a whole new mind-set toward media in general and television in particular. Next, they must actively participate in media poli-cymaking and stop deferring to policies in place, theoretically, to protect their interests. What is being presented here is a control issue, and until we personally and professionally consider the implications of where we want the locus of control, we are nowhere.

This study is a step in the direction of researching the role of media utilization in a society dominated by its communications technologies; it is time that we as citizens take control, whether as consumers or as owners/operators as well. The book aims to encourage a movement such as we have not witnessed since the 1960s, mobilizing the public toward actions and advocacy regarding its media rights and responsibilities.

It seems only appropriate to end with a quotation by George Stoney (1986, p. 11):

Without doubt the most important social phenomenon of the latter part of the 20th century has been the enfranchisement of blacks, brought into being by the civil rights movement. When the idea of access is fully implemented, when it is carried beyond cable to all electronic media as I am confident it will be one day, this movement that is absorbing so much of our energies and concern today will be seen as one every bit as important for the welfare of all Americans as was civil rights.

NOTES

1. Douglas Kellner, "Public-Access Television and the Struggle for Democracy," in Janet Wasko and Vincent Mosco (eds.), *Democratic Communications in the Information Age* (Norwood, NJ: Ablex, 1992), p. 100.

2. On September 22, 1992, the Senate voted 74–25 to establish federal regulations on cable, the House having voted for re-regulation of cable 280–128 the week before.

3. *Broadcasting* (January 29, 1989), p. 71, cited in Dominick et al. (1990), pp. 202–3.

4. Nolan Bowie points out that, according to Chapter 6 of Russ Neumann's book *The Paradox of Politics*, when individuals have the choice between entertainment and useful information (political, instructional, and educational), 96 percent of the time they choose entertainment. He adds, in an August 1993 note to me: "There should therefore be a mandate to present programs that citizens/consumers *need* rather than what they want, vis-à-vis children's programming requirements, mandated instructional and educational programming. The Government requires compulsory education of all residents and citizens. Why not TV programs?"

5. Ron Powers, "Back to the Future," *GQ* (July 1986), p. 66.

6. Pat Sparks, "Cable Access: An Untapped Resource for Human Service Organizations," *CTR* 8, no. 1, p. 7.

7. Dirk W. Koning, "The Currency of Democracy: A Community Opinion," *Grand Rapids Magazine* (May 1992), p. 48.

8. Cited in Elizabeth Kolbert, "Networks Battle the 'Channel Surfers,' " (Springfield, Massachusetts) *Union-News* (April 27, 1993), p. 25.

9. Don Conkey, "Into the Future of TV," (Springfield, Massachusetts) *Sunday Republican* (September 6, 1992), p. G1.

10. Thanks to Byron F. Marchant, legal advisor to FCC commissioner Andrew C. Barrett, for his letter and copies of the commission's actions involving video dial tone, October 9, 1992.

11. Joseph Weber, "Look, Ma—No Cable: It's Video-By-Phone," *Business Week* (November 16, 1992), p. 86.

12. Tom Hargadon, "Video Dial Tone: Let RBOCs Stick to Knitting," *New Media* (November 1992), p. 14.

13. Edmund L. Andrews, "Cable TV Battling Phone Companies," *New York Times* (March 29, 1992), p. 1.

14. Mitchell Kapor and Jerry Berman, "Building the Open Road: The NREN as a Test-Bed for the National Public Network," Washington, DC: The Electronic Frontier Foundation, 1992.

15. U.S. West, Richard Turner reported in the *Wall Street Journal*, agreed to pay $2.5 billion for more than 25 percent of Time Warner's movie studio and cable TV assets.

16. FCC News, Report No. DC–2169, "FCC Clarifies Certain Aspects of Interactive Video Data Services Rules" (Gen. Docket 91–2), July 16, 1992.

17. Fred Johnson, "Acknowledging the Conflict and Creating Dialog," *CTR*, 15, no. 3 (May/June 1992), p. 11.

APPENDIXES

Appendix 1
PACTL Audience Survey

#_____

Hello. This is Linda Fuller calling. I am a graduate student at the
University of Massachusetts in Communication Studies, interested in
learning about cable television in Longmeadow. This survey should
take about 5 to 10 minutes; is this a good time, or should I call you later?
I want you to know that your family was chosen randomly from a list of
Longmeadow residents, that this survey has only a number on it and no
identification of who you are, where you live, your telephone number,
and that all your answers will be kept in strictest confidence.

Cable TV
1.Do you currently subscribe to the Longmeadow cable?
__1.No
2.   a.If no, do you plan to get cable? __1.No __2.Yes
3.   b.Did you have cable, but cancel it? __1.No __2.Yes (Skip to #13)
__2.Yes
4.   a.If yes, how long have you been a subscriber?
        __1.Less than 6 months __2.7-12 months __3.1 year+
5.   b.What services do you get?
        __1.Basic __2.Extended basic __3.Pay services
6-9.   __6.HBO __7.HTN __8.Showtime __9.Spotlight
10. c.Why did you decide to subscribe to cable?
        __1.Better reception __2.Particular channels __3.More channels
        __4.Local programming __5.Didn't--decided for me __6.Combo
11.How would you rate the technical quality of the picture you get on
   cable compared to what you had before?
   __1.Better __2.Worse __3.About the same
12.How would you rate the quality of sound you get on cable compared to what you had before?
   __1.Better __2.Worse __3.About the same
13.Do you think Longmeadow should have an "adult entertainment"
   channel, the X-rated kind?
   __1.No
14.   a.If no, if it did would you be upset? __1.No __2.Yes
15.   b.Would you take action against having it?
               __1.No __2.Yes __3.Probably __4.Probably not
__2.Yes
16.   a.If yes, would you subscribe to "adult entertainment"?
               __1.No __2.Yes __3.Probably __4.Probably not
17.   b.Whether or not you would be a subscriber, would you take
        action to allow it in the town?
               __1.No __2.Yes __3.Probably __4.Probably not
18.   c.If you had such a channel, would you have rules in your
        household for watching it? __1.No __2.Yes

Appendix 1, continued

TV Viewing

19.How much TV would you say you watch in a typical day?
　　__1.Under an hour __2.1-3 hours __3.4-6 hours __7+ hours
20.How much TV did you watch yesterday?
　　__1.Under an hour __2.1-3 hours __3.4-6 hours __7+ hours

*When do you tend to watch TV?
21.Morning __1.No __2.Yes
22.Afternoons __1.No __2.Yes
23.Early evening __1.No __2.Yes
24.Prime Time __1.No __2.Yes
25.Late night __1.No __2.Yes
26.Weekends __1.No __2.Yes

*Next, I'm going to ask you some categories of programs, and I want
you to tell me how often you watch them: __1.Every day __2.Several
times/week __3.Only occasionally __4.Weekends __5.Never
27.__News
28.__Sports
29.__Soaps
30.__Entertainment/variety shows
31.__Action-adventure
32.__Financial programs
33.__Religious programs
34.__Educational/public TV (Channel 57)
35.__Movies
36.__Other

37.Would you say cable has changed your TV viewing habits?
　　　　__1.No __2.Yes
38.　a.If yes, do you watch more TV overall? __1.No __2.Yes
39.　b.Do you watch more sports? (ESPN) __1.No __2.Yes
40.　c.More children's programming? __1.No __2.Yes
41.　d.Musical programs? (MTV) __1.No __2.Yes
42.　e.More movies? __1.No __2.Yes
43.　f.Other types of programming? __1.No __2.Yes
44.Would you say you watch more cable channels or local ones?
　　__1.No __2.Yes __3.About the same __4.Unsure
45.When you watch TV, do you usually watch it with other people?
　　　　__1.No __2.Yes
46.　a.If yes, how many other people?__1.1 __2.2 __3.3 __4.4 __5.5+
47.　b.When you do, who usually chooses the program?
　　__1.You __2.Spouse __3.Child(ren) __4.Friend(s) __5.Consensus
48.　c.When you watch TV with other people, do you usually talk
　　　　while watching? __1.No __2.Yes
49.Do you prefer to watch TV alone or with other people?
　　__1.Alone __2.With others __3.Doesn't matter __4.Depends
50.When you watch TV, do you usually do another activity, such as
　video games, reading, knitting, exercising, etc? __1.No __2.Yes
51.How many TV sets do you have in your house?

Appendix 1, continued

      __1.1 __2.2 __3.3 __4.4 __5.5+ __6.None
*Where are your TV sets located?
52.Living room __1.No __2.Yes
53.Family room/den __1.No __2.Yes
54.Bedroom(s) __1.No __2.Yes
55.Other room(s) __1.No __2.Yes
56.Do you have any attachments for your TV set? __1.No __2.Yes
57.   a.If yes, video games? __1.No __2.Yes
58.   b.VCR? VCD? __1.No __2.Yes
59.   c.Betamax? __1.No __2.Yes
60.   d.Personal computer? __1.No __2.Yes
61.   e.Satellite dish? __1.No __2.Yes
62.   g.Other attachments? __1.No __2.Yes (specify)
63.When you choose a TV show, is it usually from: __1.Tuning in/
  switching the dials __2.TV Guide __3.Newspaper listing __4.Some-
  one's suggestion--what's on __5.Cable guide __6.Combination
64.Do you ever find TV programs as a topic of conversation?
    __1.No __2.Yes
65.   a.If yes, who with: __1.Family __2.Friends __3.People at work
    __4.People you meet casually __5.Combinations of these
66.   b.Do you ever find yourself watching a particular program so
    you can talk about it later? __1.No __2.Yes
67.Do you ever find ads a topic of conversation? __1.No __2.Yes
68.Have you ever taken action from a TV show, such as writing or
  calling a station, network, performer, or sponsor? __1.No __2.Yes
69.Have you ever found yourself talking out loud to your TV set?
    __1.No __2.Yes

  *What kinds of rules do you have for yourself about TV viewing?
70.Do you only watch certain kinds of programs, or do you prefer a
  variety? __1.No __2.Yes
71.Do you limit the amount of TV you allow yourself to watch?
    __1.No __2.Yes
72.Do you limit the times you allow yourself to watch TV?
    __1.No __2.Yes
73.Do you use TV as a reward or punishment system for yourself?
    __1.No __2.Yes
74.Do you have any particular program(s) you enjoy watching, but
  don't want anyone to know you watch? __1.No __2.Yes (specify)
75.Do you have rules for your children on TV viewing?
    __1.No __2.Yes
76.Rules for your spouse on TV viewing? __1.No __2.Yes
77.Rules for visitors on TV viewing? __1.No __2.Yes
78.Do you have rules (for category above) about particular programming? __1.No __2.Yes
79.Rules about amount of TV viewing? __1.No __2.Yes
80.Rules about times of TV viewing? __1.No __2.Yes
81.Rules about who chooses the program(s)? __1.No __2.Yes
82.Rules about activities accompanying TV viewing? __1.No __2.Yes
83.Do you ever use TV as a reward or punishment? __1.No __2.Yes
84.If you wanted to restrict TV viewing for another member of your

Appendix 1, continued

family, would you: __1.Try to reason with them __2.Just turn the
TV off __3.Try to work out a compromise
85.Have you ever found yourself identifying with particular actors or
actresses on TV? __1.No __2.Yes (try to get example)
86.Have you ever found yourself watching a show you wouldn't pick
just to be with a person to wants to watch it? __1.No __2.Yes
87.Have you ever insisted that others watch a show with you even if
they are not interested in it? __1.No __2.Yes (try to get example)

Public Access

88.Are you familiar with the public access channel, Channel 8 on
cable, with local programs? __1.No (skip to #126) __2.Yes
89.   a.If yes, how did you first learn about it? __1.Times-Mirror
__2.Found it on the dial __3.Read about in newspaper __4.
Friend/neighbor __5.Combination of above __6.Other
90.   b.How often have you watched it?
__1.Only once __2.A couple of times __3.Fairly regularly
91.   c.How regularly? __1.3+ programs/week __2.1-2 programs/
week __3.1 program every 2 weeks __4.1 program every
month __5.Other
92.Can you remember any particular program(s)? __1.No __2.Yes
93.   a.If yes, selectmen's meeting? __1.No __2.Yes
94.   b.School committee meetings? __1.No __2.Yes
95.   c.Sports on public access? __1.No __2.Yes
96.   d.Interviews? __1.No __2.Yes
97.   e.Other public access programs? __1.No __2.Yes (cite)
98.Have you every been part of public access, as a performer and/or
a producer? __1.No __2.Yes
99.   a.If yes, production? __1.No __2.Yes
100.   b.Performer? __1.No __2.Yes
101.Would you consider getting involved in PACTL? __1.No __2.Yes
102.   a.If yes, in a technical area like camerawork, editing?
__1.No __2.Yes
103.   b.Non-technical area like producing, directing, performing?
__1.No __2.Yes
104.In your opinion, if you wanted to get involved in public access,
how difficult would it be? __1.Very difficult __2.Difficult 3.Not too
difficult __4.Easy __5.Don't know
105.Do you think PACTL is run by a particular group of people?
__1.No __2.Yes
106.   a.If yes, by whom: __1.High school __2.Selectmen __3.Town
citizens __4.Combination __5.Other
107.   b.Do you think they want new people to get involved?
__1.No __2.Yes
108.Do you think PACTL should be limited to Longmeadow people
and Longmeadow interests? __1.No __2.Yes __3.Depends
109.Do you think special interest groups like pro-abortionists, envi-
ronmentalists, anti-nukes should be allowed to air their programs
on public access? __1.No __2.Yes __3.Only if opposite sides are
presented __4.Depends

Appendix 1, continued

110.Do you think controversial shows should be encouraged?
        __1.No __2.Yes __3.Depends
111.Do you think controversial programs should be aired at a particular hour? __1.No __2.Yes
112.Do you think public access has increased your knowledge of
Longmeadow town government? __1.No __2.Yes
113.Have you ever watched any of the Selectmen's meetings on TV?
        __1.No __2.Yes
114.   a.If yes, how often have you seen them? __1.Only once __2.
        Several times __3.Fairly regularly __4.Regularly
115.   b.Have you ever talked with selectmen about issues you heard
        aired on the channel? __1.No __2.Yes
116.Do you know any people involved with PACTL? __1.No __2.Yes
117.   a.If yes, have you talked with them about it? __1.No __2.Yes
118.   b.Have you ever commented to people that you saw them or
        their names associated with a particular show?__1.No__2.Yes
119.   c.Have you ever watched just to see if you recognize people
        you know on Channel 8? __1.No __2.Yes
120.Do you think PACTL has increased a sense of community in
Longmeadow? __1.No __2.Yes
121.Do you think programming on public access should be mostly:
        __Educational __2.Entertainment __3.Combination of both
122.Would you be willing to contribute to fund-raising costs of
PACTL? __1.No __2.Yes __3.Depends
123.Have you ever used the channel for an emergency, such as locating a dog or stolen car? __1.No __2.Yes (cite)
124.If you ever wanted or needed to use the access channel for an
emergency, how difficult do you think it would be? __1.Very difficult __2.Difficult __3.Not too difficult __4.Easy __5.Don't know
125.Do you have any program suggestions for PACTL?__1.No __2.Yes
126.Have you seen or received the PACTL newsletter?__1.No __2.Yes
127.Have you heard people talk about PACTL? __1.No __2.Yes
128.   a.If yes, has the conversation been mostly positive?
        __1.No __2.Yes
129.   b.Have you usually been familiar with what they are talking
        about regarding public access? __1.No __2.Yes

   *Thanks for all your opinions. Now I'd like to get some information
about you.

Demographics
130-1.In what year were you born? _____
132.Gender __1.Male __2.Female
133.Race __1.Caucasian __2.Black __3.Asian __4.Other (specify)
134.Religion __1.Catholic __2.Jewish __3.Protestant __4.Other (specify) __5.None __6.Refused
135.What is your current marital status? __1.Married __2.Widowed
__3.Separated __4.Divorced __5.Never married __6.POSSLQ
136.How many children under age 18 live in your house?
    __1.1 __2.2 __3.3 __4.4 __5.5+ __6.None

Appendix 1, continued

137.How many people besides yourself over age 18 live in your
house? __1.1 __2.2 __3.3 __4.4 __5.5+ __6.None
138.Are you currently employed? __1.No (__a.Laid off __b.Disabled
__c.Looking for work __d.Student __e.Retired __f.Houseperson
__g.Volunteer) __2.Yes
139-141.If yes, occupation: _____ (NORC code)
142.Is your spouse employed? __1.No (__a.Laid off __b.Disabled
__c.Looking for work __d.Student __e.Retired __f.Houseperson
__g.Volunteer) __2.Yes
143-145.If yes, spouse's occupation: _____ (NORC code)
146.What range best describes your total family income last year?
(Over/under $50,000):__1.Less than $25,000 __2.$25,000-$49,999
__3.$50,000-$74,999__4.$75,000-$99,999 __5.$100,000-$199,999
__6.$200,000-$499,999 __7.$500,000+ __8.Refused
147.What was the highest grade of school you attended? __1.Elemen-
tary school __2.HS __3.College/nursing school __4.Grad __5.Other
148.How long have you lived in Longmeadow? __1.Less than 6 mos
__2.6 mos-2 years __3.3-5 years __4.6-12 years __5.13-25 years
__6.26-40 years __7.41+ years __8.Refused
149.Can you think of some major problems or needs of Longmeadow? __1.No __2.Yes (amplify)
150.Would you say you're active in town activities? __1.No __2.Yes
151.Are you very involved in volunteer work in general?
__1.No __2.Yes
152.　a.If yes, how often do you volunteer? __1.At least once/week
__2.At least once/month __3.Infrequently
153.　b.What kind(s) of volunteer work? __1.Church/temple __?
Town __3.Boards __4.Hospitals __5.Schools __6.Combinations
154.Are you a registered voter? __1.No __2.Yes
155.　a.If yes, do you usually vote? __1.No __2.Yes
156.　b.What is your party designation? __1.Democrat __2.Republi-
can __3.Independent __4.Depends __5.Refuse
157.In general, would you say you're happy living in Longmeadow?
__1.No __2.Yes

Thank you very much for participating. Do you have any further
comments to make about television in general, public access cable
television in Longmeadow in particular, and/or this survey?

Source: Linda K. Fuller, "Public Access Cable Television: A Case Study on Source, Contents,
Audience, Producers, and Rules-Theoretical Perspective." Unpublished doctoral dissertation, University of Massachusetts, 1984.

Appendix 2
Solicitation for Book Information

COMMUNITY TELEVISION IN THE UNITED STATES
A Sourcebook on Public, Educational, and Governmental Access

by Linda K. Fuller
Media Dept, Worcester State College, Worcester, MA

A Survey of Access Centers and Related Organizations

Name and title of respondent:
Access center or organization:
        Address:
        Phone/FAX:

History/background:

Structure:
        Management entity:
        Services (PEG, LO, leased, etc.):
        Channels:
        Staff:

Finances:
        Source(s) of revenue:
        Annual operating budget:

Programming and production:
        Studio(s) and remote(s):
        Equipment/facilities:
        Kinds of programming:
        Schedule (please include example):
        Unique programs:

Community relations:
        Target market:
        Training:
        Volunteers:
        Number of subscribers:
        Audience surveys:

Appendix 3
National Affiliations

Advertising Council
261 Madison Avenue
New York, NY 10016
  Tel. 212/922-1500

The Alliance for Communications Democracy
394 Oak Street
Columbus, OH 43215
  Contact: Carl Kucharski
  Tel. 614/224-2288

The Alliance for Community Media
666 11th Street NW, Suite 806
Washington, DC 20001
  Contact: T. Andrew Lewis, Executive Director
  Tel. 202/393-2650, FAX 202/93-2653

Alliance for Cultural Democracy
PO Box 2478
Champaign, IL 61820
  Tel. 618/423-3711

The Alliance for Public Technology
901 15th Street NW, Suite 230
Washington, DC 20005

Alternative Media Information Center/"Media Network"
39 West 14th Street, Suite 403
New York, NY 10011
  Contact: Dan Derosu
  Tel. 212/929-2663

American Association of Retired Persons (AARP)
601 E Street, NW
Washington, DC 20049
  Contact: Kenneth Vest, Director, Communication Resources
  Tel. 202/728-4752

American Council for the Arts
1 East 53rd Street
New York, NY 10022
  Tel. 212/223-2787

American Film Institute
2021 N. Western Avenue
Los Angeles, CA 90027
  Contact: Cathy Phoenix
  Tel. 213/856-7600

Appendix 3, continued

American Library Association (ALA)
Office for Intellectual Freedom
50 East Huron Street
Chicago, IL 60611
  Tel. 312/280-4223

Association of Independent Video and Filmmakers
625 Broadway
New York, NY 10012
  Contact: Karen Helmerson
  Tel. 212/473-3400

The Benton Foundation
1710 Rhode Island Avenue NW, 4th floor
Washington, DC 20036
  Contact: Larry Kirkman, Executive Director
  Tel. 202/857-7829

Cable Television Information Center
1800 N. Kent Street, #1007
Arlington, VA

The Cable Televison Public Affairs Association
414 Main Street
Laurel, MD

Center for Constitutional Rights
666 Broadway, 7th floor
New York, NY 10012
  Tel. 212/473-3400

The Center for Democratic Renewal
PO Box 50469
Atlanta, GA 30302-0469
  Contact: Don Christensen, Coordinator

Center for Media and Values
1952 S. Shenandoah
Los Angeles, CA 90034
  Contact: Elizabeth Thoman, Executive Director
  Tel. 213/559-2944

Center for Media Education
1012 Heather Avenue
Takoma Park, MD 20912
  Tel. 301/270-3379

Consumer Federation of America
1424 16th Street NW, Suite 604
Washington, DC 20036
  Tel. 202/387-6121

Appendix 3, continued

Creative Coalition
1100 Avenue of the Americas, 15th floor
New York, NY 10036
  Tel. 212/512-5515

Cultural Environment Movement
PO Box 31847
Philadelphia, PA 19104
  Contact: George Gerbner

Electronic Frontier Foundation
1.) 155 Second Street
Cambridge, MA 02141
  Tel. 617/864-1550

2.) 666 Pennsylvania Avenue SE, Suite 303
Washington, DC
  Contact: Andrew Blau
  Tel. 202/544-9237

FAIR (Fairness & Accuracy In Reporting)
130 West 25th Street
New York, NY 10001
  Tel. 212/633-6700

Federal Communications Commission
1919 M Street NW
Washington, DC 20554
  Chair: Alfred C. Sikes
  Tel. 202/632-7000
        *Office of Plans and Policy 202/653-5940
        *Mass Media Bureau 202/632-6460
        *Common Carrier Bureau 202/632-6910

The Freedom Forum
1101 Wilson Boulevard
Arlington, VA

The Freedom Forum Media Studies Center
2950 Broadway
New York, NY 10027
  Contact: Everette E. Dennis, Executive Director

Funding Exchange
666 Broadway
New York, NY 10027

Appendix 3, continued

Global Information Network
777 United Nations Plaza
New York, NY 10017

The Hollywood Policy Center
10536 Culver Blvd.
Culver City, CA 90232
  Tel. 310/559-9334

The Independent Television Service
PO Box 65797
St. Paul, MN 55175
  Contact: Lawrence M. Sapadin, President

The Institute for Alternative Journalism
2025 I Street N., Suite 1118
Washington, DC
  Tel. 202/887-0022

The International Radio and Television Society
420 Lexington Avenue, Suite 1714
New York, NY 10170-1010
  Contact: Stephen B. Labunski, Executive Director
  Tel. 212/867-6650

The Kitchen
Center for Video, Music, Dance, Performance, Film, and Literature
512 W. 19th Street
New York, NY 10011
  Contact: Eric Latzky

Media Access Project
2000 M Street NW, Suite 400
Washington, DC 20036
  Tel. 202/232-4300

Media Coalition
900 Third Avenue, Suite 1600
New York, NY 10022
  Tel. 212/891-2070

Media Network
39 West 14th Street, Suite 403
New York, NY 10011
  Tel. 212/929-2663

The Nation Institute
72 Fifth Avenue
New York, NY 10011
  Tel. 212/242-8400

Appendix 3, continued

National Academy of Cable Programming
1724 Massachusetts Avenue, NW
Washington, DC 20036
  Contact: Nancy Larkin, VP, Community Relations
  Tel. 202/775-3611

National Alliance of Artists' Organizations
918 F Street, NW
Washington, DC 20004
  Tel. 202/347-6350

National Alliance for Media Arts and Culture
1212 Broadway, #816
Oakland, CA 94612
  Contact: Mimi Zarsky

National Association of Broadcasters
1771 N Street NW
Washington, DC 20036
  Tel. 202/429-5300
  Contact: Richard V. Ducey, Research and Planning

National Association of College Broadcasters/U-Net
71 George Street, Box 1824
Providence, RI 02912
  Contact: Glenn Guttmacher, Executive Director
  Tel. 401/863-2225

National Association of Telecommunications Officers and Advisors
c/o National League of Cities
1301 Pennsylvania Avenue NW
Washington, DC 20004
  Tel. 202/626-3160

National Black Programming Consortium
929 Harrison Avenue, Suite 104
Columbus, OH 43215
  Tel. 614/299-5355

National Cable Television Association
1724 Massachusetts Avenue, NW
Washington, DC 20036
  Tel. 202/775-3550

National Campaign for Freedom of Expression
1402 3rd Avenue, Suite 421
Seattle, WA 98101
  Tel. 800/477-6233

Appendix 3, continued

National Center for Nonprofit Boards
1225 19th Street, NW, Suite 340
Washington, DC 20036
 Tel. 202/452-6262

National Citizens Committee for Broadcasting
PO Box 12038
Washington, DC

National Coalition Against Censorship
275 7th Avenue
New York, NY 10001
 Tel. 212/807-6222

National Coalition of Independent Public Broadcasting Producers
1 Donna Avenue
New York, NY 10956
 Tel. 914/634-5251

National Community Network
3200 Cherry Creek South Drive, Suite 500
Denver, CO 80209
 Contact: Jim Dickson, President
 Tel. 303/778-5555

National Council of Churches/Dept. of Communication
475 Riverside Drive, Room 850
New York, NY 10115
 Tel. 212/870-2048

National Federation of Community Broadcasters
666 11th Street NW, Suite 805
Washington, DC 20001
 Contact: Lynn Chadwick, President
 Tel. 202/393-2355

National Gay and Lesbian Task Force
1734 14th Street, NW
Washington, DC 20009
 Tel. 202/332-6483

National Institute Against Prejudice & Violence
31 South Greene Street
Baltimore, MD 21201
 Contact: Robert Purvis
 Tel. 301/328-5170

National Missing Children's Locate Center
PO Box 1707
Gresham, OR 97030
Contact: Marilyn S. Mann, President

Appendix 3, continued

National Videotape Exchange
c/o Thurston Community TV
2940 Limited Lane
Olympia, WA 98502

Public Broadcasting System (PBS)
475 L'Enfant Plaza, SW
Washington, DC 20024
 Tel. 202/488-5000

Public Interest Video Network
1642 R Street, NW
Washington, DC 20009
 Tel. 202/797-8997

Recording Industry Association of America
1020 19th Street, NW, Suite 200
Washington, DC 20036
 Tel. 202/775-0101

Third World Newsreel
335 West 38th Street, 5th floor
New York, NY 10018
 Tel. 212/947-9277

United Church of Christ
700 Prospect Avenue, #800
Cleveland, OH 44115-1100
 Contact: Beverly J. Chain, Director, Office of Communications

US Telecommunications Experts Center
University of Nebraska at Omaha
International Center for Telecommunications Management
Omaha, NE 68182
 Contact: Michael Jensen

Video Software Dealers Association
303 Harper Drive
Mooretown, NJ 08057
 Tel. 609/231-7800

Women Make Movies
225 Lafayette Street, #206
New York, NY 10012
 Contact: Jennifer Scott

Appendix 4
NFLCP Public Policy Platform Summary

1.People need access to cable televison and other communications systems to increase and enhance interactions within all communities and nations of the world. The NFLCP encourages efforts within and between communities of all nations to provide and advance free speech and free access to information through public access to cable television and other communication systems.

2.The NFLCP supports government regulation of cable services to ensure protection of the public interest.

3.The NFLCP recognizes the authority and responsibility of local franchisers to negotiate and enforce cable franchises in the public interest. With respect to access channels, local franchisers should:
   a.require the dedication of public, education, and governmental access channels in sufficient numbers to meet community needs and interests;
   b.ensure that PEG access programming is available to the public on the lowest cost tier, and actively promoted; and
   c.provide sufficient resources for public access operations.

4.The NFLCP supports the development of public access activities with the following characteristics:
   a.public access channels and operating resources are administered by a democratically controlled, community-based, non-profit access organization which operates independently of the cable operator and the franchiser;
   b.time on access channels is allocated on a first-come, first served basis, without charge, for non-commercial programming which is locally produced or locally sponsored;
   c.public access operating resources are allocated on a first-come, first-served basis, for non-commercial programming which is locally produced or locally sponsored;
   d.the individual producer(s) and sponsor(s) of public access programming retain full editorial control of, and full responsibility for, the content of their programs.

5.The NFLCP supports the use of cable franchise fees for cable-related purposes, i.e., support of PEG access activities, enforcement of cable franchise provisions, and research and development in cable communications.

6.The NFLCP supports the right of every person and organization to lease cable channel time and related services for any legal commercial purposes, without censorship or abridgement, under non-discriminatory terms, and at reasonable rates.

7.The NFLCP supports decentralization of the control of media through legislative and regulatory actions limiting ownership of cable systems

Appendix 4, continued

by owners of other media, and limiting horizontal and vertical integration of media ownership.

8.The NFLCP supports legislative and regulatory actions which provide PEG access to video distribution systems under any regulatory or legal structure, to ensure that all members of the public will have fair and realistic opportunities to speak, and to hear a diviersity of other voices.

9.The NFLCP supports equal opportunity policies in all aspects of cable communications, and advocates affirmative action programs that address employment, ownership training, physical access, and service delivery.

10.The NFLCP advocates governmental regulation to protect the individual cable subscriber's privacy with respect to viewing practices.

Appendix 5
NFLCP Public Policy Platform, Complete Text (approved by delegates to the 1987 convention)

Preamble

Developing technologies and applications of communications media in our society have tremendous potential for human development. The NFLCP is committed to encouraging the fulfillment of this potential. We encourage all efforts to increase use of technology to enhance interaction among people and their communities and oppose any efforts that will place limitations on access to technology, information, or media, or that will arbitrarily define ownership control of transmission systems in a way that will limit access of providers and users of information.

Introduction

Purpose. The NFLCP platform is intended to serve as a statement of unity of public policy issues that affect local community programming on cable systems, as well as other forms of communications delivery. Second, it will serve as a guideline for NFLCP actions taken on behalf of its members.

Definitions

*Local community programming refers to public, educational, government, and leased access, as well as local origination. Such programming may be transmitted via coaxial cable, over the air transmission devices or other transmission media.

*Public, educational and government access refer to a means by which those respective sectors of the community can utilize cable communications on a non-commercial basis to community within a community.

*Leased access refers to third party use of cable on a paid, contractual basis.

*Local origination (L.O.) refers to programming produced by the cable operator.

Basic   Principles

The NFLCP Public Policy Platform grows out of our belief in the First Amendment rights of free speech, access to information, community control of local access resource and the widest possible diversity of information sources and services to the public, with an emphasis on localism and the decentralization of communications media.

Freedom of Speech. Access to cable communications is founded on the principle of freedom of speech as expressed by the First Amendment of the US Constitution. In our society, telecommunications, particularly television, are the predominant media for communications and access to those media is essential for freedom of speech to be a practical reality. Effective access to cable communications includes the freedom to determine the form of expression.

Access to Information. Access to information is essential to the vitality and maintenance of democratic society. It is as important to

Appendix 5, continued

hear as to speak. The NFLCP recognizes that current cable communications technology is an infrastructure used for enterprise; however, that use of the electronic spectrum should not in any way restrict or deny the right of all citizens to obtain access to information from diverse and often antagonistic sources.

Community Control of Access Programming. The NFLCP supports any activity which develops the potential for local use of telecommunications resources in the public interest and encourages the development of such resources in diverse ways. Each community must determine the organizational structure best suited to meet the needs of its citizenry. To date, NFLCP finds that a democratically controlled, nonprofit access organization is the preferred structure for achieving the communications goals envisioned by our principles. The NFLCP supports the creation of such community based, nonprofit organizations to facilitate and administer local access resources.

Diversity of Programming. People rely on electronic media for news, information, entertainment, cultural experiences and, in general, a link to their community and the world. In order to fully participate in our society, citizens need televison programming that offers the widest range of viewpoints, experiences and services. Because some communications needs are unique to specific segments of our society, corresponding television 'narrowcasting' is essential to fully realize the potential of the television medium. Diversity of communication sources is essential to the First Amendment right of freedom of speech. Each citizen's right to originate programming supersedes any telecommunication enterprise right of editorial control.

Localism and Decentralization of Media. In order that telecommunications serve the public interest fully, local communications needs must be met. Multifaceted communities benefit by an exchange of ideas, information services and experiences. This exchange is essential for a community that depends on active citizens for its vitality. The expanded and enlightened community communications have been ignored by mass electronic media. The NFLCP strongly advocates the use of cable communications to achieve uniquely local and nondiscriminatory programming.

Role of Govt Regarding Community Access to Cable Comm.

Telecommunications, which has become an essential part of community life, warrant the intervention of all levels of government to ensure that this resource will be safeguarded to provide for maximum benefit to all citizens. This responsibility is founded in that citizens have given elected representatives and appointed officials the right to further safeguard the public interest. The actions of all levels of government should fully reflect the principles of freedom of speech, access to information, diversity of programming, diversity of ownership, localism and the decentralization of media. The NFLCP recognizes that local, state and federal government has responsibility for regulation because of the following characteristics of the cable industry:

Public interest. Cable communications operate in the public domain. Private and public property are utilized for the benefit of the

Appendix 5, continued

industry. Broadcast signals use the public airwaves; interstate and local carriers (including satellites) use microwave frequencies; cable systems use state and local rights of way. Use of public resources should be planned and regulated by public agencies with meaningful input from the public and with meaningful provisions for access to such resources now and in the future.

Monopoly Service. In a given locale, the cable system operates as a de facto monopoly. This market structure warrants protection of producers and consumers of communications services that are not affiliated with the operator or its parent corporation.

Control of Information. Cable operators have some rights of editorial control and thus have the potential to limit the number and type of services carried on their systems. Local programming and access to local/regional/national information and expression on the cable communicaiton system are essential to the public interest.

Community Service Potential. Since marketplace forces are deficient in meeting the fullest range of community communications needs, government planning and regulation are necessary; citizen participation is essential. Local government has the right and the responsibility, as established by the Cable Communications Policy Act of 1984 (CCPA), to negotiate a cable franchise in the public interest and protect its citizens by actively enforcing the terms of the cable franchise, including requirements for PEG access, LO, leased access, interconnection, institutional networks, universal service and interactive service.

While the federal government has the responsibility for ensuring a consistent development of public interest use of cable communications, the NFLCP also believes that the federal government should realize its necessary limitations. Some areas appropriate for federal action include establishing technical standards, mandating interconnection, protecting privacy and consumer rights and requiring access and affirmative action. The actions taken by the federal government, which supports the basic needs and rights of citizens, should not preclude state and local governments from assessing and acting on the needs and interests of their residents. Likewise, state governments should not preclude local governments from assessing and acting on the needs and interests of their residents.

State and Local Govt Support for Community Programming
The purposes of the CCPA include assuring that cable systems are responsive to the needs and interests of the local community, and assuring that cable communications provide and are encouraged to provide the widest possible diversity of information sources and services, consistent with the First Amendment rights of the public as viewers and speakers.

The CCPA establishes guidelines for the exercise of federal, state, and local authority with respect to the regulation of cable systems, and for the implementation of national policy concerning cable communications.

The CCPA establishes, as a national policy, that franchising authorities may require the designation or use of channel capacity for

Appendix 5, continued

public, educational or governmental use and may enforce franchise requirements regarding the provision or use of such channel capacity; and the CCPA prohibits cable operators from exercising editorial control over such channels.

State and local governments have the authority and, therefore, the responsibility to encourage and support the development of community uses of local cable systems. In order to act consistently with this authority and responsibility, as established by the CCPA and the First Amendment, and as a matter of sound public policy, state and local governments should take the following affirmative actions:

a.)Ensure that personnel, training, equipment and facilities, and channel capacity are available at levels that are appropriate to foster the development of access programming in the community.

b.)Provide a stable base of financial support for local programming efforts in a manner that encourages growth and development of the medium and maintains editorial control by the producer.

c.)Establish structural arrangements for the provision and management of access which implement the basic principles and definitions set forth in the NFLCP Public Policy Platform.

d.)Protect consumer interests in cable, in particular, by ensuring that viewers have access to locally produced programming by providing that PEG access is available on the lowest cost tier, actively promoted.

Use of Franchise Fees. The NFLCP supports the use of franchise fees for cable-related purposes. This includes, but is not limited to: support of community based nonprofit access organizations; franchise enforcement and regulation; and long range planning, research and development in cable communications. Using franchise fees for cable-related purposes is sound public policy and is consistent with the NFLCP's basic principles of freedom of speech, access to information, diversity of programming, community control of access resources, localism, and decentralization of media.

Crossownership and the Centralization of Media. The NFLCP supports regulatory and legislative initiatives that seek to limit crossownership, centralization of media, and horizontal and/or vertical concentration of local media control. This amalgamation adversely affects the development of free, diverse local telecommunications.

Leased Access. Franchised cable television systems are the only multichannel video grade transmission services available to the general public and, therefore, contain some aspects of a 'common carrier.' These systems currently operate as de facto monopolies, limiting the development of multiple user options. Every person and organization must have the right to lease channel time and support services of any legal use, whether sponsored or paid by subscribers, without censorship or abridgement at nondiscriminatory terms and at reasonable rates.

Affirmative Action. To ensure that access be available to all, the NFLCP supports and encourages an equal opportunity, nondiscriminatory policy on the basis of age, sex, religious beliefs, ethnic background, political beliefs, sexual preferences, national origin, physical ability or condition, educational status or economic circumstances, by government, public interest organizations, industry, educational institutions and individuals, including community access

Appendix 5, continued

ownership, employment and other economic opportunities.

In addition, the NFLCP advocates the development and implementation of an affirmative action plan program that addresses employment, ownership, training, minority business enterprises, equal physical access and the delivery of services as it relates to all Equal Opportunity Commission categories.

Privacy

The NFLCP advocates governmental regulation to ensure consumer privacy. Individual, identifiable subscriber data gathered by cable operators could be misused by the cable operator and third parties. Regulation should mandate the following:

a.) protection of individuals from uses of individually identifiable data made without the individual's knowledge and authorization;

b.) prohibition of cable company use of data derived from transactions between cable users and any third party;

c.) subscribers' rights to identify, obtain, review and correct all information about themselves that is accessible to third parties;

d.) destruction of individually identifable information acquired through the cable system after a reasonable period of time; and

e.) responsibility for the security of information concerning subscribers will be ascribed to the cable company. Civil and criminal penalties are necessary for unauthorized disclosure and theft of individually identifiable information.

Conclusion

The NFLCP supports efforts by public interest organizations, local and state regulatory authorities, and local, state, and federal legislative action which assures that the concepts of public access to production resources and channels on cable communications systems be applied to the daily operations of all forms of telecommunications available to citizens. These forms of telecommunications include, but are not limited to: cable communications, satellites, commercial and noncommercial broadcasting, low power television, non-broadcast telecommunication technology and data bases.

Appendix 6
Cooperatives and Collectives

Alternative Views
PO Box 7279
Austin, TX 78713
  Contact: Frank Morrow
  Tel. 512/474-2107

Appalshop
306 Madison Street
Whitesburg, KY 41858
  Contact: Carolyn Sturgill
  Tel. 606/633-0108

ASIFA (Association Internationale du Film d'Animation)
790 N. Milwaukee Avenue
Chicago, IL 60622
  Contact: Deanna Morse, President
  Tel.312/243-8666

Bay Area Video Coalition
1111 17th Street
San Francisco, CA 94107
  Contact: Luke Matthew Hones, Program Director
  Tel. 415/861-3282

Flying Focus Video Collective
2305 NW Kearney, #231
Portland, OR 97210
  Contact: Liz Stiller
  Tel. 503/321-5051

Latino Collaborative
280 Broadway, Suite 412
New York, NY 10007
  Tel. 212/732-1121

The 90's
400 N. Michigan Avenue, #1608
Chicago, IL 60611
  Contact: Patrick Creadon
  Tel. 312/321-9321

Not Channel Zero
PO Box 805
Wakefield Station
Bronx, NY 10466
  Contact: Cyrille Phillips
  Tel. 212/966-4510

Appendix 6, continued

Paper Tiger Television/Deep Dish Television
339 Lafayette Street
New York, NY 10012
  Contact: Caryn Rogoff
  Tel. 212/473-8933

Paper Tiger Television/West
797 Hampshire Street
San Francisco, CA 94110
  Contact: Carla Leshne
  Tel. 415/695-0931

Public Interest Video Network
1642 R Street, NW
Washington, DC 20009
  Tel. 202/797-8997

Testing the Limits Collective
31 West 26th Street, 4th floor
New York, NY 10010
  Tel. 212/545-7120

Union Producers and Programmers NETwork (UPPNET)
c/o UFCW Local 1442
PO Box 1750
Santa Monica, CA 90406
  Contact: Fred Carroll
  Tel. 213/395-9977

Video Data Bank
1.) 37 S. Wabash Street
Chicago, IL 60603
  Contact: Nell Lundy, Special Projects Coordinator
  Tel. 313/899-5172
2.) 22 Warren Street
New York, NY 10007
  Tel. 212/233-3441

Video Project
5332 College Avenue, #101
Oakland, CA 94618
  Tel. 415/655-9050

Appendix 7
Civic, Social, Local, and Academic Organizations

American Association of Retired Persons (AARP)
601 E. Street, NW
Washington, DC 20049
  Contact: Kenneth Vest, Director, Communication Resources
  Tel. 202/782-4752

American Civil Liberties Union (ACLU)
122 Maryland Avenue, NE
Washington, DC 20002
  Tel. 202/544-1681

Anti-Defamation League
823 United Nations Plaza
New York, NY 10017
  Tel. 212/490-2525

The Appalachian Council Job Corps
363 S. Dearborn Street, Suite 1208
Chicago, IL 60604
  Contact: Windy Spencer
  Tel. 312/427-5775

The Alliance for Cultural Democracy
c/o Braufman
327 Summer Street
Boston, MA

Audio-Visual Resources for Social Change
American Friends Service Committee
2160 Lake Street
San Francisco, CA 94121
  Tel. 415/752-7766

Black Entertainment Television
1232 31st St, NW
Washington, DC 20007

Center for Constitutional Rights
666 Broadway, 7th floor
New York, NY 10012
  Tel. 212/614-6432

Center for Global Education
Augsburg College
731 21st Avenue South
Minneapolis, MN 55454

Appendix 7, continued

Chicago Access Corporation
322 S. Green Street
Chicago, IL 60607
  Contact: Barbara Popovic
  Tel. 312/738-1400

Citizens Communications Center
Georgetown University Law Center
600 New Jersey Avenue, NW
Washington, DC 20001
  Tel. 202/662-9535

DIVA-TV
c/o ACT-UP
135 West 29th Street, 10th floor
New York, NY 10001
  Tel. 212/564-2437

Downtown Community Television
87 Lafayette Street
New York, NY 10013

Education Satellite Network
Missouri School Boards Association
2100 I-70 Drive SW
Columbia, MO 62503-0099
  Contact: Terri Baur, Director

El Salvador Media Project
335 West 38th Street, 5th floor
New York, NY 10018
  Tel. 212/714-9118

Electronic Arts Intermix
536 Broadway, 9th floor
New York, NY 10012

Emergency Education Network (EENET)
National Emergency Training Center
16825 South Seton Avenue
Emmitsburg, MD 21717-9985

Executive Communications
3120 William Pitt Way
Pittsburgh, PA 15238-1360
  Contact: Gregory A. Pasi, Director

Film in the Cities
2388 University Avenue
St. Paul, MN 55114

Appendix 7, continued

Frameline
Box 14792
San Francisco, CA

Gay and Lesbian Alliance Against Defamation (GLAAD)
150 West 26th Street, Suite 503
New York, NY 10001
  Tel. 212/807-1700

Institute for Alternative Journalism
100 E. 85th Street
New York, NY 10028
  Tel. 212/799-4822

Institute for Media Analysis
145 West 4th Street
New York, NY

The Charles F. Kettering Foundation
5335 Far Hills Avenue, Suite 3000
Dayton, OH 45429
  Contact: Bruce Adams

Little City Foundation-Media Arts Center
4801 West Peterson Avenue
Chicago, IL 60646
  Contact: Maggie Lee
  Tel. 312/282-2207

The John D. and Catherine T. MacArthur Foundation
140 South Dearborn Street, Suite 1100
Chicago, IL 60603-5285
  Contact: Linda Feldman, Media Program Advisor

Media Access Project
2000 M Street, NW, Suite 400
Washington, DC 20036
  Contact: Andrew J. Schwartzman, Executive Director
  Tel. 202/232-4300

Media Alliance
356 West 58th Street
New York, NY 10019
  Tel. 212/560-2912

Media Coalition
900 Third Avenue, Suite 1600
New York, NY 10022
  Tel. 212/891-2070

Appendix 7, continued

Media Democracy Project
c/o Made in USA Productions
330 West 42nd Street, Suite 1905
New York, NY 10036
  Tel. 212/695-3090

NASA Educational Services
Oklahoma State University
300 North Cordell
Stillwater, OK 74078-0422
  Contact: Rick Collin, Videoconference Coordinator

Native American Public Broadcasting Consortium
Box 83111
Lincoln, NE
  Contact: Lawrence Spotted Bird, development and marketing mgr

Neighborhood Film/Video Project
3701 Chestnut Street
Philadelphia, PA

Northwest Coalition Against Malicious Harassment, Inc.
Box 16776
Seattle, WA 98116
  Contact: Bill Wassmuth

Pacific Islanders In Communication
1221 Kapi'olani Blvd., #6A-4
Honolulu, HA 96814
  Contact: Martha S. Carrell, President, Board of Directors

People for the American Way
2000 M Street NW, Suite 400
Washington, DC 20036
  Tel. 202/467-4999

Response Television Corporation
PO Box 3358
Iowa City, IA
  Contact: Wm. Drew Shaffer, President

San Francisco Community Television Corporation
1095 Market Street, #704
San Francisco, CA

Satellite Communications for Learning (SCOLA)
2500 California Street
Omaha, NE 68178
Tel. 402/280-4063

Appendix 7, continued

<u>Sawed on TV</u>
2075 South 13th Street
Milwaukee, WI 53204
  Contact: Rob Danielson
  Tel. 414/384-7083

<u>Southwest Alternate Media Project</u> (SWAMP)
1519 W. Main Street
Houston, TX

<u>Squeaky Wheel</u>
372 Connecticut Street
Buffalo, NY
  Contact: Lisa Sporledger

<u>TV Dinner</u>
67 Grand Avenue
Rochester, NY 14609
  Contact: Cecil Felton, Executive Director
  Tel. 716/288-1492

<u>The Union for Democratic Communications</u> (UDC)
Department of Communication
585 Manoogian Hall
Wayne State University
Detroit, MI
  Contact: Jackie Byars

<u>United Way of America</u>
701 North Fairfax Street
Alexandria, VA 22314
  Tel. 703/836-7100

<u>Video Gallery</u>
2712 Millwood, #L
Columbia, SC

<u>Videoteca del Sur</u>
84 East 3rd Street, #5A
New York, NY 10003
  Contact: Pedro Zurita

<u>Visual Communications</u>
263 S. Los Angeles Street, #307
Los Angeles, CA

Appendix 7, continued

<u>Andy Warhol Foundation for the Visual Arts, Inc</u>.
22 East 33 Street
New York, NY 10016

<u>Women's Access Coalition</u>
6 Bowdoin Park
Dorchester, MA 02122

<u>X*Press Information Services, Inc</u>.
Denver Corp. Center
4700 S. Syracuse Parkway
Denver, CO 80237
   Contact: Rosetta Rogers, Director, Special Projects

Appendix 8
Mainstream and Alternative Media

Adbusters Quarterly
Media Foundation
1243 W. 7th Avenue
Vancouver, Canada
  Contact: Kalle Lasn, publisher

AlterNet
2025 Eye Street, NW, #1118
Washington, DC
  Contact: Kelley Culmer

Angles: Women Working in Film & Video
PO Box 11916
Milwaukee, WI

Broomstick
3543 18th Street, #3
San Francisco, CA

Daughters of Sarah
3801 N. Keeler
Chicago, IL

Equal Means
2515 Ninth Street, #3
Berkeley, CA

Felix: a Journal of Media Arts and Communication
PO Box 184
Prince Street Station, NY

Feminist Bookstore News
456 14th Street, #6
San Francisco, CA

Feminist Teacher
Ballantine 422
Indiana University
Bloomington, IN

Feminist Studies
Women's Studies
University of Maryland
College Park, MD

Appendix 8, continued

Fighting Woman News
6741 Tung Avenue W.
Theodore, AL

Frontiers
Mesa Vista Hall
University of New Mexico
Albuquerque, NM

Heresies
PO Box 1306
Canal Street Station, NY

Hikane
PO Box 841
Great Barrington, MA

Hot Wire
5210 N. Wayne
Chicago, IL

Kalliope
3939 Roosevelt Blvd.
Florida Community College
Jacksonville, FL

The New VOICE
45 Dream Lane
Cohasset, CA
    Contact: Loretta J. Metcalf, Publisher/Editor

North Shore Woman's Newspaper
PO Box 1056
Huntington, NY

Teen Voices--see Women Express, Inc.

Third Text
303 Finchley Road
London, England

Utne Reader
1624 Harmon Place, #330
Minneapolis, MN
    Contact: Eric Utne, President and editor-in-chief

Appendix 8, continued

Visions
551 Tremont Street, #212
Boston, MA
  Contact: Carl Germann

Women Express, Inc.
JFK Station
Box 6009
Boston, MA
  Contact: Alison Amoroso, Executive Director

Womyn's Press
PO Box 492
Eugene, OR
  Contact: J.R. David and Jonni Erickson

Note: for a complete listing of "Working Press of the Nation," contact
National Register Publishing, PO Box 31, New Providence, NJ 07974-9903,
tel. 800/521-8110, FAX 908/665-3560. It publishes four volumes:
  1.Newspaper Directory
  2.Magazines & Internal Publications Directory
  3.TV & Radio Directory
  4.Feature Writers, Photographers, & Professional Speakers

Appendix 9
Businesses and Foundations Related to Community Television

A&E (Arts & Entertainment) Classroom
PO Box 1610
Grand Central Station, NY

Black Entertainment Television
1700 North Moore Street, #2200
Rosslyn, VA
   Contact: Craig M. Muckle, Director of P/R and Communications

Brewster/Ingraham Consulting Group
6 Puritan Road
Acton, MA
   Contact: Sharon Ingraham

The Buske Group
2015 J Street, #28
Sacramento, CA
   Contact: Sue Buske

Cable in the Classroom
1900 N. Beauregard Street, #108
Alexandria, VA

The CMR Group (Communications/Media Relations)
22330 Victory Blvd., #104
Woodland Hills, CA

CNN Newsroom
Turner Broadcasting
1 CNN Center
Box 105366
Atlanta, GA
   Contact: Lori Konopka, CNN P/R Coordinator

Communication for Change
147 W. 22nd Street
New York, NY
   Contact: Katie Corrigan

Communications Support Group
PO Box 10968
Santa Ana, CA

Appendix 9, continued

Copen & Lind
22 Ward Street
Amherst, MA
  Contact: Genya Copen

Kettering Foundation
200 Comons Road
Dayton, OH
  Contact: Bob Daley

John D. and Catherine T. MacArthur Foundation
140 S. Dearborn Street, #1100
Chicago, II.
  Contact: Linda Feldman, Media Program Advisor

Miller & Holbrooke
1225 19th Street, NW
Washington, DC
  Contact: Joe VanEaton

Moss & Barnett
4800 Norwest Center
90 S. 7th Street
Minneapolis, MN
  Contact: Adrian E. Herbst

National Community Network
3200 Cherry Creek Drive S., #500
Denver, CO
  Contact: Jim Dickson, President

National Council for Research on Women
Sara Delano Roosevelt House
47-49 E. 65th Street
New York, NY

Retirement Research Foundation
The Center for New Television
1440 N. Dayton Street
Chicago, IL

Spiegel & McDiarmid
1350 NY Avenue, NW
Washington, DC
  Contact: Jim Horwood

Andy Warhol Foundation for the Visual Arts
22 E. 33rd Street
New York, NY

Appendix 9, continued

X*Press Information Services, Ltd.
4700 S. Syracuse Pkwy, #1050
Denver, CO
　　Contact: Rosetta Rogers, Director of Special Projects

　　Note:　In case you want/need to contact the major television
networks, here are their addresses:
ABC
77 West 66th Street
New York, NY 10023

CBS
51 West 52nd Street
New York, NY 10019

Fox Broadcasting Company
PO Box 900
Beverly Hills, CA 90213

NBC
30 Rockefeller Plaza
New York, NY

Appendix 10
Educational Organizations Related to Community Television

Education Satellite Network
2100 I-70 Dr., SW
Columbia, MO
  Contact: Jeanie Rhoades, ESN Support Assistant

Educational Communications Center
Bob Dole Hall
Kansas State University
Manhattan, KS
  Contact: Barbara Newhouse, Associate Director, Academic Programs

Executive Communications, Inc.
3120 William Pitt Way
Pittsburgh, PA

Instructional Television For Students
California State University/Chico
Chico, California
  Contact: Ralph F. Meuter, Dean for Regional and Continuing Education

Learning by Satellite
Oklahoma State University
Norman, OK
  Contact: Leigh Beaulieu, Manager

Louisiana Education Resource Network (LERN)
Southern University
610 Texas Street, #307
Shreveport, LA

Lubbock Educational Access
1323 E. 24th Street
Lubbock, TX

Mass LearnPike
Massachusetts Corporation for Educational Telecommunications
University Park at MIT
38 Sidney Street, #300
Cambridge, MA
  Contact: Beverly Simon, Director of Communications and Membership

Mind Extension University
9697 East Mineral Avenue
Englewood, CO
  Contact: Andrea Montoni, Public Relations Director

Appendix 10, continued

<u>National Aeronautics and Space Administration</u> (NASA)
(Washington office, for education)
300 E. Street, SW
2nd floor, Room 2L15
Washington, DC
  Contact: Rick Collin, Videoconference Coordinator

<u>Northern Virginia Youth Services Coalition</u> (NVYSC)
12011 Govt. Center Pkwy, #210
Fairfax, VA
  Contact: Beverly Salera, Executive Director

<u>Satellite Learning</u>
1837 Algoa Friendswood Road
Alvin, TX

<u>Satellite Scholar</u>
2347 South Avenue W.
Missoula, MT
  Contact: Greg Bell

<u>Talcott Mountain Science Center for Student Involvement</u>
Montevideo Road
Avon, CT
  Contact: Ginna Crosby, Development/Public Relations

<u>TI-IN</u>
121 Interpark, #300
San Antonio, TX
  Contact: Laura Adams, Marketing Manager

Appendix 11
PACTL Producers Survey

A.Background
　1.How did you happen to get involved with PACTL?
　　a.History/background
　　b.Individual, or as a member of a group
　2.When, where did you first hear about it?
　　　(Friend; newspaper; TV; group, can't remember)
　3.Prior to working with Channel 8, did you have any experience
　　or training with TV?
　4.Did you feel at all obligated to get involved? Did anyone push you
　　to make contact?
　5.Do you usually like to be involved in projects as they are first
　　evolving?
　6.How did you make your contact with PACTL--telephone, came to a
　　meeting, joined alone or with a group.

B.Content
　1.Did you have a particular program in mind when you first came
　　to PACTL? Or, did you just want to get involved and see where
　　your expertise might fit in?
　2.Did you actually do your original idea?
　3.What else have you done? (Learn about all programs: how many,
　　type, how long they lasted, and what capacity for each one).
　4.Did you quit any programs you had started? Did you continue
　　reluctantly with any?
　5.Were most of your programs the same type, or did you diversify?
　6.Did any of your programs have to be negotiated, either with the
　　trustees or staff or performers?
　7.Did you make an effort to present both sides for any controversial
　　topics that were brought up? Were you concerned about not of-
　　fending any particular segment of your audience?

C.Audience
　1.Did you think about what particular kind of audience would like
　　your program(s)?
　2.What kind of people do you think your program(s) appealed to?
　　Did you think about appealing to a wide or a specialized audience?
　3.Do you think there is much of an audience for your kind of
　　show(s)?
　4.What age group(s) did you want to appeal to? What interests?
　5.What kind of feedback have you received from people in town
　　after your show?
　6.Do you think people who saw your show(s) related to it/them?

Appendix 11, continued

D.<u>Personal responses</u>
  1.In general, what has been your overall reaction to working with PACTL?
  2.What kinds of things did you learn from working with PACTL:
    a.Technical and/or non-technical training?
    b.Anything about yourself?
    c.Anything about Longmeadow?
    d.Anything about your fellow citizens?
  3.How did you feel about your show(s)?
  4.How did you get along with PACTL staff? With other volunteers?
  5.Do you think having been part of this/these production(s) has increased your status in any way?
  6.Do you think this experience will help a future resume or career in any way? Did you do it for that reason in the first place?
  7.What do you think your program(s) did for the town in general or people in particular? Do you think it helped create a general consensus in the town?
  8.Did this experience fulfill any wider goals of yours?
  9.Would you say you tried to come in with a particular agenda? If yes, do you think you kept to it?
  10.What do you envision to be your future involvement with the PACTL?

E.<u>Demographics</u>
  1.Age
  2.Gender
  3.Race
  4.Marital status
  5.Education
  6.Household composition
  7.Religion
  8.Occupation/employment
  9.Other volunteer experience
  10.Future career goals

Source: Linda K. Fuller, "Public Access Cable Television: A Case Study on Source, Contents, Audience, Producers, and Rules-Theoretical Perspective." Unpublished doctoral dissertation, University of Massachusetts, 1984.

Appendix 12
PACTL Producer Comments on Learning about Self

01 Came not knowing anything, but have learned it all. Everything from production techniques to getting along with different kinds of people.

02 Too ready to commit myself.

03 I learned that I had effective creative talents that had previously been untapped.

04 Peter Principle: I took on too much.

05 Want to get into graphic design.

06 Bite off more than I can chew.

07 Always learn about myself.

08 Always involved in birth processes.

09 Growth experience--I can become involved in technical areas.

10 Very fulfilling--gap in my life from retirement.

12 Realized glaring mistakes--it changed my vision.

13 Don't have the patience to volunteer here--too much hassle.

14 I learn easily, especially technical skills.

15 Already knew I was a procrastinator.

18 Do things with my whole heart, then walk away. I'm marvelous with people--could forget about the camera.

19 Hope I'm not a quitter.

20 Fun to project your interests.

22 My technical interests are limited by having to work with people.

23 Learned what I want to do: teach video.

24 Surprised at how uncomfortable I was in front of the camera.

Appendix 12, continued

25 Pioneer effect: I learned more technical stuff than I thought I ever could. This is my hobby.

27 Don't like working with TV cameras.

28 How much I like organization--this was too frustrating. Not so sure it's a good idea to work with inexperienced people.

29 Very free hand here--why I continue.

30 My plans are bigger than my capacity.

31 I can do more than I thought.

32 Learned I could really do it.

33 I could do it. Learned how a show is put togther; what you see isn't what's going on.

35 How impatient I am.

38 I need to be more patient.

39 I need total involvement.

40 I always get into things over my head.

41 Knew I could do it, but never had the chance before.

Source: Linda K. Fuller, "Public Access Cable Television: A Case Study on Source, Contents, Audience, Producers, and Rules-Theoretical Perspective." Unpublished doctoral dissertation, University of Massachusetts, 1984.

Appendix 13
SCC Public-Access Television User Phone Questionnaire

(Ask to speak to person on list.)
Hello, my name is _____. I'm calling on behalf of Suburban Community
Channels. We are conducting a brief quality check on the coursework
and facilities offered at our White Bear Lake and Oakdale locations.

1.I understand that you have made use of some of our instructional
programs, equipment or cablecasting facilities in the past 3 years; is
that correct?
    1.Yes 2.No--Terminate and thank.

2.I will read a list of Community Access programs and facilities. Please
indicate all that you have used in the last 3 years:
    1.Instructional courses--if no, terminate   2.Studio equipment
    3.Production van 4.1/2" video equipment checkout 5.3/4"

3.You indicated that you have taken some instruction from SCC--where:
    1.White Bear Lake 2.Oakdale 3.Both

4.Did you find that the courses were offered at a time of day and a day of
the week that were convenient for you?
    1.Yes 2.No--ask which serves needs better, weekends or nights

5.After taking your course(s) in (Q#3), did you feel that you could
handle the video equipment?
    1.Yes 2.No--why not? Probe and clarify.

6.Do you feel your instructor was responsive to your needs & questions?
    1.Yes 2.No--why do you say that? Probe and clarify.

7.Do you feel that the length of time spent by the instructor and the
amount of detail was enough for your needs?
    1.Yes 2.No

8.If you could change the course so that it would have served your needs
better, what changes would you have made? Probe and clarify.

 (If "instructional courses" is checked in Q#2 above, but no other boxes,
ask Q#9 and then skip to Q#16; otherwise, skip Q#9 and go to Q#10.)

9.You said that you have taken courses from SCC but also indicated that
you have never made use of any of their equipment or facilities. Why,
and what could SCC do to help you? Probe and clarify.

10.You indicated that you have used some of the community-access video
equipment. Was the equipment you needed available the first time you
went to use it?
    1.Yes 2.No

Appendix 13, continued

11.Was the equipment that you checked out in working order?
    1.Yes 2.No--ask, How did you resolve this problem? Probe/clarify.

12.Did you find that your training allowed you to use the equipment?
    1.Yes 2.No

13.Were the checkout and return procedures fast and easy?
    1.Yes 2.No--ask, How could they be made better? Probe/clarify.

14.Were you able to complete your project using the White Bear Lake or Oakdale equipment?
    1.Yes 2.No

15.Is there any other equipment you'd like to see SCC make available?
    1.Yes--ask, what other equipment?   2.No

16A.The last time you made use of public access televison, were you representing an organization or doing work for yourself alone?
    1.Myself   2.An organization

16B.Does your organization need any technical support or people to assist you in order to do your productions?
    1.Yes--ask, what type of help? Probe/clarify. 2.No

17.Which do you prefer--producing your own shows or helping someone else to produce theirs?
    1.My own shows   2.Helping someone else   3.No preference

18.There are many ways for people to find out about community-access televison. How did you first find out about it? Was it by:
    1.An announcement in a cable company bill
    2.An item in a local newspaper
    3.Another member in an organization you belong to
    4.A direct mailing from SCC
    5.Some other way (specify)
    (Do not read):   6.Can't remember

Finally, I'd like to ask some information about yourself:
19.In what suburb are you now living?

20.Are you currently:
    1.Working part-time 2.Working full-time 3.Not working outside the home   4.A Student

21.Are you:
    1.15-18yrs old 2.19-25 3.26-34 4.35-54 5.55 or over 6.Refused

Those are all my questions. Thank you very much for your cooperation.

Source: Version of SCC questionnaire, courtesy of Jan Rosenthal, P/R Dir.

Appendix 14
Case Studies of Community Television Operations

Access Center of Kalamazoo
230 E. Crosstown Pkwy.
Kalamazoo, MI
    Contact: Joan Burke, executive director

Allen County Public Library (ACPL)
900 Webster Street
Fort Wayne, IN
    Contact: Rick Hayes, station manager

Austin Community Television (ACTV)
PO Box 1076
Austin, TX
    Contacts: Rosalind Brinkley, Community Services Officer
              Douglas Kellner, Department of Philosophy, U. Texas/Austin
              Frank Morrow, producer, Alternative Views

Calaveras Community Television
PO Box 152
Avery, CA 95224
    Contact: Paul A.E. Moeller, Director, Operations and Training

Columbus Community Access
394 Oak Street
Columbus, OH
    Contact: Carl Kucharski

Grand Rapids Cable Access Center (GRTV)
50 Library Plaza
Grand Rapids, MI
    Contact: Dirk Koning, Executive Director

Hudson Community Access Television
502 Second Street, #301
Hudson, WI
    Contact: Kathleen Greenwood

International Mobile Video
PO Box 338
Sierra City, CA 96125
    Contact: Dave Bloch

Middlebury Community Television (MCTV)
 PO Box 785
Middlebury, VT
    Contact: Nelda Holder, Executive Director

Appendix 14, continued

Missoula Community Access Television (MCAT)·
500 N. Higgins
Missoula, MT
  Contact: Mary Canty, assistant director

Multnomah Community Television (MCTV)
26000 SE Stark Street
Gresham, OR

Northwest Community Television (NWCT)
6900 Winnetka Avenue, N.
Brooklyn Park, MN
  Contact: Mike Johnson, assistant executive director

Philadelphia Citizens for Public Access Cable Coalition
454 W. Earlham Terrace
Philadelphia, PA 19144
  Contact: Keith Brank

Portland Cable Access
2766 NE Martin Luther King, Jr. Blvd.
Portland, OR
  Contact: Deborah M. Luppold, general manager

Public Access Cable Television of Longmeadow, MA (PACTL)
Grassy Gutter Road
Longmeadow, MA 01106
  Contact: Emily Bent, Executive Director

Queens Public Access Television (QPTV)
41-61 Kissena Blvd, #2077
Flushing, NY
  Contact: Liz Bartucci, community outreach assistant

Sierra Buttes Cable Television (SCTV)
PO Box 496
Sierra City, CA 96125
  Contact: Tim Smith

Wilbraham Cable Televison (WTV)
PO Box 652
Wilbraham, MA 01095
  Contact: Frank Flanagan

Yakima Community Television
Department of Community & Economic Development
City Hall
Yakima, WA 98901

Appendix 15
Community Access to Dominant Media: A Model

Public access centers have a critical role to play in the evolution of communities and in the ways that communication occurs in the community's daily life. Fundamental changes are occurring in the way in which we share information, thoughts, visions and dreams.

The foundation for public access television is strong and well laid. But it is not good enough. But it is not enough. As has been seen, we shouldn't build our entire house on a single foundation. We must plan for additions based on community needs and lay foundations for those.

And try not to get caught in the growth trap of instition. Institutions, remember, are often bastions that retard and inhibit change. We must champion change and accommodate its aberrations. We must attack technology to break it down to its simplest components and make it available to anyone. This is a narrative of the pioneering efforts of one medium size cable access center's attempt to evolve into a multi-disciplinarian media access center.

The city: Grand Rapids, Michigan, population about 180,000, with a metro community of 400,000. United Arts Entertainment serves 110,000 cable subscribers with 60% penetration. The city has three VHF network affiliates, two independent UHFs, one UHF affiliate, one local PBS, and one LPTV. There are about 40 AM and FM radio stations. The broadcast market, which includes the neighboring communities of Kalamazoo and Battle Creek, ranks 39th in the nation.

In 1980, a non-profit corporation was established to contract with the city to manage a public access channel on cable. 2% of cable revenues were provided to fund it. The corporation, called the Grand Rapids Cable Access Center, Inc. (GRCAC), consists of nine board members elected from the membership-at-large. They hire an executive director to manage the day-to-day activities.

In order to meet diverse access needs, GRCAC, Inc. will soon be changing its name to the Grand Rapids Media Access Center, Inc. (GRTV). The Media Access Center will consist of these four initial divisions:

GRTV is public access television, providing free training, equipment check-out and cablecasting of local programming. In this division, over $250,000 in video equipment is available at no charge.
CAN, the Community Access network, will be an additional access channel on cable to allow programming from over two dozen local institutions (art museum, public museum, district court, parks, colleges, zoo, etc.) wired for

Appendix 15, continued

live reverse audio/video and switched by telephone onto the channel. CAN will also program the best of local, national and international access and 'hop the birds' by peeking in on satellite transmissions.

WYCE 88.1FM is a 1,000 watt community station on the air 18 hours a day, seven days a week, staffed by volunteers. An eclectic format mixes musical genres with each selection. Training occurs for on-air shifts, production and writing. We plan to pick up "Pacifica News" nightly and continue to feature local musicians. A local radio theater club hopes to present live, local radio theater every Sunday night.

Middletown Film Collective includes 3,400 films, 600 of which are features, local archives of film and video works, two 16mm camers for training and check-out, film editing station, a cleaning and repair unit, 8 and Super 8mm films and 35mm slides to video tape and screenings from the collection.

A fifth division will eventually include access to computers (we have Apple, IBM, Targa and Amiga) for computer graphics, desktop publishing, data banks, FAX, bulletin boards, training, modems, etc.

The obvious goal for us is to provide a one-stop for all non-commercial access needs. This year we are searching for a new facility for the Media Access Center. The public access division is exploring the idea of purchasing old homes in several parts of town to have small regional center for training, production and live transmission. Interconnection is already possible for cable and FM simulcasts.

If information truly is the currency of democracy, then we want to be the mint where you can print your own 'money.' As information becomes a commodity for capitalistic advancement, socio-economic groups 'South of the loop' will suffer. Low cost access to information will be extremely valuable.

Once the visions are in place and all provide various training components, we will explore the prospects of forming a Media Studies Institute and apply for recognition from the state for support and accreditation as an alternative media school.

Source: Dirk Koning, *CTR* 13, no. 1 (Spring 1990), p. 8.

Appendix 16
WTV Project Proposal Form

DATE: _____

NAME: _____
           (please print or type)

ADDRESS: _____

PHONE: (home)_____ (business)_____

      Please submit a brief outline of the program(s) which you and/or your organization would like to produce for public access.

TITLE: _____

SUBJECT:
(if more room is needed, please use the back of this form)

- -

      (please do not write below this line)
Proposal reviewed by: _____ Date: _____
Date contacted: _____ By whom: _____
Date of meeting: _____ Project begun: _____
Project completed: _____ Cablecast date: _____
Comments:

Note: WTV—Wilbraham Public Access Television, Wilbraham, MA

Appendix 17
WTV Application Request for Cablecast/Statement of Compliance

REQUESTED DATE: _____
ADDITIONAL TIMES: _____
NAME: _____   TELEPHONE NO: _____
ADDRESS: _____
ORGANIZATION: _____   TELEPHONE NO: _____
PROGRAM TITLE: _____   # OF SERIES: ____
ADEQUATE LEADER: _____   Preferred: 90; SEC. Minimum10 SEC.
AUDIO RECORDED ON: Channel 1: _____   Channel 2: _____
PROGRAM LENGTH: _____   FORMAT IS VHS ONLY
TAPE OWNERSHIP: Wilbraham PA _____   User _____

The undersigned (the "Applicant") hereby applies to Wilbraham
Public Access Cable TV Committee (the "Committee") for use of the
designated system wide program channel (the "Channel"). The
Applicant hereby acknowledges and agrees that such use shall be in
accordance with the following terms and conditions:

1.The Committee shall provide the Producer with video production and
editing equipment as deemed necessary for the production of video
programs for airing over Wilbraham's Access Channel.

2.All other obligations, arrangements, and responsibilities in
connection with the program shall be the Applicant's, including, but
not limited to:
    i.Determining the subject matter of the program
    ii.Arranging for guests, as appropriate, for the program
    iii.Scheduling appropriate times and dates for cablecast
    iv.Obtaining all necessary clearances, waivers and consents
        from all persons and entities required for cablecasting
    v.Coordinating the production of the program

3.The Applicant's use of the Wilbraham Cable Access facility and the
Access Channel is as an independent contractor. The Committee has no
control over the content of the program, and the Applicant, limited only
by the FCC imposed restrictions enumerated in paragraph 6 hereof, has
absolute control over the content of the program.

4.Neither the Committee, the Access Coordinator, the Town of
Wilbraham, nor any volunteers of the Access Channel shall be liable for
any liability, loss, damage or other injury arising out of, or caused by,
any matter or material supplied or spoken by the Applicant or any of its
officers, agents or employees or any material supplied or spoken by any
person or entity which is cablecast over the Access Channel during the
cablecast of the program.

5.The Applicant shall indemnify and hold harmless the Committee, the
Access Coordinator, the Town of Wilbraham and any volunteers of the

Appendix 17, continued

Access Channel from any and all liability, loss, damage or other injury (including reasonable attorney's fees and all costs incurred in defending any claim) arising out of, or caused by, any matter or material supplied by or spoken by the Applicant or any of its officers, agents or employees or any material supplied or spoken by any person or entity cablecast over the Access Channel during the cablecast of the program, including, but not limited to, claims based on a failure to comply with applicable laws, rules, regulations or other requirements of local, state or federal authorities; claims based on libel, slander, invasion of privacy or infringement of a common law or statutory copyright; claims based on a breach of contractual or other obligations owing to third parties by the Committee; and for any other liability, loss or damage arising out of, or caused, by the Applicant's use of the Access Channel.

6. Any program which contains any of the following is prohibited:
*any material which constitutes libel, slander, invasion of privacy or publicity rights;
*obscene or indecent material (i.e., any material which is defined as obscene under applicable local, state, or federal law);
*any advertising material designed to promote the sale of commercial products or services, including advertising by or on behalf of candidates for public office;
*the direct or indirect presentation of lottery information (i.e., any advertising or information concerning any lottery, gift enterprise, or similar scheme offering prizes dependent in whole or in part upon lot or chance or any list drawn or awarded by means of any such lottery, gift enterprise, or scheme when such list contains any or all prizes);
*materials which require appropriate rights from broadcast stations, networks, sponsors, music licensing organizations, performers, representives, copyright holders and any other persons as may be necessary to cablecast on the Access Channel unless the Public Access User can present written authorization for the use of such materials;
*programming that violates the program content of the Town of Wilbraham or any state or federal laws;
*direct solicitation for goods, services, or funds for personal gain.

7. The Applicant has read the Wilbraham Public/Educational Cable Access Policy Manual governing use of the Access Channel and agrees to abide by the terms and conditions therein and herein.

8. The FCC requires the Committee to maintain and to make available for public inspection, a record of all persons and entities applying for use of the Access Channel and Agrees that this Application may be used as such record.

ACCESS USER SIGNATURE: _____
DATE: _____
Wilbraham Public Access Cable TV Committee authorized rep: _____

Note: WTV—Wilbraham Public Access Television, Wilbraham, MA

Appendix 18
WTV Procedures for Producers

Dear Public Access Producer:

The following pages will provide you with the procedures you are to follow in order to access the Public Access Channel, its equipment and facility. Please refer to the policy manual if you have policy questions.

Everything you wish to do, such as reserving equipment or editing time, picking up or returning equipment, editing, or broadcasting will take place during those times when the Public Access Room is open for business. The only exception will be the initial step of having your project approved.

The following steps should provide you with all the necessary information you will need to bring your Public Access video project to a successful completion.

STEP 1: SUBMITTING YOUR PROJECT PROPOSAL FORM
To have your project proposal form approved, submit it to a member of the Access Committee. Upon approval of your project, it will be recorded under your name in the producer project proposal log book located in the Public Access room.

STEP 2: RESERVING THE CAMCORDER AND SUPPORT EQUIPMENT
Call the Public Access room at 599-0940 during its hours of operation. The coordinator on duty will reserve a camcorder system for you.

Note: Policy states that you show the coordinator the blank tape that you will use. If you need a blank tape, you may purchase it through the Access Channel. Current cost is $10.25. Make out check to: "Town of Wilbraham."

STEP 3: PICKING UP AND RETURNING THE CAMCORDER SYSTEM
Unless otherwise noted, pick up your reserved camcorder on a Monday night and return it on the following Monday night.

STEP 4: RESERVING TIME FOR EDITING
Call the Public Access Room during its hours of operation. The coordinator on duty will reserve time for you.

STEP 5: RESERVING A BROADCAST DATE/TIME
Upon completion of your master tape, leave your "broadcast/ statement of compliance" form and master tape with coordinator. Retain all talent and/or premises release forms and other pertinent information. Make sure tape is properly identified; time of program must be listed. If you desire, you may be present on the night your program is to be aired.

Note: WTV—Wilbraham Public Access Television, Wilbraham, MA

Appendix 19
WTV Application for Equipment

TODAY'S DATE: _____   DATE EQUIPMENT REQUESTED: _____
CHECKOUT DATE: _____ TIME: _____ RETURN DATE: _____ TIME: _____
NAME: _____   PHONE: _____
ADDRESS: _____   ZIP CODE: _____
ORGANIZATION: _____   PHONE: _____
ADDRESS: _____   ZIP CODE: _____

IF REQUEST IS DENIED, REASON FOR DENIAL: _____

COORDINATOR'S SIGNATURE: _____

 In consideration for the use of televison production Equipment,
provided by Wilbraham Public Access Channel (WTV-46) for community
access programming, the Applicant hereby agrees as follows:

 1. I have read and am thoroughly familiar with the contents of the
Wilbraham Public/Educational Cable Access Policy Manual.

 2. I agree to exercise reasonable care in the use of the Equipment and to
at all times keep the Equipment in a safe place. I understand that
Wilbraham Public Access Channel will repair damage to the Equipment
resulting from normal wear and tear under ordinary use. However, I
agree to pay the costs of any repair or replacement of Equipment or
materials resulting from misuse, loss, theft or vandalism while the
Equipment is in my possession or control. I agree to return the
Equipment at the time stated. I agree to pay the Wilbraham Public
Access Cable TV Committee ON DEMAND the cost for repairs or
replacement, costs which will be determined by the current market
value. I agree to pay reasonable attorney's fees and collection costs
incurred by Wilbraham Public Access Cable TV Committee in collecting
or attempting to collect any sums due under this agreement.

 3. I agree that the intended use of the Equipment is to produce a
program(s) for the Town of Wilbraham's Access Channel, and that,
unless otherwise stated, the Equipment will not be used in any way for
personal profit or remuneration. I further agree that the Equipment
will not be used in violation of US Copyright Laws, and that
programming will comply with all the related ordinances of the Town of
Wilbraham and the Commonwealth of Massachusetts.

 False or misleading statements made in this application are grounds for
forfeiture of the right to use public access Equipment and Facilities.

 I recognize that this application is non-transferable.

_____   _____
 Applicant's signature   Date

Note: WTV—Wilbraham Public Access Television, Wilbraham, MA

Appendix 20
WTV Equipment Check-out Form

<u>OUT</u>   <u>IN</u>   <u>SERIAL #</u>   <u>DESCRIPTION</u>

CAMERA SYSTEM
_Camcorder (AG 450) with carry case
_AC Adapter with charging connector
_Lens cleaning kit
_Earphone
_A/V cable with converter plug
_300Ω - 75Ω transformer cable
_Battery pack 1 2 3

Tripod with connector block
AC extension cord, 25 feet 1 2 3
AC power strip
Lavelier mike (audiotechnica pro-7)
Handheld unit (audiotechnica pro-46)
Microphone cable, 16 feet
Desk stand with microphone holder
XLR plug to tini plug adaptor cable

Lighting equipment (lower VP-97)
_Pro-light: barn doors, 12' power cord
_V-lights (2)
_Umbrella and tota frame
_Tota frame
_Tripods (3)
_Stand with stud link
_Tota clamp

GDA lamps 1 2 3
GCA lamps 1 2 3

Producer's name: _____
Check-out date: _____   Time: _____
Agree: _____
Check-in date: _____   Time: _____
Agree: _____

Note: WTV—Wilbraham Public Access Television, Wilbraham, MA

Appendix 21
WTV Premises Taping Release

PUBLIC ACCESS PRODUCER: _____

PREMISES TO BE TAPED: _____

OWNER: _____

DATES OF TAPING: _____

    Owner consents to permit the Public Access Producer identified above to make videotape recordings of the owner's premises. Owner hereby assigns and releases any of Owner's rights to the reproduction, exhibition, broadcast and/or distribution of said videotape.

    In connection with such videotape recordings, Producer will hold Owner harmless from any damage to the Premises caused by the Producer, and for injury to any person on the site of the above premises caused by the Producer.

    Owner warrants that s/he has the legal right and power to grant the Producer the rights granted herein.

NAME: _____
BY: _____
ADDRESS: _____
DATE: _____

Note: WTV—Wilbraham Public Access Television, Wilbraham, MA

Appendix 22
WTV Talent Release Form

PUBLIC ACCESS PRODUCER: _____

I hereby assign all rights and release from liability the above Producer(s) and the Wilbraham Public Access TV Committee from the recording, reproduction, exhibition, telecasting and distribution of my visual image and voice for nonprofit use.

SIGNED: _____

DATE: _____

I certify that I am the parent and/or guardian of _____, a minor under the age of eighteen years. I hereby consent that any videotapes which have been or are about to be made by the above producer(s) may be used for the purposed explained above.

SIGNED: _____
                          (parent or guardian)

ADDRESS: _____

DATE: _____

Note: WTV—Wilbraham Public Access Television, Wilbraham, MA

Appendix 23
WTV Bulletin Board Information Sheet

WTV-46 will broadcast public service announcements about events which are of community interest. Please provide a brief, typewritten description of the event by filling in the information below. Due to technical restrictions, your description must be limited to 25 words or less. Any description exceeding this limitation will not be broadcast. Please submit your information at least seven days in advance of the scheduled event.

Description of event: _____

Date(s) of event: _____ Time (s): _____

Location of event: _____

Sponsor of event: _____

Contact person: _____ Telephone #: _____

Submit information to: WTV-46
Public Access Bulletin Board Information
Minnechaug Regional High School
Wilbraham, MA 01095
or
WTV-46
PO Box 652
Wilbraham, MA 01095

WTV-46 YOUR COMMUNITY CHANNEL

Note: WTV—Wilbraham Public Access Television, Wilbraham, MA

Appendix 24
Access in the 1990s: A Modest Manifesto

Refuse to be defined by the dead language of the cable franchise, which is based on abstract political jurisdictions that are designed to cut off communication by definition. Instead, work the networks of real communication that define real community.

Create legal arguments to justify your refusal to be confined to the franchise.

Diversify funding, using the franchise as a core.

Build close working relationships with the various networks of community-based organizations. They are another form of real community. Learn to recognize the difference between genuine community groups and those that are just fronts for the powers-that-be, then give preference to the genuine ones.

Understand that arts organizations have become central organizations in the community. Understand that many of them are under the same kind of pressures as access when it comes to censorship.

Don't fight the market for programming. Define the difference between commercial, corrupt programming and programming that can be sold to other outlets. Become a go-between for producers and the market. Consider principled spinoffs from access, where the values of community media can begin showing up in commercial programming. Consider using public funds to start local production efforts that are flexible in the sense that they can be distributed in a number of venues.

Stop worrying about independent producers making a few dollars from the work they do in access. Encourage them to sell/distribute their work after it runs in your community. Access needs producers who make good community televison, and they will not stick around if their efforts are restricted to Bush-style volunteerism.

Forget the narrow mission statements in the franchise regarding television. Become diverse community media centers. Become the primary site for media education and media training. Immediately start courses in computer literacy, home video, organizational uses of the new phone systems, and digital photography. Do not define your organization only in terms of television.

Abandon the pseudo-neutral approach to training and education that claims to be avoiding imposing a style or visual language on the community. Develop a training approach that allows people to understand how communication is fundamentally implicated in oppression. Learn what is undemocratic about the forms of communication that have developed from exploitative practice and counter it with new forms. Open these issues up to explicit debate within the center and the community.

Find and implement legal arguments for all of the above. Be as clever and ruthless in this as the cable companies that were working to rid themselves of access.

Source: Fred Johnson, *CTR* 13, no. 1 (Spring 1990), p. 5.

Glossary

AARP—American Association of Retired Persons, the largest organization of older Americans in the United States. Located at 1909 K Street NW, Washington, DC, the nonprofit, nonpartisan organization boasts a membership of more than 23 million.

Access—dedicated cable television channels made available by operators for local public programming on a first-come, first-served basis.

Access support—the personnel, training, equipment, and promotional activities provided by the cable operator to help PEG access.

Administrative management—a managerial approach that emphasizes the efficiency and effectiveness of the total organization.

Alphanumeric—letters and numbers, symbols and punctuation marks.

Ascertainment—FCC regulations that require licensed broadcasters to determine the interests, needs, and issues of the communities they represent.

Aspect ratio—the ratio of a picture height to its width, which in video is 3:4.

Asynchronous—nonreal time. For example, two activities, such as transmission and receiving of a message, do not occur simultaneously.

Audio cue—a sound (word, musical note, noise, and the like) used as a point of reference in selecting various editing points.

Basic cable—a minimum accounting of services a subscriber receives, which typically includes PEG access channels.

Bicycle—the process of exchanging taped programs with other television facilities.

Blocking—the positioning and movement of actors and cameras by a director for each scene and shot.

Broadcasting—as defined by the Communications Act of 1934, the dissemination of communication meant to be received directly by the public or by the intermediary of relay stations, as found in radio and television.

Bulletin Board—electronically generated video screen(s) cablecasting community messages and program announcements.

Camcorder—the combination of a camera and video recorder in a single unit both physically and electronically.

CATV—Community Antenna Television Systems, the early name for cable television, a system introduced in the 1950s whereby an area receives distant television signals via coaxial wire, boosted by a local cable company.

Character generator—a typewriter-like device that is used to transfer alphanumeric information (lettering, color, spacing) onto a television screen.

Churn—in cable television, subscriber tendency to cancel shortly after contracting for services.

Closed circuit—a private transmission system confined to wire or microwave in limited locations, not available for reception on standard receiving equipment off the air.

Coaxial cable—cable that consists of a central wire core surrounded by a layer of plastic, metal-webbed insulation topped with an outer layer of plastic.

Color bars—standard test signal which is used as a reference when setting up video equipment.

Common carrier—communications channels whose services are open to the public for hire to handle interstate and international communications electronically.

Communications Act of 1934—an act of Congress that created the Federal Communications Commission.

Community access—alternative term used for "public access."

"Compunications"—a description of the merger of communications and computing from a term coined by Anthony O. Oettinger.

Control room—the place where audio and video recording and switching equipment is located; staffed by the director and other crew persons during a production, it is usually located adjacent to a studio.

Convergence—the bringing together of distinct media technologies into a single electronic computer-driven environment.

Copyright—legal protection for writers, publishers, producers, and other media artists to keep their works from being reproduced.

Counter-programming—the scheduling of a television program appealing to a different audience from the one(s) trying to attract them.

Credits—a list of technical and/or creative people who have participated in or been responsible for a program, usually scrolled at the beginning or end of it.

Crew—technical personnel in a video production, like camera operators or sound recordists.

CTR—*Community Television Review*, the official publication of The Alliance for Community Media (formerly NFLCP).

Cut—the electronic equivalent of splicing pieces of audiotape or film together.

Cyberspace—the illusion of reality that is created when computer-generated stimuli replace the naturally occurring stimuli around us.

DBS (direct broadcast satellites)—high-powered satellites capable of beaming signals directly to small home antennas.

Database—electronically stored information collections, often with interrelated files managed and stored by a central system.

Dedicated line—a telecommunications link reserved expressly for private use by a single individual, company, or group of companies.

Dial-access—a receiving system where the viewer "dials up" a requested program, which is then automatically started up and fed to that location.

Digital video effects—sophisticated visual video transitions like flips, rolls, page turns, tumbles, flyaways, or pushes.

Dissolve—a video transition where one frame fades out while another one fades in, usually to show extremes of time or space.

Documentary—a program using creative interpretation of actuality footage.

Downlink—the apparatus used to receive transmission from a communications satellite.

Dubbing—the erasing of an audio track and the replacing of it with new words, sounds, or music; also, making copies of a tape.

Edit master—the final version of an edited program, prepared for duplication.

Editing—a process in which portions of a television production are selected and fit together into a program.

Educational access—dedicated cable channel for local educational programming, whether based/operated within the local school system or imported via satellite from another source.

Electromagnetic waves—electrical impulses, made up of energy traveling through space at the speed of light, that transmit broadcast signals.

Electronic mail—also known as "E-mail," typed messages that flow to and from computer users.

Establishing shot—the first camera shot in a sequence, introducing time, theme, and location.

Facsimile— also known as "fax," a medium whereby textual and/or graphic information is transmitted from sender to receiver.

FCC—Federal Communications Commission, a regulatory agency established by the Communications Act of 1934 to oversee broadcast communication in the public "interest, convenience, and necessity."

Fiber optics—thin strands of glass used to carry data communication for a thousand or more cable channels.

First Amendment—a constitutional guarantee in the Bill of Rights that reads: "Congress shall make no law respecting an establishment of religion, or prohibiting the free exercise thereof; or abridging the freedom of speech, or of the press; or the right of the people peaceably to assemble, and to petition the Government for a redress of grievances."

501(c)3—legal non-profit status granted to service organizations.

Franchise—the granting of rights to provide cable television service to an area by means of a legal agreement between a government entity and a cable company.

Gatekeeper—a media professional, such as a journalist, producer, or editor, in charge of determining what information constitutes "news."

Glitch—a lapse in the video image, usually unintentional.

Government access—dedicated cable channel for local governmental programming.

Graphics—visual design information, typically computer-generated for a television production.

Grazing—a method of television viewing made possible by remote-control devices that allows continuous rapid scanning of all available channels.

Hard copy—a document which is printed.

HDTV (high-definition television)—large-screen television.

Headend—location of the local signal generation for a cable system.

Home video—personal media such as video playback or playback/record cassette equipment and/or videodiscs in the home.

Information Age—the period following the agricultural and industrial ages in which social and economic development and much of the labor force are concentrated in information industry sectors.

Information technology—microelectronics-based combinations of computing and telecommunications for the acquisition, processing, storage, and dissemination of vocal, pictorial, textual, and numerical data.

Interactive television—also known as "two-way television," an arrangement made possible on cable systems where signals can be sent from the headend to the television set and vice versa.

Lavalier—a kind of microphone that is attached to clothing or is worn around the neck of on-air television personalities.

Libel—information that is published or broadcast that can damage an individual's good name or reputation, or that can lessen the esteem, goodwill, or respect due that person.

Log—a written record of videotape footage.

Logging—the process of reviewing a tape and marking down a detailed description of each shot, camera movement, and scene prior to editing.

Lottery—a contest involving prize(s), chance, and consideration.

Magazine format—a program format that consists of a number of feature stories shot in different styles, then pieced together.

MMDS (multichannel, multipoint distribution services)—communication systems using microwave relays to transmit television signals from a master omnidirectional antenna to smaller microwave ones.

Microwave—very short wave, usually measured in gigahertz (billions of cycles per second), of higher frequency than standard broadcast transmissions.

Modulator—basic signal generator used to feed access signal(s) to the headend.

MSO—multiple system operator, who owns and/or operates more than one cable television system.

Multimedia—a single technical standard and network of universally available, standardized audio, video, image, and/or data communication.

Narrator—a speaker off-camera who relates a story or relevant commentary to what is happening on-screen.

Narrowcasting—telecasting to a specific target niche.

Noncommercial television—broadcast stations that operate on budgets derived from sources other than the sale of advertising time.

Off-the-air—message(s) received from a broadcast on a standard radio or television channel.

Omnidirectional microphone—one that can receive sounds equally from all directions.

"On location"—video productions "out in the field," or outside the parameters of the studio.

On-the-air—"live" transmission.

Panning—a camera shot where the lens crosses the length of a scene.

Pay cable—television channels that are added to basic cable, for an additional subscriber fee.

Pay-per-view (PPV)—a system allowing subscribers to cable television to pay a one-time fee to watch a specific program.

PEG access—dedicated public, educational, and governmental cable television access channels.

Penetration—percentage of potential television households that actually subscribe to a particular cable system.

Photo op—an "opportunity" for a photographic session, usually set up by politicians.

Photographer—a person using a camera, also called a shooter, videographer, or videojournalist.

Pixillation—the cutting out of a certain number of frames within a sequence, producing a fast-motion, kinetic, jumpy effect.

Portapak—battery-operated video equipment used in field productions that is capable of operating on battery power.

POSSLQ—person(s) of opposite sex sharing living quarters.

Postproduction—the activities involved in finishing a program, such as editing, mixing, and duplicating the original footage.

Preproduction—the planning activities that are undertaken before a program is shot.

Pretest—a preliminary assessment of attitudes and/or actions before application of a major test.

Producer—the person responsible for overseeing all aspects of a television production, including tape content.

PSA—public service announcement, a short informational production offered by a nonprofit organization in the public interest.

Public access—the right of all community members to free, uncensored use of a dedicated cable channel for programming on a first-come, first-served basis.

Public domain—data that is not copyrighted and therefore may be used freely without permission, like certain music.

Qube—the 1977 Columbus, OH, experiment in commercial two-way cable television. The first of its kind, Qube allowed viewers to respond to television programs, select pay-per-view programs, and vote on referenda—until it went out of business in 1979.

RAM (random-access memory)—impermanent computer memory where information can be transferred in and out.

Random sampling—survey selection process whereby each unit of the selected whole has an equal chance of being used.

Raw footage—tape footage that is still unedited.

"Real time"—video recording or transmission of an actual event as it is happening.

Request for proposals (RFP)—a governmental invitation for submission of a proposal to establish a cable television system.

Reverse feed—the capacity of sending or receiving signal(s), found in "live" cablecast locations.

ROM (read-only memory)—permanent computer memory.

Rough cut—the unedited version of a videotape.

Satellite—orbiting space station capable of receiving and transmitting audio, video, and data signals, sending them on to earth stations.

Script—a written copy containing the video and audio information that constitutes a production, including camera, audio, and timing.

Shoot—the term for a television production.

Slander—spoken information that can damage an individual's good name or reputation.

Software—program material.

Sponsor—person or group who arranges cablecasting of preproduced tapes through an access facility.

Storyboard—a sequence of pictures/sketches for camera shots, used in production planning.

Switcher—a panel in the control room that contains various buttons for video inputs and devices for producing effects.

Talent—a person or persons who appear "on camera."

Talking heads—the term for a (typically boring) television program consisting only of static shots of people talking.

Target market/target niche—a particular group identified by its demographic and/or psychographic characteristics, such as urban preteens, single mothers, golfers, country and western fans.

Telco—abbreviation for a telephone company, whether a carrier, manufacturer, or local operator.

Telecommunication—electronic communication that can consist of one-way and/or two-way, wired and/or unwired communications systems.

Tiering—cable television system whereby operators lump different channels or services into tiers, charging subscribers additional fees to receive certain kinds of programming beyond the "basic" offerings.

Tripod—a three-legged camera support, often mounted in a studio, to keep the camera still.

VCR (videocassette recorder)—telecommunications equipment that uses videotape to record and play back television programs or parts.

Video—the picture portion of a telecast.

Video dial tone—a telecommunication service allowing video telephone calls.

Video toaster—a set of hardware and software that allows producers to incorporate special effects into their productions by means of four basic functions: transitions, 3-D animation, computer artwork, and character generator functions.

Virtual reality—computer-simulated "reality" interacting with more than one of the senses, typically touch, sound, and sight.

Voiceover—narration that is dubbed over video shots.

Zapping—the use of a remote-control pad to change television channels, usually to avoid advertisements.

Zipping—fast-forwarding VCRs through advertisements in recorded programs.

Zoom—a fancy camera movement going from a wide shot to a close-up by adjusting the camera lens.

References

Achtenberg, Ben. 1974. *The Cable Book: Community Television for Massachusetts?* Cambridge, MA: Urban Planning Aid.

Adams, Michael H. 1992. *Single-Camera Video: The Creative Challenge*. Dubuque, IA: William C. Brown.

Adler, Richard, and Walter S. Baer. 1974. *The Electronic Box Office: Humanities and Arts on the Cable*. New York: Praeger.

Agosta, Diane, with Caryn Rogoff and Abigail Norman. 1990. *The Participate Report*. New York: Media Program for the New York State Council on the Arts.

Agostino, Donald E., and Susan Tyler Eastman. 1989. "Local Cable Programming." In Susan Tyler Eastman, Sydney W. Head, and Lewis Klein, *Broadcast/Cable Programming: Strategies and Practices*, 3rd ed., pp. 347–69. Belmont, CA: Wadsworth.

Allen, Johnny Mac. 1986. "Cable Television: Strategic Marketing through Community Relationships." Paper presented at the annual convention of the California Association of Community Colleges. Anaheim, CA.

American Association of Retired Persons. 1986. *Community Television: A Handbook for Production*. Washington, DC: NFLCP.

Anderson, Chuck. 1975. *Video Power: Grass Roots Television*. New York: Praeger.

Andorka, Frank H. 1989. *A Practical Guide to Copyrights and Trademarks*. New York: World Almanac.

Andrews, Edmund L. 1992. "Cable TV Battling Phone Companies." *New York Times* (March 29):1+.

Anshien, Carol M., et al. 1973. "Public Access Report." New York: New York State Council on the Arts.

Atkin, David, and Robert LaRose. 1991. "Cable Access: Market Concerns amidst the Marketplace of Ideas." *Journalism Quarterly*, 68, no. 3 (Fall):354–62.

Aufderheide, Patricia. 1991. "Public Television and the Public Sphere." *Critical Studies in Mass Communication*, 8:168–83.

———. 1992. "Public Television and the Public Interest." *Journal of Communication*, 42, no. 1 (Winter):52–65.

———. 1993. "Public Access Cable Programming, Controversial Speech, and Free Expression." Unpublished paper.

Badeaux, Floyd. 1991. "Commentary: Local Government Cable Television." *Public Management*, 73, no. 4 (April):19–20.

Baer, Walter S. 1973. *Cable Television: A Handbook for Decisionmaking*. Santa Monica, CA: Rand.

Baer, Walter S., Michael Botein, Leland L. Johnson, Carl Pilnick, Monroe E. Price, and Robert K. Yin. 1974. *Cable Television: Franchising Considerations*. New York: Crane, Russak.

Barber, Benjamin R. 1984. *Strong Democracy: Participatory Politics for a New Age*. Berkeley, CA: University of California Press.

Barron, Jerome A. 1973. *Freedom of the Press for Whom? The Right of Access to Mass Media*. Bloomington: Indiana University. Press.

Beck, Kristen. 1983. *Cultivating the Wasteland: Can Cable Put the Vision Back in TV?* New York: American Council for the Arts.

Beecher, Andy. 1986. "The Early Days of Government Access." *CTR*, 9, no. 2:15–18.

Belsie, Laurent. 1993. "Soon: Get a Movie, Buy Goods Via TV." *Christian Science Monitor* (April 12):6.

Bender, Eileen T., et al. 1979. *Cable Television: Guide to Public Access*. South Bend: University of Indiana.

Berger, Joseph. 1993. "Forum for Bigotry? Fringe Groups on TV." *New York Times* (May 23):29+.

Bergman, Robert E., and Thomas V. Moore. 1990. *Managing Interactive Video/ Multimedia Projects*. New York: Educational Technology Publications.

Berner, Richard Olin. 1976. *Constraints on the Regulatory Process: A Case Study of the Regulation of Cable Television*. Cambridge, MA: Ballinger.

Berrigan, Frances J. (ed.). 1977. *Access: Some Western Models of Community Media*. Paris: UNESCO.

Besen, Stanley M., Willard G. Manning, Jr., and Bridget M. Mitchell. 1977. *Copyright Liability for Cable Television: Is Compulsory Licensing the Solution?* Santa Monica, CA: Rand.

Bicknell, Nancy. 1984. "L. O. and Survival: New Ways of Thinking." *CTR* (Spring):9–11.

Bittner, John R. 1991. *Broadcasting and Telecommunication: An Introduction*, 3rd ed. Englewood Cliffs, NJ: Prentice-Hall.

Blau, Andrew. 1991. "Hit Pause, Then Search: Looking Forward after Twenty Years of Access." *CTR* (June/July):6–7.

———. 1992. "The Promise of Public Access." *The Independent* (April):22–26.

Booth, Stephen A., and Frank C. Barr. 1992. "Pieces of 8: Small 8mm Video Camcorders Take the Technological Lead." *Popular Mechanics* (October):65–67.

Bortz, Paul I., Mark C. Wyche, and James M. Trautman (eds.). 1986. *Great Expectations: A Television Manager's Guide to the Future*. Washington, DC: National Association of Broadcasters.

Bowe, Marisa. 1991. " 'Underground' Video." *Video Times* (Spring):52–57.

Brenner, David, with Monroe Price and Michael Meyerson. 1990. *Cable Television and Other Nonbroadcast Video: Law and Policy*. New York: Clark and Boardman.

Bretz, Rudolf. 1975. "Public Access Cable Television: Audiences." *Journal of Communication*, 25, no. 3 (Summer):22–32.

————. 1976. *Handbook for Producing Educational and Public Access Programming for Cable Television.* Englewood Cliffs, NJ: Educational Technology Publications.

Buske, Susan. 1983. "Statement of Susan Buske, Executive Director, NFLCP, Hearing before the Subcommittee on Communications, the Committee on Commerce, Science, and Transportation, United States Senate, Ninety-Eighth Congress, First Session on S.66 to Amend the Communications Act of 1934, February 16 and 17," pp. 157–61. Washington, DC: United States Government Printing Office.

Buske, Sue Miller. 1986. "The Development of Community Television." *CTR* (Summer):12.

Cable Communications Policy Act of 1984 (Public Law 98–549). Washington, DC: U.S. Government Printing Office.

Calhoun, Richard. 1972. "Public Television Channels in New York City: the First Six Months." New York: Center for Policy Research.

Cantor, Muriel G. 1971. *The Hollywood TV Producer: His Work and His Audience.* New York: Basic Books.

Cardona, Mary Bennin (ed.). 1992. *The 1992 NFLCP Yellow Pages.* Washington, DC: NLFCP.

Carey, John. 1993. "Looking Back to the Future: How Communication Technologies Enter American Households." In John V. Pavlik and Everette E. Dennis (eds.), *Demystifying Media Technology: Readings from the Freedom Forum Center*, pp. 32–39. Mountain View, CA: Mayfield.

Carpenter, Polly. 1973. *Cable Television: A Guide for Education Planners.* Santa Monica, CA: Rand.

Carpenter-Huffman, Polly, Richard C. Kletter, and Robert K. Yin. 1974. *Cable Television: Developing Community Service.* New York: Crane, Russak.

Center for Analysis of Public Issues. 1971. *Public Issues.* Supplement no. 1 (July). Princeton: Center for the Analysis of Public Issues.

Center for Democratic Renewal. 1992. *When Hate Groups Come to Town: A Handbook of Effective Community Responses*, 2nd ed., revised and updated. Atlanta, GA: Center for Democratic Renewal.

Christensen, Gary L. (ed.). 1985. *The New Era in CATV: The Cable Franchise Policy and Communication Act of 1984.* New York: Practicing Law Institute.

Clifford, Terry. 1982. "Vanity Video." In Robert Atwan, Barry Orton, and William Vesterman, *American Mass Media: Industries and Issues*, 2nd ed. New York: Random House.

Clift, Charles, and Ron Garay. 1986. "Yesterday's Tomorrows: Past Visions of Cable's Future." Paper presented to the Popular Culture Association. Atlanta, GA.

Connors, Tracey D. 1988. *The Non-Profit Organization Handbook.* New York: McGraw-Hill.

Controversial Programming Committee, NFLCP. 1991. *Controversial Programming: A Guide for Public, Educational and Government Access Television Advocates.* Washington, DC: NFLCP.

Deep Dish Directory—A Resource Guide for Grass Roots Television Producers, Programmers, Activists and Cultural Workers. 1986, 1988. New York: Paper Tiger TV.

Devine, Robert H. 1991. "Marginal Notes: Consumer Video, the First Amendment and the Future of Access." *CTR* (June/July):8–11.

Dominick, Joseph, Barry L. Sherman, and Gary Copeland. 1990. *Broadcasting/Cable and Beyond: An Introduction to Modern Electronic Media.* New York: McGraw-Hill.

Doty, Pamela. 1975. "Public Access Cable TV: Who Cares?" *Journal of Communication,* 25, no. 3 (Summer):33–41.

Downing, John. 1991. "Community Access Television: Past, Present and Future." *CTR* (August):6–8.

Dworkin, Ronald. 1992. "The Coming Battles over Free Speech." *New York Review of Books* (June 11).

Eastman, Susan Tyler, Sydney W. Head, and Lewis Klein. 1989. *Broadcast/Cable Programming: Strategies and Practices,* 3rd ed. Belmont, CA: Wadsworth.

Elmer-Dewitt, Philip. 1993. "Building the On Ramp to the Electronic Highway." *Time* (May 31):52–53.

Engelman, Ralph. 1990. "The Origins of Public Access Cable TV, 1966–1972." *Journalism Monographs* (October).

Enos, J. Clive III. 1979. "Public Access Cable Television in New York City: 1971–5." Unpublished doctoral dissertation, University of Wisconsin-Madison.

Faber, Mindy. 1990. *A Tool, A Weapon, A Witness: The New Video News Crews.* Chicago: Randolph Street Gallery.

Ferguson, Marjorie (ed.) 1986. *New Communication Technologies and the Public Interest: Comparative Perspectives on Policy and Research.* Beverly Hills, CA: Sage.

Flanagan, Joan. 1982. *The Grass Roots Fundraising Book: How to Raise Money in Your Community.* Chicago: Contemporary Books.

Frederiksen, H. Allan. 1972. *Community Access Video.* Menlo Park, CA: Nowells.

Fuller, Linda K. 1984a. "Public Access Cable Television: A Case Study on Source, Contents, Audience, Producers, and Rules-Theoretical Perspective." Unpublished doctoral dissertation, University of Massachusetts.

———. 1984b. "Toward a Reconceptualization of Television: The Potential Impact of Access." Paper presented to the International Communication Association. San Francisco.

———. 1984c. "Developing Survey Instruments for Assessing Community Programming." *CTR,* 7, no. 1 (Spring):18.

———. 1984d. "Television Of the People, By the People, For the People: Public Access." Paper presented to the International Television Studies Conference. London.

———. 1985a. "Access and First Amendment Rights." *Northeast Regional Report* (Winter):8.

———. 1985b. "Program Producers of Public Access." Paper presented to the Popular Cultural Association. Louisville, KY.

———. 1985c. "Measuring Your Local Programming Audience." Workshop for NFLCP, Boston.

———. 1986. "The Constitutionality of Cable Technology." In Ray B. Browne and Glenn J. Browne, *Laws of Our Fathers: Popular Culture and the U.S. Constitution,* pp. 123–31. Bowling Green, OH: Bowling Green State University.

————. 1987. "Constructing New Approaches to Cable Technology." Paper presented to the Communication Association of Massachusetts. Milton, MA.

————. 1988. "Considerations and Case Studies of Community Access Television in the United States." Keynote speech, Junta de Andalucia, Unión de Consumidores de España, RTVA. Seville, Spain.

————. 1989. "Access to Grassroots Media: Public Access Cable Television in the U.S." Paper presented to the Union for Democratic Communications. New York.

————. 1990. "Producers of Programming for Public Access: A Nonprototypical Profile." *Medienpsychologie*, Jg. 2, Heft 4:302–14.

————. 1991a. "The Potential Impact of New Technologies on Access." Paper presented at the NFLCP spring conference. East Hartford, CT.

————. 1991b. "Balancing Special Interest Groups." Paper presented at the Northeast Region NFLCP Conference. Greenfield, MA.

————. 1992. "Outreach to Underrepresented Groups." Workshop for NFLCP Conference. St. Paul, MN.

————. 1993a. "Management of Community Television." Workshop for Northeast Regional Convention, The Alliance for Community Media. Pittsfield, MA.

————. 1993b. "US Community Television: Concerns, Controversies, and Case Studies." Paper presented to the International Association of Mass Communication Researchers. Dublin, Ireland.

————. 1993c. "If Interactive Video Is the Goal, What Is the Best Educational Means to Achieving It?" *Telematics & Informatics*, 10, no. 4:379–89.

Geller, Henry. 1974. *The Mandatory Origination Requirement for Cable Systems*. Santa Monica, CA: Rand.

Geller, Henry, with Alan Ciamporcero and Donna Lampert. 1987. "The Cable Franchise Fee and the First Amendment." *Federal Communications Law Journal*, 39.1.2 (May).

Gillespie, Gilbert. 1975. *Public Access Cable Television in the United States and Canada*. New York: Praeger.

Ginsburg, Douglas H. 1979. *Regulation of Broadcasting: Law and Policy Toward Radio, Television, and Cable Communications*. St. Paul, MN: West.

Goss, Patricia Bellamy. 1978. "A Policy Analysis of Subscriber Reaction to Cable Television Access Programming in New York City." Unpublished doctoral dissertation, New York University.

Greene, Alexis. 1982. "Is Public Access TV Doing Its Job?" *New York Times* (August 22):H1.

Greenfield, Jeff. 1992. "The Videotaping of Darn Near Everything." *TV Guide* (July 25):17–19.

Grundfest, Joseph. 1976. *Citizen Participation in Broadcast Licensing Before the FCC*. Santa Monica, CA: Rand.

Guinary, Donald L. 1975. *Citizens' Groups and Broadcasting*. New York: Praeger.

Hamburg, Morton I. 1979. *All about Cable: Legal and Business Aspects of Cable and Pay Television*. New York: Law Journals Seminars-Press.

Hardenbergh, Margot. 1986. "Defining Public Access in the Eighties." *CTR*, 9, no. 4:6–7.

Hargadon, Tom. 1992. "Video Dial Tone: Let RBOCs Stick to Knitting." *New Media* (November):14.

Head, Sydney W., and Christopher H. Sterling. 1990. *Broadcasting in America: A Survey of Electronic Media*, 6th ed. Boston: Houghton Mifflin.

Heeter, Carrie, and Bradley S. Greenberg. 1988. *Cableviewing*. Norwood, NJ: Ablex.

Heller, Neil. 1989. *Understanding Video Equipment*. White Plains, NY: Knowledge Industry.

———. 1992. *Managing a Video Production Facility*. White Plains, NY: Knowledge Industry.

Herbst, Adrian E. 1992. *Restrictions on Public Access Channels: Candidates on Access in an Election Year*. Minneapolis: Moss & Barnett.

Hewitt, John. 1992. *Sequences: Strategies for Shooting News in the Real World*. Mountain View, CA: Mayfield.

Hill, Chris, and Barbara Lattanzi. 1992. "Media Dialectics and Stages of Access." *Felix*, 1, no. 2 (Spring):97–105.

Hipsman, Irwin. 1986. "Access Management Structures—A Primer." *CTR*, 9, no. 4:8.

Hollins, Timothy. 1984. *Beyond Broadcasting: Into the Cable Age*. London: BFI.

Hollowell, Mary Louise. 1975. *Cable Handbook: A Guide to Cable and New Communications Technologies*. Washington, DC: Communications Press.

Hong, Peter. 1990. "Fires, School Board Meetings, and Accidents—24 Hours A Day." *Business Week* (December 17):32.

Horton, Howard. 1982. "The History of Access." Paper presented to the NFLCP Conference. Boston, Massachusetts (November).

Ianacone, Evonne. 1980. *Changing More Than the Channel: Citizen's Guide to Forming a Media Access Group*. St. Louis: Media Access Group.

Iudica, Doreen E. 1991. "Local Access Cable Shows Come of Age." *Boston Globe* (April 15):W1+.

Jacobson, Robert E. 1977. *Municipal Control of Cable Communications*. New York: Praeger.

Jesuale, Nancy, and Ralph Lee Smith. 1982. *CTIC Cablebooks*. Volume 1: *The Community Medium*. Arlington, VA: Cable Television Information Center.

Jesuale, Nancy, Richard M. Neustadt, and Nicholas P. Miller. 1982. *CTIC Cablebooks*. Volume 2: *A Guide for Local Policy*. Arlington, VA: Cable Television Information Center.

Johnson, Leland L. 1975. *Expanding the Use of Commercial and Noncommercial Broadcast Programming on Cable Television Systems*. Santa Monica, CA: Rand.

Johnson, Nicholas, and Gary Gerlach. 1972. "The Coming Fight for Cable Access." *Yale Review of Law and Social Action*, 2 (Spring):217–25.

Johnson, Rolland C., Donald E. Agostino, and Kenneth J. Ksobiech. 1974. *The Columbus Video Access Center: A Research Evaluation of Audience and Public Attitudes*. Bloomington: Institute for Communication Research, Dept. of Radio-TV, Indiana University.

Jones, Glenn R. 1988. *Jones Dictionary of Cable Television Technology*, 3rd ed. Englewood, CO: Jones 21st Century.

Kahin, Brian. 1984. "Rethinking Public Access Networking: Vertical, Horizontal, Hard, and Soft." *CTR*, 7, no. 4:31–32.

Kahin, Brian, and W. Russell Neuman. 1985. "Community Programming and the

Principle of Access." Unpublished proposal, in association with NFLCP and Francis Spiller Associates.

Karwin, Tom. 1986. "Public Policy: It's Time for States to Regulate Uses of Franchise Fees." *CTR*, 9, no. 4:24+.

Karwin, Thomas, with Jan Sanders, Fred Johnson, and the NFLCP Public Policy Committee. 1988. *Cable Access Advocacy Handbook*. Washington, DC: NFLCP.

Kellner, Douglas. 1992. "Public-Access Television and the Struggle for Democracy." In Janet Wasko and Vincent Mosco (eds.), *Democratic Communications in the Information Age*, pp. 100–113. Norwood, NJ: Ablex.

Kletter, Richard C. 1973. *Cable Television: Making Public Access Effective*. Washington, DC: National Science Foundation.

Kolbert, Elizabeth. 1993. "Networks Battle the 'Channel Surfers.'" (Springfield, Massachusetts) *Union-News* (April 27):25.

Koning, Dirk. 1990. "Community Access to Dominant Media: A Model." *CTR*, 13, no. 1 (Spring):6.

Kotler, Phillip. 1982. *Marketing for Non-Profit Organizations*. Englewood Cliffs, NJ: Prentice-Hall.

Kreiss, Robert A. 1981. "Deregulation of Cable Television and the Problem of Access Under the First Amendment." *California Law Review*, 54 (July):1001–1150.

Krupnick, Michael A. 1990. *The Electric Image: Examining Basic Television Technology*. White Plains, NY: Knowledge Industry.

Ksobiech, Kenneth J., et al. 1975. *The Columbus Video Access Center: A Research Analysis of Public Reaction*. Bloomington: Institute for Communication Research, Dept. of Radio-TV, Indiana University.

Kucharski, Carl. 1990. "Where Do We Go from Here? The Musings of an Access Codger." *CTR*, 13, no. 3 (Fall):4–7.

———. 1991. "Access and Government Contracts." *CTR*, 13, no. 4 (Winter):4.

Landro, Laura. 1982. "Public Access TV in New York Tends Toward Sex, Sadism." *Wall Street Journal* (December 20):1.

Ledingham, John A. 1982. "Characteristics of Cable Access Centers in the Top 100 Media Centers." Paper presented to the Thirty-second Annual Conference of the International Communications Association. Boston.

LeDuc, Don R. 1973. *Cable Television and the FCC: A Crisis in Media Control*. Philadelphia: Temple University Press.

Longworth, Allison. 1976. "Public Access—Cable Television's Uncharted Waters." *Journal of Educational Communication*, 1, no. 5 (March–April):14–16.

Lyle, Jack, and Douglas B. McLeod. 1993. *Communication, Media and Change*. Mountain View, CA: Mayfield.

Manzi, Stephen, and Ivano Brugnoli. 1990. "Confessions of Access Producers in Search of Fame and Fortune." *CableVision* (March 12).

McCoy, Charles. 1993. "Microsoft Corp. Explores TV Alliances with Time Warner, TCI, Other Firms." *Wall Street Journal* (June 14):B4.

McNeil, Donald R. 1990. *Wiring the Ivory Tower: A Round Table on Technology in Higher Education*. Washington, DC: Academy of Educational Development.

Meyerson, Michael. 1985. "The Cable Communication Policy Act of 1984: A Balancing Act on Coaxial Wires." *Georgia Law Review*, 19 (Spring):543–622.

Meyrowitz, Joshua. 1985. *No Sense of Place: The Impact of Electronic Media on Social Behavior*. New York: Oxford University Press.

Miller, Phil. 1990. *Media Law for Producers*. White Plains, NY: Knowledge Industry.

Morris, Charles R., et al. 1972. "Public Access Channels: The New York Experience." New York: Center for the Analysis of Public Issues.

Mueller, Wally. 1989. "Controversial Programming on Cable Television's Public Access Channels: The Limits of Governmental Response." *DePaul Law Review* 38:3 (Summer).

Newcomb, Horace M., and Robert S. Alley. 1982. "The Producer as Artist: Commercial Television." In James S. Ettema and D. Charles Whitney, *Individuals in Mass Media Organizations: Creativity and Constraint*, pp. 69–89. Beverly Hills, CA: Sage.

NLFCP Public Policy Committee. 1991. *Controversial Programming: A Guide for PEG Access TV Advocates*. Washington, DC: NFLCP.

Nicholson, Margie. 1990. "Cable Access: A Community Communications Resource for Nonprofits." Washington, DC: Benton Foundation.

Novak, Glenn D. 1984. "Public Access Cable Television: Extending the Production Laboratory for College Students." Paper presented at the annual meeting of the Speech Communication Association. Chicago.

Olenick, Arnold J., and Phillip R. Olenick. *Making the Nonprofit Organization Work: A Financial, Legal and Tax Guide for Administrators*. Englewood Cliffs, NJ: Institute for Business Planning.

On the Cable: The Television of Abundance. 1971. Report of the Sloan Commission on Cable Communications. New York: McGraw-Hill.

Oringe, Robert S., and Sue Miller Buske. 1987. *The Access Manager's Handbook: A Guide for Managing Community Television*. Stoneham, MA: Focal Press.

Orton, Barry (ed.). 1982. *Cable Television and the Cities: Local Regulation and Municipal Use*. University of Wisconsin-Extension.

Ostling, Douglas J. 1990. *Access Producers Handbook*. (NFLCP.)

Othmer, David. 1973. *The Wired Island: The First Two Years of Public Access to Cable Television in Manhattan*. New York: Fund for the City of New York.

Park, Rolla Edward. 1979. *Audience Diversion Due to Cable Television: Supporting Data*. Santa Monica, CA: Rand.

Peck, Abe. 1985. *Uncovering the Sixties: The Life and Times of the Underground Press*. New York: Pantheon.

Peck, Diana (ed.). 1980. *The Cable TV Franchising Primer*. Kettering, OH: NFLCP.

Perry, Robert. n.d. "Obscenity Law and Cable Communications." *CTR*, 8, no. 2:12–13.

Phillips, Mary Alice Mayer. 1972. *CATV: A History of Community Antenna Television*. Evanston, IL: Northwestern University Press.

Pilnick, Carl. *Cable Television: Technical Considerations in Franchising Major Markets*. Santa Monica, CA: Rand.

Pilnick, Carl, and Walter S. Baer. 1973. *Cable Television: A Guide to the Technology*. Santa Monica, CA: Rand.

Pine, Evelyn. 1986. "Exchanging Tapes Creates New Communities." *CTR*, 9, no. 1:28–29.

Pollack, Andrew. 1993. "VCR's Are Facing Two Revolutions." *New York Times* (March 7):F9.

Pool, Ithiel De Sola, and Herbert E. Alexander. 1973. "Politics in a Wired Nation." In Pool, Ithiel De Sola (ed.), *Talking Back: Citizen Feedback and Cable Technology*. Boston: MIT Press.

Powell, Bill. 1993. "Eyes on the Future." *Newsweek* (May 31):39–41.

Price, Monroe. 1990. "Congress, Free Speech, and Cable Legislation: An Introduction." *Cardoza Arts & Entertainment Law Journal*, 8:225–31.

Price, Monroe E., and Michael Botein. 1973. *Cable Television: Citizen Participation After the Franchise*. Santa Monica, CA: Rand.

Price, Monroe E., and John Wicklein. 1972. *Cable Television: A Guide for Citizen Action*. Philadelphia: Pilgrim Press.

Pringle, Peter K., Michael F. Starr, and William E. McCavitt. 1991. *Electronic Media Management*, 2nd ed. Boston: Focal Press.

Public Access Operating Rules and Procedures, 2nd ed. Washington, DC: NFLCP.

Purvis, Robert. *Bigotry and Cable TV: Legal Issues and Community Response* (Institute Report No. 3). 1990. Baltimore: National Institute Against Prejudice and Violence.

Radspinner, Diana Braiden. 1986. "Educational Access: We've Only Just Begun." *CTR*, 9, no. 4:15+ .

Raymond, Michele. 1980. "Does Access Imply Excess? Or, Who Will Pay for Local Programs?" *TV Communications* (February 15):68–73.

Rice, David M., Michael Botein, and Edward B. Samuels. 1980. *Development and Regulation of New Communications Technologies*. New York: Communications Media Center, NY Law School.

Rivkin, Steven R. 1973. *Cable Television: A Guide to Federal Regulations*. Santa Monica, CA: Rand.

ROAR. The Paper Tiger Television Guide to Media Activism. 1991. New York: Paper Tiger Television Collective.

Rogers, Michael. 1993. "A Simple Guide to the Television Technology of the Future." *TV Guide* (January 23):27–30.

Roman, James W. 1983. *Cablemania: The Cable Television Sourcebook*. Englewood Cliffs, NJ: Prentice-Hall.

Ronka, Bob. 1981. "Cable TV: Preserving Public Access." *Los Angeles Law Review*, 4 (March):8–13.

Rood, Thomas Richard. 1977. "Cable Television: A Status Study of Services and Community Access Programming Practices in the State of Michigan." Unpublished doctoral dissertation, Wayne State University.

Ross, Leonard. 1974. *Economic and Legal Foundations of Cable Television*. Beverly Hills, CA: Sage.

Rowland, Linda M. 1992. "The Camera's Rolling at Minnechaug High School and all over Wilbraham." *The Reminder* (September 15):4.

Ruston, William F. 1980. "Public Interest and Access Programming: You Were There with 'Over a Barrel.' " *Public Telecommunication Review*, 8, no. 1 (January/February):12–14.

Sanchez, Ernest. 1986. *Copyright and You: A Primer for Producers on Copyright and Fair Use*. Washington, DC: NFLCP.

Schaffer, William Drew, and Richard Wheelwright (eds.). 1983. *Creating Original Programming for Cable TV*. Washington, DC: Communications Press.

Schmidt, Benno C., Jr. 1976. *Freedom of the Press vs. Public Access*. New York: Praeger, 1976.

Schwartz, Barry, and Jay Garfield Watkins. 1973. "The Anatomy of Cable Television." In Schwartz, Barry N. (ed.), *Human Connection and the New Media*, pp. 80–87. Englewood Cliffs, NJ: Prentice-Hall.

Schwartz, Robert. 1982. "Public Access to Cable Television." *The Hastings Law Journal* (March).

Sedano, Michael V. 1975. "Cable Television, Public Access, and the Speech Teacher." Paper presented to the Annual Meeting of the Western Speech Communication Association. Los Angeles.

Senate Committee on Investigations and Taxes Report. 1984. "Adult Illiteracy in New York State—A Hidden Disgrace." Albany, NY: New York State Senate.

Shamberg, Michael. 1973. *Guerrilla Television*. New York: Raindance.

Shanks, Bob. 1977. *The Cool Fire: How to Make It in Television*. New York: Vintage Books.

Shapiro, Andrew O. 1976. *Media Access: Your Rights to Express Your Views on Radio and Television*. Boston: Little, Brown.

Shearer, Cynthia. 1986. "Who Do We Think We Are? Images of Ourselves in Public Access Television." Unpublished paper.

Singleton, Loy A. 1986. *Telecommunications in the Information Age*, 2nd ed. Cambridge, MA: Ballinger.

Sinofsky, Esther Rit. 1984. *Off-Air Videotaping in Education: Copyright Issues, Decisions, and Implications*. New York: R. R. Bowker.

Smith, Ralph Lee. 1972. *The Wired Nation. Cable Television: The Electronic Communications Highway*. New York: Harper and Row.

Sparkes, Vernone M. 1979. "The Users of Cable Television Access Channels: A Study of the Diffusion and Adoption of a Communications Innovation." Paper presented to the Sixty-second Annual Meeting of the Association for Education in Journalism. Houston, TX.

Stoney, George. 1986. "Public Access: A Word About Pioneers." *CTR*, 9, no. 2:7–11.

Strong, William S. 1990. *The Copyright Book: A Practical Guide*, 3rd ed. Cambridge, MA: MIT Press.

Talbot, Mary. 1993. "Low Budgets, Lots of Grit." *Newsweek* (May 10):66–67.

Tate, Charles (ed.). 1971. *Cable Television in the Cities: Community Control, Public Access, and Minority Ownership*. Washington, DC: The Urban Institute.

TeMaat, Agatha (ed.). 1986. *ITV Utilization Ideabook*. Bloomington, IN: Agency for Instructional Technology.

Tierney, John. 1993. "Will They Sit by the Set, or Ride a Data Highway?" *New York Times* (June 20):1 +.

Townsend, George R., and J. Orrin Marlowe. 1974. *Cable: A New Spectrum of Communication*. Spectrum Communications.

Tuchman, Gaye. 1974. "Assembling a Network Talk-Show." In Gaye Tuchman (ed.), *The TV Establishment: Programming for Power and Profit*, pp. 119–35. Englewood Cliffs, NJ: Prentice-Hall.

Turner, Richard. 1993. "Hollywood Is Seeing the Future, and It Is Interactive Show Biz." *Wall Street Journal* (May 19):1 +.

Using New Communications Technologies: A Guide for Organizations. 1986. Washington, DC: The Media Institute.

Van Eaton, Joseph, and William Earley. 1988. "Controversial Programming and Access: An Outline of Basic Issues and Approaches Under the First Amendment." Paper delivered in Dayton, OH.

Vassoler, Kiki, Deborah A. Reino, and Alfred Vizzone. n.d. *Cable Television Sample Surveys: Ascertaining Your Community on Cable Television Matters.* n.p.

Wade, William. 1991. *Nonprofit Management Reports.* Rockville, MD: The Taft Group.

Wenner, Lawrence A. 1976. "Cable Television and the Promise of Public Access." Paper presented at the University of Iowa.

Windish, Joe. 1990. "A Studio Control Room Goes Mobile." *CTR*, 13, no. 1 (Spring):12–14.

Winston, Brian. 1986. *Working with Video.* New York: Watson-Guptill.

Wolf, Barbara. 1986. "Cable Access and Social Change: Eight Case Studies." *CTR*, 9, no. 1 (Spring):18–21.

Woodward, Charles C., Jr. 1974. *Cable Television: Acquisitions and Operation of CATV Systems.* New York: McGraw-Hill.

Wurtzel, Alan. 1975. "Public Access Cable Television: Programming." *Journal of Communication*, 25, no. 3 (Summer):15–21.

Wurtzel, Alan H. 1974. "The Electronic Neighbor: A Source and Content Analysis of Public Access Channel Programming on a New York City System." Unpublished doctoral dissertation, New York University.

Yin, Robert K. 1973a. *Cable Television: Applications for Municipal Services.* Santa Monica, CA: Rand.

———. 1973b. *Cable Television: Citizen Participation in Planning.* Santa Monica, CA: Rand.

Zelmer, A. C. Lynn. 1979. *Community Media Handbook.* Metuchen, NJ: Scarecrow Press.

Zoglin, Richard. 1993. "When the Revolution Comes What Will Happen to . . ." *Time* (April 12):56–58.

Index

272 *Index*

Arts programming, 77–78
Asian programming, 49, 58, 75, 110
ASIFA. *See* Association Internationale
du Film d'Animation
Association Internationale du Film
d'Animation (ASIFA), 55–56
Association of Independent Television
Stations, 46
Association of Independent Video and
Filmmakers, 44
Atkin and LaRose, 15, 25
Atlanta, Georgia, 106, 147
Auburn, Massachusetts, 78
Audiences, 12–15, 90, 112, 149, 152
Aufderheide, Patricia, 1, 18, 24–25, 29,
34, 99, 100, 189
Austin, Texas, 78, 101, 148, 150–52
Avon, Connecticut, 88

Badeux, Floyd, 96
Baer, Walter S., 10, 22, 31, 34
Baer and colleagues, 10
Bailey and Connett, 165
Bakersfield, California, 112
Baltimore, Maryland, 95, 106
Barnouw, Erik, 100
Barron, Jerome A., 4, 33, 100
Bartlett, Scott, 125
Bay Area Video Coalition, 50
Beck, Kristen, 144–45
Beecher, Andy, 91, 125
Behrend, Sam, 102
Bellingham, Massachusetts, 163
Belsie, Laurent, 177
Bender, Eileen T., and colleagues, 10,
11
Benton Foundation, 42, 45, 142
Berg, Lisa, 163
Berger, Joseph, 100
Berkeley, California, 78
Berks Community Television, 171
Berner, Richard Olin, 10
Berrigan, Francis J., 7
Besen and colleagues, 10, 23
Bicknell, Nancy, 8
Bill Cosby on Prejudice, 101
Bittner, John R., 6
Black Entertainment Television, 63

Blau, Andrew, 7, 98, 188
Bloch, Dave, 120, 122, 156
Bloomington, Indiana, 69
Boehm, Andy, 95
Boise, Idaho, 80
Borg, Carl, 81
Borrup, Tom, 42
Bortz and colleagues, 11
Boston, Massachusetts, 43, 90, 147,
163
Bowe, Marisa, 17, 53
Bowie County, Maryland, 77
Brand, Keith, 171
Brea, California, 92
Brenner and colleagues, 10
Bretz, Rudolf, 12
Brewster-Ingraham Consulting Group,
61–62
Broadcasting, 178
Bronx, New York, 82
Brooklyn Park, Minnesota, 152–53
Broomstick, 60
Bucks County, Pennsylvania, 148
Buffalo, New York, 107
Bulletin Board, 96
Burlington, Vermont, 164
Burns, Red, 17
Buske, Sue Miller, 16, 42, 77, 126–27,
136
Buske Group, The, 62

Cable Act of 1992, 99, 183, 190
Cable Communications Policy Act of
1984, 24, 28–29, 100, 142, 183, 190
Cable in the Classroom, 63, 64
Cable Television Advertising Bureau,
45
Cable Television Information Center,
45, 77
Cable Television Public Affairs Associa-
tion, 45–46
Cabletime, 59
Cableview, 59
Cablevision, 59
Cablewatch, 59
Calaveras Community Television, 153–
54
Caldicott, Helen, 151

About the Author

LINDA K. FULLER is an Assistant Professor in the Media Department of Worcester (Mass.) State College and a board member of her town's cable TV commission. She is the author of *The Cosby Show: Audiences, Impact, and Implications* (Greenwood Press, 1992), *Chocolate Fads, Folklore, & Fantasies* (1993), and *Media-Mediated Relationships* (forthcoming); a co-author of *Communicating Comfortably* (1000), *Communicating Quotably* (1993), and *Communicating about Communicable Diseases* (forthcoming); and a co-editor of the multi-volume series *Beyond the Stars: Studies in American Popular Film* (1990–).